THE
COMPROMISED
CHURCH

THE
COMPROMISED
CHURCH

The Present
Evangelical Crisis

JOHN H. ARMSTRONG
GENERAL EDITOR

CROSSWAY BOOKS • WHEATON, ILLINOIS
A DIVISION OF GOOD NEWS PUBLISHERS

Cover design: Brian Ondracek

First printing, 1998

Printed in the United States of America

ISBN 1-58134-006-0

Library of Congress Cataloging-in-Publication Data
The compromised church : the present evangelical crisis / John H.
  Armstrong, general editor.
      p.   cm.
  Includes bibliographical references and index.
  ISBN 1-58134-006-0
    1. Evangelicalism—United States. 2. Christianity and culture—
United States.   I. Armstrong, John H. (John Harper), 1949-
BR1642.U5C644   1998
277.3'0829—DC21   98-21366

11	10	09	08	07	06	05	04	03	02	01	00	99	98
15	14	13	12	11	10	9	8	7	6	5	4	3	2	1

For the reformation of the church and the revivial of biblical Christianity in an increasingly dark time in history when integrity in both life and doctine is the crying need of evangelical Christianity.

And for my daughter-in-law, Adriana, who is an obvious answer to my prayers, and whose gentle and humble spirit, combined with her love for Christ, consistently brings joy to my life.

CONTENTS

THE
CONTRIBUTORS

GENERAL EDITOR

John H. Armstrong (B.A., M.A., Wheaton College; D.Min., Luther Rice Seminary) is founder and president of Reformation & Revival Ministries in Carol Stream, Illinois. He served as a Baptist pastor for twenty-one years before becoming a conference speaker and editor of *Reformation & Revival Journal*, a quarterly publication for church leadership. He was the general editor of *Roman Catholicism: Evangelical Protestants Analyze What Unites & Divides Us* and *The Coming Evangelical Crisis: Current Challenges to the Authority of Scripture and the Gospel*. He is the author of *Can Fallen Pastors Be Restored?*, *A View of Rome*, *Five Great Evangelists*, and *When God Moves*. He has contributed to numerous other books and periodicals.

OTHER CONTRIBUTORS

Arturo G. Azurdia III (B.A., Cal State University, Hayward, California; M.Div., American Baptist Seminary of the West; D.Min., Westminster Seminary in California) is senior pastor of Christ Community Church, Cordelia, California. He serves as an instructor in Bible exposition and theology at Grace School of Theology and Ministry, Pleasanton, California. A forthcoming book on preaching will be published in 1998.

Gerald Bray (B.A., McGill University; M.Litt., D. Litt., University of Paris-Sorbonne) is professor of Anglican studies at Beeson Divinity School, Birmingham, Alabama, and is an ordained minister in the Church of England. He is author of *The Doctrine of God*, *Biblical Interpretation*,

The Contributors

and *Creeds, Councils and Christ*. He has contributed to numerous publications and serves as editor of *The Churchman*.

Derke P. Bergsma (A.B., Calvin College; B.D., Calvin Theological Seminary; M.A., Northwestern University; Drs., Free University of Amsterdam; Rel.D., Chicago Theological Seminary) is professor of practical theology at Westminster Theological Seminary in California. He is an ordained minister in the United Reformed Church and is author of *Predestination: Islam and Calvinism* and *Redemption: The Triumph of God's Great Plan*.

R. Scott Clark (B.A., Nebraska; M.Div., Westminster Theological Seminary in California; D.Phil., candidate, University of Oxford) is academic dean and assistant professor of church history at Westminster Theological Seminary in California. He is a minister in the Reformed Church in the United States, in which he served as a pastor for several years. He is co-editor of *Protestant Scholasticism: Essays in Reassessment* and is a contributor to several periodicals.

Edmund P. Clowney (B.A., Wheaton College; Th.B., Westminster Theological Seminary; STM, Yale Divinity School; D.D., Wheaton College) is adjunct professor of practical theology at Westminster Theological Seminary in California and is a former president of Westminster Theological Seminary (1966-1982) in Philadelphia. A former pastor and church planter, he is author of ten books including *Called to the Ministry, Christian Meditation, The Unfolding Mystery: Discovering Christ in the Old Testament*, and *The Church*.

Mark E. Dever (B.A. Duke University; M.Div., Gordon-Conwell Theological Seminary; Th.M., Southern Baptist Theological Seminary; Ph.D., Cambridge University) is senior pastor of Capitol Hill Baptist Church, Washington, D.C. A frequent conference speaker, he serves as contributing editor to the *Cambridge Papers*. He has contributed to numerous periodicals and is visiting professor at both Beeson Divinity School and Southern Baptist Theological Seminary.

Sinclair B. Ferguson (M.A., B.D., Ph.D., University of Aberdeen) is a former professor of systematic theology at Westminster Theological Seminary in Philadelphia. He is currently senior pastor of St. George's—Tron Parish Church, Glasgow. He is author of numerous books including *John Owen and the Christian Life, The Holy Spirit, Deserted By God?*, and *Grow in God's Grace*.

The Present Evangelical Crisis

R. Albert Mohler, Jr. (B.A., Samford Univ.; M.Div., Ph.D., Southern Baptist Theological Seminary) serves as the ninth president of Southern Baptist Theological Seminary. Formerly the editor of *The Christian Index*, he was general editor for *Gods of the Age or God of the Ages?* Dr. Mohler was named one of *Time* magazine's most promising leaders age forty and under in the December 5, 1994, issue.

Phillip Graham Ryken (B.A., Wheaton College; M.Div., Westminster Theological Seminary; Ph.D., Oxford University) serves as associate minister for preaching at Tenth Presbyterian Church, Philadelphia. His academic work was done in historical theology. He is an avid observer of American culture.

Paul R. Schaefer, Jr. (B.A., University of Pennsylvania; M.T.S., Emory University; D.Phil., Oxford University) is associate professor of religion and philosophy at Grove City College in Pennsylvania. He has taught at Northwestern College and Philadelphia Theological Seminary and also served on the ministerial staff of Tenth Presbyterian Church, Philadelphia.

Stephen J. Wellum (B.A., Roberts Wesleyan College; M.Div., Ph.D., Trinity Evangelical Divinity School) is assistant professor of theology at Northwest Baptist Theological College and the Associated Theological Schools of Trinity Western University, Langley, B.C. Before teaching, he was a pastor in South Dakota.

Donald S. Whitney (B.A., Arkansas State University; M.Div., Southwestern Baptist Theological Seminary; D.Min., Trinity Evangelical Divinity School) is assistant professor of spiritual formation at Midwestern Baptist Theological Seminary. An ordained Southern Baptist minister, he served two churches before his present teaching position and is author of *Spiritual Disciplines for the Christian Life, How Can I Be Sure I'm a Christian?*, and *Spiritual Disciplines Within the Church*.

Monte E. Wilson (B.A., Bethany College; M.R.E., D.Min., Bethany Seminary) is director of Global Impact, a ministry that teaches developing nations how to apply biblical truth to every area of life. He is also the editor of *Classical Christianity*, a teaching publication designed to introduce ecumenical orthodoxy to the evangelical church.

ACKNOWLEDGMENTS

The editor would like to once again thank the board of Reformation & Revival Ministries, Inc., for their support and genuine friendship in the work that Christ has given to me as His servant. Each of these eleven men gives of himself in various ways to make my ministry possible—Bruce Bickel, Bob Mulder, Don Anderson, Wendell Hawley, Kent Hughes, Richard Johnson, Mark Talbot, John Sale, Tom Shaw, Irv Queal, and Andy Froiland.

Thanks also to Rev. Jules Polachek, Executive Director of Reformation & Revival Ministries, whom God has given to labor with me in this cause for Christ and His Kingdom. Your ministry to me frees my heart so that projects such as this can be completed with much joy.

I am also served by a competent office manager, Micha Babbitt, who helps me keep on track much of the time. I am also profoundly grateful for Dr. Wendell Hawley, my Executive Consultant, whose prayer and counsel make every ministry effort flow more effectively.

The greatest appreciation of all must go to my wife, Anita, who has again supported me in a writing and editing project. When I felt like giving up once or twice, you helped me see things one day at a time. Thanks too for all the typing and proofing you did on this particular project. Though your name is not on the cover of this book, you and I know how much you actually did to help me finish it. I would certainly find life very difficult without your presence to cheer and encourage me. God has highly favored me through your life.

This book has also had the full support of Dr. Lane Dennis, who is much more than a publisher. Lane, you are my friend, a very dear brother, and a genuine encourager in the great fight of faith. Stay the course, my brother. God is using your publishing labors for great good! It is a privilege to finally have a book published by Crossway.

Acknowledgments

The original idea for this project came from R. Scott Clark, academic dean at Westminster Theological Seminary in California. While teaching at Wheaton College for two years, Scott and I became good friends and shared a number of lunch meetings. One such meeting resulted in a napkin filled with writing that planted the seed in my mind and resulted in this finished book. Thanks for the encouragement, Scott.

An edited volume such as this often has problems in regard to deadlines, editing, and other related matters. Though this effort has been a bit more trying than others, one could not have had thirteen better contributors than those who have written essays for this particular volume. Several of you are publishing in this kind of forum for the first time. I genuinely hope it will not be the last. Your gift has helped me communicate a profound concern for and to the church.

May Christ's name be exalted in the church, and may this volume truly help many in their understanding of and efforts for reforming the churches.

SOLI DEO GLORIA

EDITOR'S PREFACE

JOHN H. ARMSTRONG

Since this present volume is a type of sequel to my earlier book, *The Coming Evangelical Crisis: Current Challenges to the Authority of Scripture and the Gospel* (Moody Press, 1996), I am taking several risks in presenting it.

First, there are several excellent books now available that seek to demonstrate how American evangelicals have forsaken their biblical and theological heritage. Each of these books makes a contribution that is useful in its own way. *The Coming Evangelical Crisis* was generally reviewed favorably and seems to have helped many to get a clearer perspective on the task that lies ahead of us in reforming the church. Another volume with a similar theme might be too much of the same thing.

Second, edited volumes such as this often do not capture the attention of the average person. They appear to be unduly academic to many. This volume does not try to speak down but rather to lift up. It might well put some off for this very reason, even though we have worked to make it readable.

Third, this particular volume does not have as many recognizable names among the contributors as the earlier volume did. This is true for several reasons. In this present volume many of the writers were chosen precisely because they had done considerable work in the field in which I asked them to contribute. Some of the essayists already have books in the very subject they address in this present work. This means that several of the authors are extremely competent communicators in the area I assigned to them. Several more had even done research for academic degrees in the subjects I asked them to tackle. For this reason I think they

Editor's Preface

have given to many new readers material that will be immensely profitable if it is carefully and reflectively read.

I have made it a practice in my ministry to look for new authors who have something to say that might not otherwise be heard, at least not as widely as this book might afford. I think the church in our time needs to be far more cognizant and appreciative of the many gifted servants it presently has who do not have widely recognizable names.

In spite of these risks, I felt compelled to plan and edit this particular volume for several reasons.

First, the crisis that the earlier book spoke of as "coming" is clearly here. The evidence for this crisis can be seen in the evangelical church at large, not just in the wider culture. While multitudes are trying to rescue America or to take our society to an era supposedly better than the present one, I am convinced that the Word of God calls Christians to work for the "reforming of the church."

Second, if we can get Christian leaders to consider the role of Scripture and the Gospel once again, which the first book sought to do, we will then have to directly address a number of matters that concern the life and ministry of the average evangelical congregation. If the evangelical crisis is truly "in the church," then we must understand how this came about and how we can begin to pursue the kind of change that leads to genuine biblical reformation.

This present volume is not meant to be a text on ecclesiology. It is actually a treatise for our times. Its focus will be, however, upon particular aspects of ecclesiology. There are many excellent books that are more definitely theology books dealing with ecclesiology proper. One exceptionally well written book is *The Church* (InterVarsity, 1995), written by the author of Chapter 1 in this present volume, Dr. Edmund P. Clowney. For the reader who wants to pursue this theme, I recommend that work.

What we actually attempt in this present work is an overview of several pressing issues that touch the very life of the church day in and day out. When church growth, marketing, and revivalism dominate the present church scene, as they no doubt do, then both the image and self-knowledge of the typical church needs keen minds and warm hearts to challenge its leadership to think more clearly about what we are doing and why we are doing it. This book seeks to do exactly that. It does so by addressing several theological concerns that directly affect the evangelical church

The Present Evangelical Crisis

from within. David Wells sets the tone by looking at our times in his help-ful introduction. We then take up various matters, including the life and practice of the church and those who lead the church (i.e., "office bear-ers"). We will also take an engaging, and perhaps controversial, look at worship. We will survey the loss of the sacraments. We will examine anew church discipline and preaching. We also seek to show how several pres-ent trends have not served the church particularly well—e.g., a present emphasis upon spirituality rather than godliness, and a decades-long pre-occupation with small groups in a not altogether healthy manner. All of these areas must be biblically reformed if we would lead congregations toward renewed health.

In addition, we will look at the ministry of the Gospel itself. What should the work of the minister really be? Is the pastor to be a rancher or a shepherd? What is needed today if we would train and support sound ministers of the Word? How are such men called to Christian ser-vice? Do any models in church history speak to our particular time?

Each essay is complete in itself, and yet the whole book has a purpose that clearly unites it. My prayer, as general editor, is that many readers will come to understand that the church presently faces severe problems. At the same time I am convinced that sound solutions for these problems are found both in Scripture and in the history of the Christian church. May the reader be stirred to love and good works and, with me, long practi-cally and passionately for the reformation of the church in our day. A growing number long to see better days for the church. "May that num-ber increase" is my sincere and earnest prayer.

INTRODUCTION:
THE WORD IN THE WORLD

DAVID F. WELLS

If there is an evangelical crisis, one apparently has to look for it; and if one finds it, there are those who say that one is imagining things. The appearance certainly is that the evangelical world is humming like a finely tuned machine. It seems not to be at a crucial turning point, and its future seems not to be clouded with uncertainty at all.

Everywhere in *Christianity Today*, for example, one is met with the reassuring sense that all is well. Even the internal debates that ruffle its pages from time to time are not the sort that would ever threaten to rend the body. Besides, the magazine is at pains to stay above the fray. It is no surprise, therefore, that from its perch it sees nothing alarming in any direction. *Leadership* likewise hoists aloft its sails on a sea that is placid and calm. Occasionally the murkier sides to ministry heave into sight, but for the most part it devotes itself to being a perky, upbeat effort to latch onto the latest trends and not allow its feet to get entangled in biblical matters. Fortunately, *Leadership* has Peter Drucker to make sense for us out of the practice of ministry. Who knows, one wonders, where the evangelical world would be if it had only the apostle Paul? Such a fate is almost too dreadful to contemplate.

The truth is that in garden-variety evangelicalism there is no sense of crisis at all. And why should there be? When one looks at the evangelical presses, they are all in high gear. They are not only churning out books, but some are also showering us with a rich profusion of religious paraphernalia. The devout of the Middle Ages would have turned green with envy had they been able to see what we now have. When one turns

Introduction: The Word in the World

to television, new evangelists have taken the place of the old. However, the shadowy business of bringing blessing and cash into unseemly proximity with one another has gone on without skipping a beat. When one takes to the road, "new paradigm" churches are springing up like mushrooms everywhere. They do not always look like the old thing. Gone, very often, are the familiar church buildings, and in their place are those that look more like low-slung corporate headquarters or country clubs. Inside, a cyclone of change has ripped out the crosses, the pews, the eighteenth-century hymns, the organs, and the biblical discourses. In their place are contemporary songs, drums, cinema-grade seats, light discourses, professional singers, drama, and humor. But there is no sense of crisis about any of this. Quite the reverse. The appearance is that these churches have reality by the tail.

To speak of a crisis, then, is to take on some uphill work. It is akin, perhaps, to the difficulty of injecting a note of caution about the stock market at the very moment when corporate profits are spectacular and the Dow Jones Average has just climbed to new and unprecedented heights. Those in the throes of a rip-snorting party, be it economic or religious, usually find notes of caution a bit irritating and even offensive. I therefore wish to explore this difficulty a little, both with respect to the wider culture and to post-War evangelicalism, before taking up the main theme of this essay. I do so because it is important to establish the context within which any talk about a crisis must be understood.

THE CRISIS IN CONTEXT

In America, in the twentieth century in particular, we have had to calculate anew the costs and benefits of being modern. There is something to be said on both sides of the equation. On the one side of the ledger have to be weighed the innumerable benefits. Since 1930, for example, our life span has increased by two decades, thanks to astonishing advances in medicine and technology ranging from vaccines for polio and measles, to the discovery of DNA, to the widespread use of antibiotics, to gene splicing and implanted cardiac defibrillators. We also have every effort and time-saving gadget imaginable, from dishwashers, to washing machines, to vacuum cleaners, to freezers. It now seems inconceivable that only half a century ago, in 1940, most houses lacked what we now consider elementary

The Present Evangelical Crisis

amenities—for example, refrigeration and central heat; 30 percent did not even have running water. In the 1950s, when Levitown was built, one of its most popular features was the unheard of benefit that each house came with its own washing machine. Since then assembly lines have poured a tidal wave of products into showrooms, malls, and catalogs. The result is that today, in some ways, we live a pampered life that has no precedent. We have more than any other generation—more money, more goods, more comforts, more choices, more protections, and more freedoms.

On the other hand, we also have to weigh the invisible costs that have to be paid for this abundance. We are consumer beings now, and our own internal rhythms are tied into the marketplace as never before. Market insecurity rattles our very being even as the constant trends, fashions, and tastes that this market generates become the unforgiving standards by which we feel compelled to live. If ours is a world constantly in change, so we as people are constantly in change too, moving from job to job, place to place, desire to desire, viewpoint to viewpoint, and perhaps from spouse to spouse. The quotient of what changes to what does not has been dramatically and painfully transformed in our time. And one of the consequences of this is that by every measure anxiety today is at unprecedented levels, as is depression.

The most telling metaphor for all of this may be the storage locker, which since the 1970s has become a major business. Easy to build and easy to maintain, storage bins provide rentable space that is more lucrative than that in apartment buildings. The storage locker, in fact, tells the story of America in a number of ways. America is about the gathering of "stuff" that, in time, overwhelms the owner. It is also about phases of life broken by dislocations between which we find the storage locker. It is there between broken marriages, moves, career changes, and children coming and going. The books, tables, clothes, and bicycles that are piled into these lockers are the residue that remains from many of life's changes, changes of all kinds—temporary and permanent, planned and unplanned, happy and sad.

The turbulence in our modern life, the bewildering sense of uprootedness that it leaves behind, is simply the most obvious of the costs of being modern, but there are others that are less tangible but no less debilitating. For while modern life fills us up with its goods and trinkets, it also empties us out. Ours is a generation adrift on the high seas of techno-

Introduction: The Word in the World

logical innovation but bereft of rudder or compass. The religious norms, the moral beliefs, the cultural expectations that once provided some sense of order and propriety in society have all but disappeared. We now have much, but we also have little. The problem is partly that we have wanted too much, for our appetites of consumption are unrestrained; but the larger problem is that we have also wanted too little—too little of what is true and right.

There are, then, two sides to being modern. There are enormous benefits that are matched by corresponding costs. Those who write of this cultural crisis are often misjudged. For them to say there is a cultural crisis is apparently belied by the remarkable transformation of our world wrought by our virile economy, our technological finesse, our inventiveness. Indeed, to speak of a crisis is to appear ungrateful for all of this, to be overly cynical and even downright pessimistic. It cuts against the grain of the American spirit, against its upbeat optimism, its perennially cheerful assessment of its own prospects, its can-do confidence, and its desire to be liked.

The same dynamic is present in the evangelical world too, and the same danger attends those who speak to it. There is no question that when we compare our situation today with what pertained in the early post-War years, we are in a vastly improved position. Then, evangelicalism was on the fringes, religiously and societally, but now it is in the center. Then, churches were small, for the most part, and comparatively few in number, but now they have benefited from the enormously successful evangelism that has occurred. This growth may have slowed more recently, but there can be no doubt that there has been an explosion of believing in recent decades. Christian schools and colleges have grown in number and quality, as have seminaries; and since the early 1970s there has been an explosion of voluntary associations, Christian organizations, and new ministries. For these and many other reasons, the appearance is of boom times religiously speaking. But if we have much, I believe that we now also have little—too little of what is true and right. Our appetite for truth, as well as for what is morally right, is being lost. Evangelical abundance on the surface, and boundless evangelical energy, conceals a spiritual emptiness beneath it. It is because of this emptiness that a major crisis is now in the making.

In one respect, there is nothing particularly novel about the decline

The Present Evangelical Crisis

of the evangelical church in our time. Spiritual life is always flowing and then ebbing. The tide comes in, and then it goes out. In the book of Judges we see this unmistakable pattern. There are six cycles, and the rhythms are identical: each one is initiated by Israel's sin (3:7; 3:12; 4:1; 6:1; 8:33-35; 10:6); each declension is attended by suffering under the hand of God (3:8; 3:12; 4:2; 6:1; 8:33-36; 10:7-8); this suffering softened the hearts of God's people so that they began to seek Him in prayer (3:9; 3:15; 4:3; 6:6; 10:15); God then raised up a deliverer to restore them (3:9; 3:15; 4:4-23; 6:11-16; 10:1-2). The tide went out each time because of sin, and God brought it back in again each time because of grace.

It is a basic and elementary lesson that the book of Judges teaches, and yet one has to ask why the spiritual condition of God's people at that time, which was so clear to the author of the book, was lost on them. The answer, I believe, is that the sin that alienates God often disguises its nature and buys legitimacy off the surrounding culture. The worship of Baal began to seem natural and normal. What became odd was the refusal to embrace the pagan gods and goddesses. Indeed, in every age where a mass departure from God and His truth has happened, the reasons for it seem entirely normal and self-evident. That is why the ebbing of spiritual life appears to be so innocent. Indeed, it is hardly even noticed. And the telltale sign that it is happening is that the enemies of faith disappear from sight. People settle into doing what is culturally conventional at a spiritual level. This is why, in the Old Testament, the prophetic calling was such a painful and lonely thing. To those far from God, the prophet always seemed so wrong-headed, so lacking in grace, so pessimistic. Since then, nothing really has changed. In an age such as ours, when evangelicalism is mistaking its outward prosperity for inward riches and confusing truth with cultural habit and desire, even the most ordinary of people who know that something is amiss have to wonder how well their perceptions will be received.

Although the current moment is always extremely difficult to understand, I believe that the spiritual tide in the evangelical world has begun to go out. The causes for this are, no doubt, numerous. Some are internal, and some are external, and it is not easy to see their exact relationship. Does faith first decline internally, losing its doctrinal substance, its God-centered worship, its discipline, its serious preaching, and its faithful service? Thus weakened and beginning to drift, does it then fall prey

Introduction: The Word in the World

to the external allurements in the culture? Is that how it happens? Or do the external allurements first intrude upon the faith? Does one small compromise follow another, so that doctrine first loses its importance and then its shape? Or do these processes happen simultaneously? However we choose to think about this matter, both poles—culture and doctrine—have to be considered in any explanation of the decline of the church's life. It is the external entanglements, however, that are the focus of this essay, and in those that follow it is the internal dynamic that is more in view.

This essay's thesis is very simple. It is that the character of contemporary evangelicalism is changing because of its unwitting entanglement with a culture that, in its postmodern configuration, has the power to eviscerate the doctrinal substance of that faith. What explains this entanglement? It is best explained by the fact that the cognitive location of evangelical faith in the culture has changed, resulting in a disposition to adapt to that culture rather than to sustain a moral and spiritual antagonism to it. The consequence of this is that evangelicalism is being transformed into something that it should not be. In this change, we are, I believe, beginning to see the spiritual tide going out.[1]

COGNITIVE DISSIDENTS

The dynamic that explains this internal change is not hard to explain. It concerns the way in which any group preserves, or fails to preserve, its identity. In sociological language, it concerns the fate of the sect. A sect is any group of people whose view of the world is discernibly different from what pertains in the wider society. Sects in this sense can be of all kinds, ranging from the current militias to religious groups like the Branch Davidians. Regardless of the kind of group that it is, the internal dynamic is remarkably similar.

First, a distinctive language emerges within the group. This not only reflects the group's worldview, but it also serves as a badge of identification. Its use instantly marks those who are "in" and its absence those who are "out."

Second, rules about life emerge, often enforced by authoritarian leaders. These rules are important in preserving the group's cohesiveness and identity. They are there as markers for the unwary or unwise, warning them not to enter questionable territory in terms of belief, associations, or behavior. Peter Berger notes that with respect to the ideology of groups like these, it is important that they set "the conditions within which the ideas in question have a chance of remaining plausible."[2] It is the necessity of preserving what is distinctive to the group that also constitutes the members of such a sect as cognitive dissidents. They are at odds, cognitively speaking, with the society around them.

Third, all sects in this sociological sense quickly develop ways of providing mutual therapy, for doubt is often a besetting, if concealed, problem. Those whose way of looking at life is markedly different from what is taken to be "natural" and "normal" in society may have their moments when they wonder whether they are wrong. Why is it that the world can apparently get along quite well without the distinctive knowledge that they have and the meaningful associations within the group? Sects, because they are cognitive minorities, are prone to feeling threatened. They may experience loneliness. They also have to bear the opprobrium of knowing that they are considered odd. It is this inward unease, this doubt, this anxiety that constitutes the shadows that follow cognitive dissonance and for which the therapy of sympathy and association is needed (cf. Ps. 73).

It is not difficult to see that Protestant fundamentalism in the twentieth century has been, in these ways, a sect.[3] Although its stridency in the first decades of this century came to be moderated later on, its view of the world has nevertheless always been distinctive and discernibly different from what has been considered normal in society. Its sense of antithesis, both to the culture and to the liberalism within Christian faith, was sharp and painful. It developed its own religious jargon and formulated rules that rapidly became legalisms that covered everything from wearing lipstick, to dancing, to movies. It withdrew educationally, denominationally, and culturally and organized itself into enclaves from which the outside world was excluded. Within these enclaves, therapy and comfort were offered to those who, from time to time, might wonder about the world outside. And it is not hard to see how fundamentalist doctrine had both a religious and a cultural dimension, for as George Marsden notes, at the heart of the debate with the modernists was the question: "Should Christianity and the Bible be viewed through the lens of cultural development, or should culture be viewed through the lens of Scripture?"[4]

Introduction: The Word in the World

For example, that the Bible was to be viewed as inerrant and "liter-ally" true was, at a doctrinal level, a way of asserting its inspiration; but at a cultural level it was also a way of rejecting literary criticism in the universities. And this criticism was simply symptomatic of the whole drift of modern education. The belief in miracles, which was at the heart of fundamentalism, was there because it is at the heart of the Bible; but the assertion of such a belief was also an unmistakable way of rejecting the naturalistic and secular temper of the day. The belief in divine creation was, at one level, the assertion of biblical teaching; but at another, it was a deliberate rejection of Darwinianism and was a way of defying the reigning cognitive paradigm in society. Dispensational premillenialism was seen to replicate biblical teaching, but it was also a way of rejecting ideas about the progress of humanity that were at the heart of the civil *credo* that dominated public thinking until quite recently.[5] In fact, prior to Christ's return things are going to get much worse, not much better. Fundamentalist doctrine thus served both to protect biblical truth and to fend off the modern world.

In retrospect, it is clear that many dangers attend the path of cogni-tive dissonance. It is not easy to reject the reigning cognitive paradigm without stumbling into anti-intellectualism. That was a turn that funda-mentalism took.[6] Nor is it easy to sustain a moral antithesis to culture without drifting into legalism. Legalism may sometimes be as debilitat-ing to the church as the moral dangers against which the legalism has become the protection. Much of fundamentalism did become hidebound and legalistic. Fundamentalism also produced a profusion of authoritar-ian leaders who could resolve life's dilemmas with a degree of certainty that is usually beyond the reach of mere mortals. The fundamentalist landscape was filled with such figures.

In the early post-War years, evangelicals were determined that they would not repeat the fundamentalists' mistakes. They distanced them-selves from their rather rough and belligerent cousins by speaking of themselves as "neo-evangelicals." The language was Carl Henry's, though it has usually been credited to Harold Ockenga. What was "neo" about them was that they would not be anti-intellectual, separatistic, legalistic, or culturally withdrawn. They shed fundamentalist uncouth-ness, earned Ph.D's from the finest universities, sat at the ecumenical table, dispensed for the most part with dispensational premillenialism, and loosed themselves from most cultural taboos.

The final chapter has not yet been written on this experiment, but when the time comes there will be an interesting question to answer. For all the warts and flaws of fundamentalism, it did succeed in preserving the Word of God and the Gospel. Will this also be true of the evangelicals? They are undoubtedly much nicer than the fundamentalists, but in the end will they fail where the fundamentalists had succeeded? That will be a delicious piece of irony if it turns out to be true.

CHRIST AND CULTURE

On the surface, the issue seems simple enough. Fundamentalists exhibited too much of the "Christ-against-Culture" animus, and evangelicals have too much of the old liberal "Christ-of-Culture" outlook.[7] The earlier liberals, Niebuhr said, believed they "could live in culture as those who sought a destiny beyond but were not in strife with it."[8] That is what too many evangelicals are like today. From our church marketers to our respectable journals to some of our theologians,[9] there is a rush to embrace cultural norms, habits, and tastes in hope of success and in the naive belief that it is all quite harmless and can be harnessed to this or that Christian cause with impunity. So at first glance the transition from fundamentalism to evangelicalism seems like one from too much strife with culture, in the one case, to too little with it in the other.

At root, however, it is a question of how to engage the culture without losing one's soul. Fundamentalism feared losing its soul and so did not engage the culture; evangelicalism fears being different from the culture and is in danger of losing its soul.

CULTURE

The word *culture* has undergone a shift in meaning in recent decades, one that largely coincides with the emergence of a massive literature generated by assorted sociologists and cultural critics. The older meaning of *culture* grew out of the Latin word from which the English is derived, and it had an agricultural sense. A cultured person was one who had worked the soil of his or her inner life. What this meant was that a cultured per-

Introduction: The Word in the World

son was one who valued being civilized, who read great literature, listened to classical music, engaged in elevated conversation, did works of compassion, and through these means sought to cultivate the virtues as well as good taste. Culture in this sense was thought to refine and improve life.

By contrast, the word *culture* today stands for the beliefs and values that have become part and parcel of the modernized world we are building. Included as part of our culture are the assumptions, which may be hidden and unrecognized, that shape the way people see themselves and their world. It is, therefore, a morally neutered word because it embraces not simply the fine and elevated aspects of high culture, as it once did, but the good, bad, and indifferent aspects of popular culture as well. Culture is not only Bach but the Sex Pistols, not only the morally elevated but the trashy and degraded as well, not only quiet discussion of refined topics but the way the world looks from the underside of society's belly, not only art objects but the tawdry produce of a capitalist system that caters to the lowest common denominators.

This more complex understanding of culture also makes more complex how Christian faith is to relate to it. The world of consumption that we inhabit, for example, has given us a bounty that in itself cannot be judged as bad. However, this bounty may well enlarge our appetites for consuming, and these become part of our culture and its rhythms. Can we enjoy the bounty without beginning to need it at a psychological level? Can we feast at the table of plenty without coming to define life in terms of the abundance of the things possessed? Our world gives us powerful and ubiquitous technology that, in itself, is an extraordinary benefit. At the same time, living in this technological world tends to enclose us in a realm of low secular cognitive horizons where what is efficient, what works quickest at least cost, becomes the Good.

This attitude is now deeply entrenched, not only in the corporate society, but also in the church. Can we have technology without its hard-edged pragmatism? Television opens the entire world to us, bequeathing to us a virtual omniscience. It also uproots us from place by making us psychologically present to the whole world. Can we live in its world without experiencing profound psychological dis-ease in regard to our own? Can we be present to the whole world, witness its catastrophes, evil, and deprivations, and remain unscathed by it all? Today we have a

The Present Evangelical Crisis

multitude of choices that is simply without precedent, from spouses to careers to products. This is a matter for gratitude. But this variety that, from one angle, is such a benefit is, from another, part of our contemporary difficulty, for it is in such diversity that relativism simmers. Can we live amidst such pluralism and not lose our moral absolutes? In short, can we learn to be in the modern world, enjoying its bounty, its choices, its technology and television, without belonging to the worldview that it creates? That is the central question with which the church now has to wrestle, though evangelicals have been extremely slow in seeing this despite the fact that the moral and spiritual dimensions of modernity have been explored quite poignantly by many contemporary writers. Unfortunately, it is still the case that "the people of this world are more shrewd in dealing with their own kind than are the people of the light" (Luke 16:8).

It is impossible, then, to think of culture in this newer sense without thinking at the same time of modernity, of those ways of looking at life, those habits and appetites that are part and parcel of the modernization of the world and that create the spiritual and moral climate of this time. The Internet, for example, is both a tool and a cultural artifact. The complexity of considering its import to Christian faith, though, arises from the fact that its functions can be good, bad, and indifferent. As a communications device, it is good; as a bazaar of goods for shoppers it is probably indifferent; as a source of pornography and in its capacity to create virtual and alternative reality, it is dangerous. This kind of example can be endlessly repeated, and what this means is that relating Christ to culture is no simple matter because culture encompasses the whole range of both moral meaning and taste. It is high and low, elevated and debauched, good and bad. In order for the church to learn how to establish what the relation is between Christ and this understanding of culture, it is going to have to discern, in ways that are far more acute than it has to date, where matters of spiritual and moral import lie because these may come packaged in what is attractive, desirable, and alluring.

CULTURE AS WORLDLINESS

It is not difficult to see, then, that the values and perceptions that modernity creates often coincide with what the Bible has in mind when it speaks of worldliness. In biblical terms, worldliness is that system of values, that way of looking at life, that is rooted in fallen human nature but is given collective expression. It is everything external to the individual and in a society—what are taken as normative beliefs, behavior, what is or is not considered desirable—that gives plausibility to our fallenness. Indeed, it is everything in a society that gives its tacit permission to sinning (see John 8:23; 9:5; 12:31; 14:30; 15:19; 16:11; 17:16; 18:36; 1 Cor. 1:20-28; 7:31; Eph. 2:2; Jas. 1:27; 4:4; 2 Pet. 2:20; 1 John 2:15-17; 4:3-5; 5:19).

What the church has to do, therefore, is to look for correlations between worldliness as I have described it and the cultural consequences of modernization that I am sketching. At the point where they coincide, the church has to become both anti-modern and carefully self-conscious about its virtue and its cognitive processes. What might some of these points be?

The church needs to begin by recognizing how modernity works to rearrange the religious landscape. The old secularization thesis, that religion would retreat before the processes of secularization until it disappeared, may seem more plausible in Europe today than it is in America. The fact is that modernity does not necessarily eliminate religion, but it does work to rearrange it. Modernity is hostile to *biblical* faith, not necessarily to faith in general. It is quite telling, I think, that in Germany where there are 30,000 clergy of all kinds, there are 90,000 witches and fortune tellers. In France, there are 26,000 Roman Catholic priests but 40,000 astrologers. And in America today, it is clear that side by side with its growing modernity there is a gathering tide of spirituality of every kind that is seeping into society. Modernity is coexisting with these spiritualites because they are compatible with it—and in many ways biblical faith is not.

For example, modernity tends to contract all of reality into the self, and it replaces a moral way of thinking about life with one that is therapeutic. Life's great preoccupation therefore becomes, not the biblical God or even the Good that is outside the self, but the pains, ambiguities, and sense of loss that are internal to it. Getting in touch with the self, in our culture, becomes the same thing as getting in touch with truth. All of this may then spill out into a quest for spirituality, interiorized though it is, but it is a quest that is so privatized that it will not intrude itself on others, nor will it think much about moral responsibility before others because its purview is not moral at all.

The Present Evangelical Crisis

Modernity is hostile to the moral world in which the biblical discussion about sin takes place. It is hostile to the idea that God is other than our sense of ourselves in our innermost feelings, that He is objective to us, that He addresses us by the Word, that He summons us to accountability before Himself. Modernity therefore has the effect of transforming guilt into shame, and shame, our inner embarrassment about ourselves, can then be resolved simply through counseling. Thus has our moral life become secularized. This is the argument I have developed in *Losing Our Virtue.*

This rearrangement of meaning around the self, around its moods, needs, intuitions, aches, and ambiguities, has entered the church. Its presence is signaled wherever there are those who think, or act, as if the purpose of life is to find ways of actualizing the self, realizing it, and crafting it through technique or purchase, instead of restraining it out of moral considerations and in this sense putting it to death. Where Christian faith is offered as a means of finding personal wholeness rather than holiness, the church has become worldly.

There are many other forms of worldliness that are comfortably at home in the evangelical church today. Where it substitutes intuition and feelings for biblical truth, it is being worldly. Where its appetite for the Word has been lost in favor of light discourses and entertainment, it is being worldly. Where it has restructured what it is and what it offers around the rhythms of consumption, it is being worldly, for customers are actually sinners whose place in the church is not to be explained by a quest for self-satisfaction but by a need for repentance. Where it cares more about success than about faithfulness, more about size than spiritual health, it is being worldly. Where the centrality of God to worship is lost amidst the need to be distracted and to have fun, the church is being worldly because it is simply accommodating itself to the preeminent entertainment culture in the world. Is it not odd that in so many church services each Sunday, services that are ostensibly about worshiping *God,* those in attendance may not be obliged to think even once about His greatness, grace, and commands? Worship in such contexts often has little or nothing to do with God. In these and many other ways, the church today is being worldly precisely because it is also modern. And it is its modernity that conceals from its view its worldliness.

Introduction: The Word in the World

NO ENEMIES

What I have been describing is, of course, the loss of the church's needed otherworldliness and its consuming preoccupation with its this-worldly life. That is a posture that becomes increasingly at home in its culture, and therefore the enemies of Christian faith slowly fade from view. Soon there is very little that cannot be incorporated into the faith or even become the center around which that faith gets reorganized. As it becomes worldly in these ways, it also becomes anthropocentric, its God more and more immanent and less and less transcendent, its worship more horizontal than vertical, its piety more psychological than moral, its gospel more self-focused than cross-centered. It loses its capacity for reform and its ability to take its bearings upon the Word of God because this Word has lost its weight and interest. It loses its moral vision, and so the search for self-satisfaction, in organized or casual ways, replaces the life of virtue.

In such an environment, the doctrines about God fade and then fall apart, the importance of real worship becomes difficult if not impossible to sustain, the truth of God's Word becomes uninteresting and unappetizing, and Christian life becomes indistinguishable from cultural life. In differing degrees, all of this is now evident in the evangelical world. Since many of its leaders, its organizations, and its magazines are looking the other way, some have noticed nothing untoward; or worse yet, some are actively promoting what will bring the evangelical house tumbling down.

There is, however, a final irony to note. It is this: In the Old and New Testaments, the moments of great impact in the world were never those in which the people of God became indistinguishable from those in their world. When this happened it was a moment of spiritual debauchery. In order to influence the world, the people of God have to be quite *different* from it cognitively and morally. The irony is that to be relevant, the church has to be otherworldly; and when this spiritual otherness is extinguished by the ache for this-worldly acceptance, it loses the thing that it wants above all else—relevance. The church eventually discovers, to its great dismay, that it has lost its voice and no longer has anything left to say. That is the discovery that now seems to be looming ahead of the evangelical world. It is the iceberg that awaits

The Present Evangelical Crisis

the *Titanic* as those on board persuade themselves of their invincibility
and pass the days in partying.

NOTES

1. I have written on culture, modernity, and worldliness on several occasions.
To do so again has taxed my ingenuity, for I am limited as to the number of
new things I can say on these subjects. There are, therefore, some parallels
in this essay with what I have written elsewhere. See *No Place for Truth: Or,
Whatever Happened to Evangelical Theology* (Grand Rapids, MI:
Eerdmans, 1993); *God in the Wasteland: The Reality of Truth in a World
of Fading Dreams* (Grand Rapids, MI: Eerdmans, 1994); *Losing Our Virtue:
Why the Church Must Recover Its Moral Vision* (Grand Rapids, MI:
Eerdmans, 1998).

2. Peter L. Berger, *Facing Up to Modernity: Excursions in Society, Politics, and
Religion* (New York: Basic Books, 1977), p. 173.

3. Martin Marty's project of describing fundamentalism worldwide, and in
many religions, keys on the idea of fighting. Fundamentalists are militants
who fight *back* at their religious and political adversaries, fight *for* their own
worldview, fight *with* the resources that come from their worldview, fight
against outsiders, and fight *under* God. See Martin E. Marty and R. Scott
Appleby, eds. *Fundamentalisms Observed* (Chicago: University of Chicago
Press, 1991), pp. ix-x. Nancy T. Ammerman's essay on Protestant
fundamentalism in that volume (pp. 1-65) is, however, rather more nuanced
than this generic definition suggests.

4. George M. Marsden, *Fundamentalism and American Culture: The Shaping
of Twentieth Century Evangelicalism 1870-1925* (New York: Oxford
University Press, 1980), p. 229.

5. See George M. Marsden, *Understanding Fundamentalism and
Evangelicalism* (Grand Rapids, MI: Eerdmans, 1991), pp. 39-41.

6. Richard Hofstadter developed this theme in his *Anti-intellectualism in
American Life* (New York: Alfred A. Knopf, 1962), although the swath he
cut was wider than simply fundamentalism both in its historical life and in
its doctrinal parameters. More Recently, Mark Noll has spoken of the
"intellectual disaster of fundamentalism." See his *The Scandal of the
Evangelical Mind* (Grand Rapids, MI: Eerdmans, 1994), pp. 109-145.

7. H. Richard Niebuhr describes the essence of the Christ-against-Culture
position as keying in on the idea of *opposition* between Christ and culture:
"Whatever may be the customs of the society in which the Christian lives,
and whatever the human achievements which it conserves, Christ is seen as
opposed to them, so that he confronts them with the challenge of an 'either-
or' decision." (See his *Christ and Culture* [New York: Harper and Row,
1951], p. 40). The essence of the Christ-of Culture position is, of course,
agreement. In these views, "Jesus often appears as a great hero of human
culture history; his life and teachings are regarded as the greatest human
achievement; in him, it is believed, the aspirations of men toward their values

Introduction: The Word in the World

are brought to a point of culmination; he confirms what is best in the past, and guides the process of civilization to its proper goal. Moreover, he is part of culture in the sense that he himself is part of the social heritage that must be transmitted and conserved" (ibid., p. 41).

8. Ibid., p. 87.

9. Stanley Grenz has conceptualized at a formal, theological level what is simply acted upon without thought more popularly in evangelicalism. He has argued that theology has three "sources." Scripture is primary, but to this should be added tradition and culture. This is a remarkable departure from the Reformation's way of thinking. With respect to the third, he says that theologians "have repeatedly looked to the categories of society for the concepts in which to express their understanding of the Christian faith commitment" (see his *Theology for the Community of God* [Nashville: Broadman and Holman, 1994], p. 25). This is, he acknowledges, Tillich's method of "correlation." The issue, of course, is how far and in what ways cultural forms change biblical substance. On this, Grenz is far from clear. In speaking about the Gospel in a postmodern age, for example, he says that it must now become "post-individualistic," "post-rationalistic," "post-dualistic," and "post-noeticentric" (*A Primer on Postmodernism* [Grand Rapids, MI: Eerdmans, 1996], pp. 167-174). Why? What is troubling about Grenz's proposal is that it is not advanced because it is biblically true but because it is culturally plausible. This is what will appeal to postmoderns. Although Grenz is aware of how this has led into liberalism in the past, he appears to be quite unaware, as Millard Erickson notes, of the subjective notion of truth with which he is operating as well as the raw, cultural pragmatism. (See his *The Evangelical Left: Encountering Postconservative Evangelical Theology* [Grand Rapids, MI: Baker, 1997], p. 59.)

AUTHORITY:
THE CHURCH AND THE BIBLE

Edmund P. Clowney

Evangelicals will carry into the twenty-first century a full library of reflection on their twentieth-century experience.[1] Their studies have traced the rise and fall of the tide of liberalism. Early in the twentieth century those who accommodated the Gospel to the rationalism of the Enlightenment gained control of denominational headquarters and educational institutions. Fundamentalism, on the defensive, rightly saw liberal modernism as a rejection of Christianity. A wider group of evangelicals continued to define themselves by that difference. The older liberalism, on the other hand, was undercut when the Enlightenment culture it imitated slipped out from under it. For evangelicals, the turning point was 1976, the year that *Time* magazine dubbed "The Year of the Evangelicals." Some evangelicals then began to justify the unaccustomed respect thrust on them by doing what the liberals had done, gradually accommodating their message to the secular mind-set.

That scenario is at least suggestive, even if oversimplified. The success of evangelicalism is undoubted if measured in the number and growth of its movements and institutions. It is successful, too, in the number of self-described evangelicals, especially when compared with evangelicalism in England.

But is evangelicalism beginning to gain the world by losing its own soul? Is the church becoming the compromised church? What issue or issues will determine our answer to these questions? The evangelical doctrine of the church can no longer be neglected, and its recent development will help us to consider the issues.

Authority: The Church and the Bible

The issue of authority is central for the identity of evangelical witness. To be worthy of its name, evangelicalism must present the Evangel. Gospel proclamation binds evangelicals to the authority of God's revelation in Scripture; we proclaim the Lord of the Word from the Word of the Lord. Further, Scripture tells us of the saving purpose of God, His redemptive plan to claim a people for His own. The Gospel not only calls the church into existence—it announces the church as an essential part of the message. To assess their place and calling in the world, evangelicals must appeal to the standards by which the Lord will judge their service. His standards are necessarily creedal, not in the sense that any historic creed expresses them perfectly, but in the sense that the Lord has told us who He is and what He requires of us.

A quarter of a century ago a conference of evangelical scholars and leaders met for a week at Wenham, Massachusetts, to reconcile different opinions about the inspiration of Scripture. One Continental professor insisted on giving the Holy Spirit "elbow room" in inspiration. There are "bubbles," he said, in the Bible. Others held to the plenary, verbal inspiration of Scripture, maintaining that the Bible, while using ordinary language, is without error. J. I. Packer clarified the question by declaring that our doctrine of Scripture cannot be determined in advance by our own assumptions or by the "pragmatics" of our findings in biblical study. The doctrine of Scripture, like all Christian doctrine, must be derived from the Bible itself.

The question debated at the Wenham conference still remains central for evangelicals. Indeed, it was the question J. Gresham Machen addressed in *Christianity and Liberalism*.[2] Liberals followed Schleiermacher, grounding religion in experience rather than in revealed truth. Machen insisted that liberalism was not Christianity. Experience and truth have also been separated in definitions of evangelicalism. Some see it broadly in terms of Christian piety; others insist on some core agreement on doctrine.[3] D. A. Carson has rightly insisted that Christian doctrine, and especially belief about the Bible, is primary for evangelicals.[4] Indeed, debates over authority and office in the church have shown how our view of the Bible's teaching about its inspiration will affect our interpretation of its text.

No doubt the basic teaching of the Bible about itself needs reiteration more than new development. Evangelicals, however, are in danger of viewing as "fundamentalistic" a view of the Bible that is indeed fundamental to historic Christianity. The International Conference on Biblical Inerrancy sought to counter that error in the ten years of its activities from 1978 to 1987. The error has outlived that decade of effort and has now been heightened by the challenge to the interpretation of the Bible posed by postmodern pluralism. In *The Gagging of God*, Carson has addressed the hermeneutical issue, or as he calls it, "The Hermeneutical Morass."[5] His work is basically apologetic. He accepts the insights of contextual understanding but exposes the inconsistency of relativist claims. He affirms that while the statement "Jesus Christ is Lord" is uttered in a cultural setting, it declares an absolute truth, expressible in every language and culture. Carson grounds his arguments in insights that flow from his own labors as a New Testament scholar. He does not, however, attempt a "full-orbed theology constructed to trace the patterns of redemptive history."[6] While he traces major doctrines in the "plotline" of the Old Testament as well as the New, he does not develop the place of revelation and inspiration in the plotline of biblical theology.

The unfolding of biblical theology focuses on God's revelation of Himself through spoken and written words. Christianity distinctively confesses God, the absolute Person, the personal Absolute.[7] His triune Being is forever in personal fellowship. Jesus, who is God the Son incarnate, reveals divine Personhood to us and claims to have received the words He speaks in eternal fellowship with His Father in heaven (John 8:26, 47). The living God is the speaking God. God the Son in John's Gospel is the Logos, the Word who proceeds from the Father.

Throughout the progressive revelation of the Bible's plotline, God's words spoken to create, to preserve, to deliver are His life-breath, His *ruach*, vocalized. Can dead bones scattered on the valley floor live (Ezek. 37:3)? Yes, for the prophet speaks the word of the Lord's power. God's word of promise is His word of power spoken in the future tense: "I will put enmity . . ." (Gen. 3:15). The enmity is thereby put. God's saving word does not return void but accomplishes His purpose (Isa. 55:11).

Nor does Scripture separate the written Word of God from the spoken Word. God who speaks from Sinai also writes the words of His covenant on the tablets of stone with His own finger (Exod. 31:18; 32:16). The recording of the covenant terms was an essential part of covenant-making.[8] The written book of the covenant became a covenant

Authority: The Church and the Bible

"memorial"; its place was the "Ark of the Witness" that contained the tablets of witness (Deut. 31:2-26).

God's promise of saving blessing shapes the whole history of His covenant. No word of promise is too wonderful or difficult for God (Gen. 18:14; Jer. 32:27; Luke 1:37). The promise must find its fulfillment, the call its answer, the commandment its observance, the final blessing its realization. God's Word cannot be frustrated at last by human unbelief: "Let God be true, and every man a liar" (Rom. 3:4; cf. Ps. 51:4).

The written Scriptures are prophetic oracles inscribed by men who "spoke from God as they were carried along (*pheromenoi*) by the Holy Spirit" (2 Pet. 1:19-21). Quotations from the Old Testament are therefore attributed in the New to the authorship of the Holy Spirit (Acts 1:16; Heb. 3:7; 10:15). The sacred Scriptures are able to make one wise unto salvation because they are "God-breathed" (2 Tim. 3:16, *theopneustos*). The meaning of this term is not so much "inspiration" as "spiration" or "exhalation," as Warfield has shown.[9] The Scriptures as a product are the work of the Spirit.

The ascription of all word-revelation, and especially of all Holy Scripture, to the Spirit does not limit the Spirit to any one method of inspiration. "We are to think of the Spirit's inspiring activity, and, for that matter, of all His regular operations in and upon human personality, as (to use an old but valuable technical term) *concursive*; that is, as exercised in, through and by means of the writers' own activity, in such a way that their thinking and writing was *both* free and spontaneous on their part *and* divinely elicited and controlled, and what they wrote was not only their own work but also God's work."[10]

Studies to show the distinctive perspective and theological emphasis of the writers of the Gospels are necessary and illuminating to show us the richness of their witness. A viewpoint at odds with the claims of Scripture goes beyond this to find contradictory theologies in the New Testament and to read the Gospels as reporting on views in later church circles rather than testimonies to the historical Jesus, the Christ.

The structure of the divine plan in Scripture is realized in Christ who is the Son of the promise, called, chosen, and beloved. He fulfills by word and deed the whole of the covenant promise and commandment and receives the full measure of the covenant blessing (Gal. 3:16, 29; Luke 9:35; 2 Cor. 1:19-20). Through Him, the Word of God is fulfilled in the

The Present Evangelical Crisis

church, the people of the new covenant (Gal. 3:29; 4:28; Heb. 11:39-40). This is the Word that is "living and active [and] sharper than any double-edged sword" (Heb. 4:12).

Jesus claims that the Scriptures testify of Him. More than that, He understands Himself and His mission as the fulfillment of the Old Testament. If His enemies believed the writings of Moses, they would believe Him, for Moses wrote of Him (John 5:46ff.). Jesus declared that Scripture cannot be broken, that the smallest letter or touch of the pen that distinguishes a letter cannot pass until all is fulfilled (Matt. 5:18). Jesus went to the cross to fulfill Scripture and cried, "I am thirsty" not merely from His agony, but that Scripture might be fulfilled (John 19:28).

That Jesus regarded the Old Testament as the promise of His own messianic calling is evident, but it is the implication that some resist. If Jesus was indeed wrong about the Bible, He was wrong about who He was and what He came to do. So, too, were His followers, who wrote the New Testament. All the efforts to create a Jesus different than the One to whom the Scriptures bear witness will continue to fail. Not the Gospel of Thomas with its gnostic Christ, but the canonical Gospels provide the truth about Jesus, and the church has bowed before that witness.

Study of the New Testament continues to show how the convictions of the church about Jesus were deepened by inspired reflection on the Old Testament. After His resurrection, Jesus opened the minds of His disciples to understand the Scriptures. They had the key to the Old Testament Scriptures as they testified to the things that Jesus had done and said during His earthly ministry. Where the Greek Old Testament read, "Sanctify the Lord Himself" (Isa. 8:6ff.), Peter, quoting the passage, wrote, "In your hearts set apart Christ as Lord" (1 Pet. 3:14-15). The Lord of the Old Testament was now revealed as the Lord of the New, Jesus the Christ.

Those who led the New Covenant people of God into the understanding of the person and work of Christ were the apostles and the prophets associated with them. Jesus chose twelve apostles to be with Him and to be witnesses to His deeds and words. As apostles, they were "sent ones" commissioned to carry the Gospel to the nations, just as they had been sent to the villages of Israel during Jesus' ministry.

They were also foundation stones for the new form of the people of God. When Peter confessed Jesus to be the Christ, the Son of the living God, Jesus declared that he spoke by revelation from his Father in heaven.

Authority: The Church and the Bible

In turn, Jesus declared Peter to be Cephas, the "Rock" upon whom He would build His church. Jesus gave the same authority of the keys to the other disciples (Matt. 18:18). The apostles had authority as recipients of revelation (Eph. 3:7-13; Gal. 2:8-9; Rom. 1:1-6). Luke describes Peter's claim to be one of the chosen eyewitnesses of Christ's resurrection, one who ate and drank with Him after He rose from the dead and was then commissioned to preach Christ (Acts 10:41ff.). In the Book of Revelation, the names of the twelve apostles are written on the twelve foundations of the New Jerusalem (Rev. 21:14).

Paul wrote to defend his apostolic status against the claims of the "super-apostles" who challenged his authority (1 Cor. 9:1-2; 2 Cor. 10—11). His claim rests upon his unique calling, not from men, but from the risen Lord who appeared to him on the Damascus Road (Gal. 1:1; 1 Cor. 9:1; 15:8). While he is the least of the apostles, since he had persecuted the church of God, he is also the last of the apostles, for by the grace of God, the revelations granted to him as the apostle to the Gentiles put the capstone on the revelation of the New Covenant in Christ.[11]

Because of his apostolic authority, Paul could order the affairs of the churches. He required the discipline, in a formal church meeting, of a man guilty of incest, as though he were himself present (1 Cor. 5:3-5). He instructed the church in legal actions (ch. 6), in marriage (ch. 7), in matters of conscience (ch. 8), in spiritual gifts and worship (chs. 12—14), as well as in the conduct of his own ministry (chs. 1-4). Some thought him weak, but he could come with the rod of spiritual power (1 Cor. 4:21). If anyone thinks himself spiritually gifted, let him acknowledge that what Paul writes is the Lord's command: "If he ignores this, he himself will be ignored" (1 Cor. 14:38). Paul, who worked with his own hands to support his team at Corinth and revisited Lystra after being stoned there, is a steward of God's revelation (1 Cor. 4:1).

The church is apostolic, for it is founded on the teaching authority of the apostles. Yet the apostles serve the Lord. He alone is the Ruler of the church. The offices of the Old Testament all foreshadow dimensions of the full Lordship of Jesus Christ: a Prophet like Moses, a Priest like Melchizedek; a King like David. Jesus comes as Servant, fulfilling His people's side of the covenant, but He also comes as the Lord Himself, Immanuel.

Since all things are from Him and for Him, and all things hold

The Present Evangelical Crisis

together by His power, He is like no other, the One through whom the whole cosmos will be renewed and who rules over all things for the sake of His body, the church.

As the book of Acts makes particularly clear, Christ's rule over the church and for the church is not that of a titular monarch who has ceded the control of His Kingdom to others. Jesus Christ actively governs all things. When Herod Agrippa persecuted the church, Christ's judgment struck him down in the midst of his blasphemous acceptance of deification (Acts 12:20-23). The Lord Jesus who controls the nations also rules His church as its Head, governing it by His Word and Spirit. In Acts the growth of the church is described as the growth of the Word under the direction of the Spirit. The Word is the Word of Christ, in particular the Old Testament promise of Christ proclaimed in the light of the fulfillment, as we see from apostolic preaching in Acts (cf. 1 Pet. 1:11). The Spirit, given at Pentecost, is the promise of the Father and the enthronement gift of the Messiah. The Spirit guides the church in the spread of the Gospel. The Spirit and the Word of Christ are therefore never in tension (John 6:63).

Christ orders the life of His church by His authority. His yoke is easy, for His rule is perfect freedom, peace in the Father's will. His Spirit possesses the church, not less radically than demon possession, but more so. Demonic control depersonalizes, but the Spirit's possession restores and renews personality in Christ (Luke 8:30, 39). He sets us in His new community of families and the family of the church.

As the Spirit of Christ possesses us, He seals God's ownership of us. On the other hand, the Spirit is given to us as our possession. He is the foretaste of glory, for in Him we have already the supreme blessing of glory, the immediate presence of the Lord Himself. It is the presence of the Lord in the midst that constitutes the church and unites our gatherings here with the festival assembly in glory (Heb. 12:18-29). Individually and corporately, the Spirit unites us to Christ. The order that Christ provides for His church is a holy, spiritual order. Without the work of the Spirit, the order of church organization becomes meaningless or oppressive. It is designed for those who have tasted God's saving grace and enjoy common life in Christ. When men claim divine authority in the name of ecclesiastical organization, they destroy the freedom of the Spirit and bring in the worst form of tyranny—binding the conscience with the ordi-

Authority: The Church and the Bible

nances of men, subjecting the realm of the Spirit to the government of the flesh.

For this reason, too, the rule of Christ in the church cannot be defined within sociological structures that lack categories for the work of the Spirit. The church is not a democracy or a republic, nor does it offer an awkward form of government by committee. Church sessions or councils are not business boards, nor are senior pastors chief executive officers. Whatever the outward arrangements may resemble, the dynamic life of the church is the work of the Spirit from whom all the gifts come.

In the Old Covenant the people of God were formed as a family, then as a nation, but always in ways that were distinctive. God altered family customs, chose younger sons, and disrupted the family planning of weak faith (Gen. 17:18). So, too, when Israel was made a nation, God gave His peculiar people distinctive laws, a sabbatical system, and, at first, no earthly king.

In the New Covenant the church as the community of the Spirit of Christ is even more distinctive. The temptation remains to conform the church to the structures of the environment. Stanley Hauerwas, in *After Christendom?*, traces the greatest problems of the church today to the time when the church was given imperial recognition by the Roman emperor Constantine and then became the official religion of the Empire.[12] The smothering effect of that official embrace can still be seen in the state churches of Europe. In the United States, however, a different accommodation has taken place. Nathan O. Hatch has described "Evangelicalism as a Democratic Movement" and traced the development of its character back to Revolutionary times.[13] It is the democratic organization of the American churches, he argues, that accounts for their growth, as compared to the churches of Europe.

Among contemporary challenges to scriptural church order, the first, and strongest, is the American focus on individualism. The church is not seen as the body of Christ or the spiritual community of His people but as a religious club of individual Christians. The Gospel is a message for the salvation of souls but has nothing to say about ecclesiastical authority. This position is explicit in the Calvary Chapel churches in California, which have no church membership. Individualism is the unwritten assumption in most evangelical churches. In part, this is the consequence of urbanization and the splintering of denominations. Free to attend the

The Present Evangelical Crisis

church of their choice, individuals choose when and where to go. Any whiff of church discipline signals rapid departure to some other congregation where the newcomer is welcomed (no questions asked about former commitments). Brand loyalty is often stronger within parachurch organizations.

Individualism also marks religion with the modernity that grew out of the Enlightenment. It has become an axiom of American political thought that a multicultural democracy respects all religious opinions so long as they are privately held.

Recognizing American individualism, and assuming that evangelism and Christian nurture don't mix,[14] the church growth movement has redesigned Sunday morning gatherings to attract non-Christians. Unfortunately, individuals reached by the Sunday celebration show little inclination to attend a midweek service designed for participative community worship.

Individualism has also undermined the unity of the church. Denominations and sects keep multiplying. Paul's question to those at Corinth who followed him in preference to Peter or Apollos goes unanswered: "Is Christ divided? Was Paul crucified for you?" (1 Cor. 1:13). He demands that those whose hope of salvation is in their union with Christ on the cross must recognize their union with all others for whom Christ died (Eph. 4:2-6). Must it be through severe persecution that evangelicals will take seriously the apostle's words?

Separation in the church also appears in the complete independency of most evangelical churches. While some Baptist churches express their unity in denominational association, evangelical churches, whether congregational or connectional, usually operate as functionally independent. Significantly, the National Association of Evangelicals is by title a parachurch organization of individuals, although it does admit denominations to membership.

The holiness of the church stands also in peril in the contemporary evangelical church. Preaching may be moralistic, replete with suggestions for better marriages and reducing the stress of the workplace, but lacks the devotional depth of union with Christ as the source of grace and motivation for holy living. The place of Christian fellowship in reproving and rebuking one another has been recognized in small-group structures and in men's movements such as the Washington Christian Fellowship and

Promise Keepers, but formal church discipline continues to be neglected. Without effective church discipline, the clear difference in lifestyle between the church and the world will never be apparent.

Individualism also fuels resistance to the catholicity of the church among evangelicals. Evangelical interest in world missions has been met by a new era as the peoples of the world come to live in the United States. Urban evangelical churches have gained in multicultural membership. Yet individualism can also be racist. If I can attend the church of my choice with no thought of the people in my neighborhood, then I am likely, consciously or unconsciously, to seek out a church where I will feel at home among people most like myself.

The remedy to unbiblical individualism, however, is not communitarianism or socialism, making the community or society supreme. God joins His people to Himself not just corporately, but also individually. The seal of our union with Christ is the Holy Spirit, and both individuals and the church are temples of God's Spirit (1 Cor. 3:16-17; 6:17-20). Jesus called disciples individually, by name. The crowds who were added to the early church were believers (Acts 5:14). Paul greets Christians "whose names are in the book of life" (Phil. 4:3). Paul's use of the figure of the body of Christ emphasizes individuality of gifts as well as the harmonious way in which they are to function (1 Cor. 12). The body figure beautifully joins the individual to the community.

A number of recent books about the church have reacted strongly against evangelical individualism.[15] Rodney Clapp inveighs against an American Christianity that can "profess with a straight face that God exists to meet my needs."[16] For the privatized Christian, "'Spirituality' is an amorphous, ever mutable engagement between two isolated selves—the human individual and 'God,' both apart from the world, change, time, place and community." Clapp writes as a "plebeian, postmodern Christian."[17] He presents the church as a way of life together and quotes with approval the statement of Bruce Marshall "that the church's participation in God's life happens 'not primarily in the minds and hearts of individuals . . . but in the public eucharistic celebration by which Christ joins individuals to himself and so makes them his own community.'"[18] He deplores the civil religion that has made the nation-state the public, historical life of people's faith. "We do not so need a nation-state, because we already have the church." He takes Charles Colson to task because

Colson "cannot countenance the primacy of social formation in the building of character." Colson was arguing that government programs can't make people moral: "They can punish behavior; they cannot transform hearts."[19] Clapp sees Colson as embracing the liberal individualizing of religion and ignoring the role of the church as community in forming character.

Clapp also concludes that the Reformation was handicapped by the inventing of printing, since that opened the door to use of the Bible in private rather than in the social context of the church.

While Clapp loses balance in his advocacy of the community over the individual, he should be credited with revealing the depth of our own commitment to the individualism of modernity. Yet his final vision of life, sailing in the community boat, seems to leave too much at sea.[20] As a postmodern, he rejects the rationalistic grounding of thought in undeniable postulates ("foundationalism"). As culturally conditioned, we cannot lay claim to absolute truth but assert that there must be a God for Christianity to be true.[21] This is not said for the sake of the argument, but as an epistemological statement. Reformed epistemology is not locked in to foundationalism either, but finds a better way by insisting on presuppositions that begin with God's own existence. These are presupposed, not to support Christianity as one community of faith, but to ground all reason and created existence.

D. A. Carson sees a drawing together in evangelical apologetics between presuppositionalists and evidentialists and favors the presuppositional view of John Frame (a view that roots in Cornelius Van Til and his development of Christian philosophy in the Netherlands).[22] A Christian, whether postmodern or not, may well dissent from the rationalism of Rene Descartes who sought to prove the existence of God from the self-evident proposition *cogito, ergo sum*. But to reject foundationalism without finding an alternative in the divine establishment of revealed truth only substitutes for the liberal relativism of "truth for me" a postmodern relativism of "truth for my community." Because no community has access to absolute truth, Clapp says that the choice is to become either sectarian or syncretist.[23] Of the two, he chooses, as Christians must, the holistic sectarian community rather than the compartmentalized eclectic life of the polytheistic paganism.[24] But Clapp urges that while the Christian community remains a sect, it need not be a narrow one. Much is to be learned from other communities, and the Christian sect develops through time, as it struggles in and with changing cultures. As the earliest Quakers said, "We want you to follow the Spirit, which we have sought to follow, but which must be sought anew in every generation."[25]

Truth is indeed not detached but participative, as Clapp says;[26] but the participation that grasps truth is not first our participation with one another, but with the Spirit of God. Clapp says, "If I ever reject Christianity as my root narrative, it will be because I have learned enough of another narrative or code to find Christianity wanting."[27] On the other hand, he also says that we must strive "to check all other stories by the story of Israel and Jesus Christ, to live by a hierarchy of codes that always sees the Christian code as most relevant and, indeed, as uniquely and finally true."[28] He is willing to continue using the masculine pronoun for God, since he is certain "that the God of Israel and Jesus Christ is narratively (and so quite specifically) identified, so that the unsurpassable and irreplaceable name of the Christian God is Father, Son and Holy Spirit."[29]

Clapp's continuing use of "narrative" as a qualifier binds the community to its "story" and avoids the suggestion that the Bible could be a storehouse of truth, especially truth as propositionally expressed. To be sure, the words of Scripture are understood in their total context. There is a narrative, or even "metanarrative," of the unfolding of God's plan from creation to consummation.[30] But when God speaks His own name from the burning bush or from Sinai, His authority to name Himself is not drawn from His revelation; it constitutes it. Clapp sincerely professes devotion to the Triune God, but the epistemology he has developed loosens the authority of Scripture to the thrust of a story, and thereby also questions the specific authority of the King of the church as expressed in His Word.

Certainly one of the most substantial and provocative recent works on ecclesiology is *What On Earth Is the Church?* by Kevin Giles.[31] R. T. France, in his "Foreword," again identifies individualism as a great threat to evangelicalism and commends the book for tackling it "head-on."

Giles shows through New Testament scholarship (combined with commitment to his thesis) that "community" is the master New Testament term for the church. Like Clapp, he emphasizes the social definition of the church; he does so by examining the whole New Testament with the question in view. He sees hierarchical structure in the church as traceable back to Plato's *Timaeus*, institutionalized in the medieval church, and not adequately rejected in the Reformation.[32] In the New Testament he finds varying views of the church. The community he finds is one in transition. While he does not accept the details of Ernst Kasemann's lecture to the 1963 Montreal conference on Faith and Order, he responds favorably to Kasemann's view that the New Testament does not present a unified understanding of the church, but "a number of ecclesiological archetypes: and an incessant process of change."[33] He believes that the "old dogmatism" that established every doctrine of importance with a proof-text from Scripture must be abandoned, but says that there do appear "major themes and ideas that bind together the parts."[34]

Well, not all the parts, for in the Pastorals he finds a different perspective from anything earlier. The dynamic is replaced by the institutional; charismatic ministry is not mentioned; "women are to accept the authority of men and not teach in the church; the freedoms given to women in the earlier Paulines are cancelled; and 'sound teaching' and preserving the truth are the responsibilities of leaders. A struggle to see how the gospel applies to new situations is not in evidence." Instead, the church is "described as an unshakeable, stately edifice and bearer of 'the truth.'"[35] Giles says: "Whether we applaud these developments or abhor them is of no significance." This is how the churches "in Pauline circles" developed, and how the Gospel was preserved.

Yet Giles wants to curb somewhat the declarations of the Pastorals. The argument of 1 Timothy 2:13-14, he says, is *ad hominem* and cannot be taken as a continuing law for the church.[36] The Pastorals present human relations as they do only because they want to endorse the general norms of their society. People are to accept the stations their culture accords them. The real message of the Pastorals is that the church must not hinder the Gospel by being out of step with the general ordering of society.[37] Giles does not fully explore what that would mean today—in Australia or the United States!

He is sure that the fellowship that constitutes the church is egalitarian and democratic. Nevertheless, in his study of Ephesians 5:21-33, he does not try to explain away Christ's headship. He denies that "head" here means "source." Instead, he agrees that Paul is saying that the wife should be in subjection to her husband as the church is to Christ (v. 24).

Authority: The Church and the Bible

Had Paul stopped there, he says, the total submission of the wife to her husband would have been as "binding and demanding as the worst of patriarchalism."[38] But Paul did not stop there, and Giles provides a beautiful description of what Paul requires of husbands, modeled upon Christ's love for the church.

Giles, however, supports his conviction about the egalitarianism of the church by citing arguments taken from the doctrine of the Trinity. He features an argument taken from the doctrine of "perichoresis." He defines this as the residing of each person of the Trinity in the others, so that what one person of the Trinity does, the other does.[39] He cites the Athanasian creed: all the persons of the Trinity are "co-equal," "none is afore, or after other: none is greater, or less than another."[40] The differences of the persons in the Trinity are not hierarchical but are distinctions constituted by differing relations, which he likens to male and female differences in humanity.

The doctrine of the Trinity continues to be debated.[41] Does perichoresis deny the eternal generation of the Father by the Son? In any case, scriptural revelation has been formulated in the doctrine of the economic Trinity that defines different roles for the coequal persons of the Trinity in the work of salvation. It is role difference that distinguishes men and women as they serve the Lord in the family and the church. That is the distinction Paul supports from the account of creation (1 Tim. 2:15; cf. 5:14; Gen. 2:7, 22; 1 Cor. 11:8-12). Further, we cannot derive directly from the doctrine of the ontological Trinity what ordering of male/female relations God has ordained for the church in this time between the times. The church already participates in the Spirit and in the foretaste of the life to come, but still awaits the consummation glory. We are all, men and women, sons of God in Christ Jesus (Gal. 3:26), for in union with Christ, all those things that divide us and separate us from one another are transcended (Gal. 3:28).

Yet the full expression of this reality differs. Paul teaches that in Christ Gentiles are Abraham's seed, heirs of the promises given to Abraham (Gal. 3:29). They are no more Gentiles, but the Israel of God. He also teaches that union in Christ makes masters and slaves brothers (Philem. 16). The structure of slavery is subverted when the slave serves his master as he would serve Christ (Eph. 6:7) and when the master serves his Master in heaven as he cares for his slave (Eph. 6:9). Slavery is not a

The Present Evangelical Crisis

creation ordinance, but the outcome of human sin. But in the case of man and woman, the sexual difference that is transcended in Christ remains until the resurrection, when we will be like the angels in heaven, and marriage will be surpassed. Marriage, contrary to many Christian sects, is not transcended in this life, though, as Paul teaches, its abuse in male oppression is removed.

There is some analogy here with the way the sting of slavery is removed in Christ, since neither institution is attacked. But the differences are far greater than the likeness. Since marriage itself is a major image of the relation of the Lord to His people, it is in no way seen as an evil to be undermined. Rather, the relationship of marriage is transformed by the analogy that emphasizes its permanence. The duties of the husband, well explained by Giles,[42] make the husband's role as the head of the wife unlike anything advocated apart from the Gospel. Yet Giles adds a sentence that summarizes the difference in his approach to this Scripture: "Paul has subtly sought to transform the marriage relationship in his own historical situation, and in doing so set a trajectory that would culminate in the modern partnership model of marriage."[43]

These words set before us the issue for evangelicals. Will we accept in Scripture that which our age will accept and put what doesn't meet its norms on a developmental trajectory that lands us when we are accepted? Or will apostolic teaching transform our minds and our practice? Paul is surely doing more than subtly suggesting a better way than he dare articulate, given his cultural milieu. He is affirming a transformed order that gives new meaning to a husband's headship. Yet the responsibilities of the new headship are part of the transformation. Not in the order of the family, nor in the church as the family of God are we yet in resurrection glory. We need to interpret Scripture in its cultural context, but not to forget its revelatory context, written for us upon whom "the fulfillment of the ages has come" (1 Cor. 10:11). Jesus Christ, the final Word of God, has spoken. The salvation that was "first announced by the Lord, was confirmed to us by those who heard him" (Heb. 2:3). "We must pay more careful attention, therefore, to what we have heard, so that we do not drift away" (Heb. 2:1).

The issues for ecclesiology, whether of the individual and the community, of male and female, or of truth for the post-modern mind, are all transformed in Christ under His authority, His revealed Word, illumined by His Spirit. He is Lord and governs His Church by His Word and Spirit.

NOTES

1. Rather than providing a long bibliography, it may be sufficient to name some of the authors, or editors of compilations: John H. Armstrong, David W. Bebbington, Donald G. Bloesch, Charles Colson, Michael Cromartie, Donald W. Dayton, Carl F. George, Os Guinness, D. G. Hart, Stanley Hauerwas, Michael Scott Horton, James Davison Hunter, Robert K. Johnston, George Marsden, Alister McGrath, Mark A. Noll, Richard John Neuhaus, Lesslie Newbigin, Bruce and Marshall Shelley, David F. Wells.

2. J. Gresham Machen, *Christianity and Liberalism* (Grand Rapids, MI: Eerdmans, 1923).

3. Note the citation of Douglas A. Sweeney in D. A. Carson, *The Gagging of God: Christianity Confronts Pluralism* (Grand Rapids, MI: Zondervan, 1996), p. 453.

4. Carson, *The Gagging of God*, pp. 444-461. Carson presents the authority of the Bible as the formal principle of evangelicalism, and the message of the Gospel as the material position. He shows the difficulties of maintaining that clear position as doctrinal conviction ebbs.

5. Ibid., chaps. 2—3.

6. Ibid., p. 242.

7. Ibid., p. 224, citing and discussing John Frame, *Apologetics to the Glory of God* (Phillipsburg, NJ: Presbyterian & Reformed, 1994), p. 38.

8. See Meredith G. Kline, "The Two Tables of the Covenant," *The Westminster Theological Journal*, 1960, 22:133-146.

9. B. B. Warfield, "God-Inspired Scripture," in *The Inspiration and Authority of the Bible*, ed. S. G. Craig (Philadelphia: Presbyterian & Reformed, 1948), p. 277ff.

10. James I. Packer, *'Fundamentalism' and the Word of God* (Grand Rapids, MI: Eerdmans, 1959), p. 80.

11. Peter R. Jones, "1 Corinthians 15:8: Paul the Last Apostle," *Tyndale Bulletin*, 36, 1985, pp. 3-34.

12. Stanley Hauerwas, *After Christendom? How the Church Is to Behave If Freedom, Justice, and a Christian Nation Are Bad Ideas* (Nashville: Abingdon, 1991).

13. George Marsden, ed., *Evangelicalism and Modern America* (Grand Rapids, MI: Eerdmans, 1986, repr.), pp. 71-82. See also two essays by Hatch in Darryl G. Hart, ed., *Reckoning with the Past* (Grand Rapids, MI: Baker, 1995), "The Origins of Civil Millennialism in America," pp. 85-107 and "The Christian Movement and the Demand for a Theology of the People," pp. 154-179.

The Present Evangelical Crisis

14. Dr. Timothy Keller challenges this assumption at Redeemer Presbyterian Church in Manhattan.

15. The fellowship of the church as the people of God is also emphasized in other books on ecclesiology. Everett Ferguson, *The Church of Christ: A Biblical Ecclesiology for Today* (Grand Rapids, MI: Eerdmans, 1996) writes systematic theology based on the unity of canonical revelation (pp. xiv-xv). See also David L. Smith, *All God's People: A Theology of the Church* (Wheaton, IL: Victor Books, 1996). My own book presents an evangelical theology of the church from a Reformed perspective: *The Church* in *Contours of Christian Theology* (Downers Grove, IL: InterVarsity Press, 1995). I have limited my remarks to two chosen for their importance and for the definitive issue facing evangelicals.

16. Rodney Clapp, *A Peculiar People: The Church As Culture in a Post-Christian Society* (Downers Grove, IL: InterVarsity Press, 1996), p. 36.

17. Ibid., p. 12. By "plebian" he indicates his alignment with Anabaptist theology and social ethics (although he is a member of an Episcopal church). By "postmodern" he means that he does not appeal to universally self-evident truths as a base for thought (foundationalism). In this he might appear to agree with Richard Rorty and other deconstructionists. Yet he rejects Richard Rorty's liberal view of religion as private. Clapp is "*in that sense* profoundly antiliberal" (p. 219).

18. Ibid., p. 56ff.

19. Quoted on p. 69. The Clapp quote is on p. 70.

20. Ibid., pp. 181-182.

21. "Nothing else, even if supposedly 'universally' available and self-evident, can be more basic than this: For Christianity to be true, there must be a God who engages people in their history." Clapp, *A Peculiar People*, p. 182.

22. For discussion of Reformed presuppositionalism, see Richard R. Topping, "The Anti-Foundationalist Challenge to Evangelical Apologetics," *Evangelical Quarterly*, 1991, 63:1, pp. 45-60; John Frame, "The New Reformed Epistemology," Appendix 1 in *The Doctrine of the Knowledge of God* (Phillipsburg, NJ: Presbyterian & Reformed, 1987), pp. 382-400; and Carson, *The Gagging of God*, chaps. 3-4, pp. 93-191.

23. Clapp, *A Peculiar People*, pp. 145-146.

24. Ibid., p. 146.

25. Ibid., p. 156. He quotes from the epigraph to Eberhard Arnold's, *Why We Live in Community* (Farmington, PA: Plough Publishing House, 1995).

26. Clapp, *A Peculiar People*, p. 186.

27. Ibid., p. 182.

28. Ibid., p. 180.

29. Ibid., p. 214, n. 11.

30. See Carson, *The Gagging of God*, p. 191, where he defines the "jargon" term "metanarrative" as applied to the Bible: "a comprehensive 'story' that

Authority: The Church and the Bible

provides the framework for a comprehensive explanation, a comprehensive worldview." He then proceeds in two chapters to consider movements in the plotline of the Bible and relates them to religious pluralism.

31. Kevin Giles, *What On Earth Is the Church?: An Exploration in New Testament Theology* (Downers Grove, IL: InterVarsity Press, 1995).

32. Ibid., p. 215.

33. Ibid., p. 183.

34. Ibid.

35. Ibid., p. 148.

36. Ibid., p. 151.

37. Ibid.

38. Ibid., p. 143.

39. Ibid., p. 226.

40. Ibid., p. 227.

41. For the doctrine, see Wayne Grudem, *Systematic Theology: An Introduction to Biblical Doctrine* (Leicester: Inter-Varsity Press; Grand Rapids, MI: Zondervan, 1994), pp. 248-261.

42. Giles, *What On Earth Is the Church?*, pp. 143-144.

43. Ibid., p. 144.

2

EVANGELICALS LOSING THEIR WAY: THE DOCTRINE OF THE TRINITY

Gerald Bray

There is no theological theme that has made a greater impact in the twentieth century than the doctrine of the Trinity. If we could go back in time to about 1900, we would realize that although the mainline churches all professed belief in the "One in Three and Three in One," few if any gave it much prominence. A couple of centuries earlier there had been considerable controversy over unitarianism, and orthodox writers had done their best to combat that heresy. But it has to be said that their efforts, successful though they were, smacked more of defensiveness than they did of creativity. Men like Charles Hodge, for example, were generally content to repeat the standard arguments, most of them inherited from Augustine, without engaging the issue any further. That may have been enough to ward off the unitarians, but it did little or nothing to inspire evangelical Christians with a deep sense of the importance of trinitarian thinking. In particular, there was no revival of Trinitarianism connected with the Great Awakening of the eighteenth century, with the result that although the doctrine has been maintained by evangelicals, it has not played a very central part in their thinking.

THE TRINITY AND RECENT THEOLOGICAL DEVELOPMENTS

For most of the nineteenth and early twentieth centuries, conservative Reformed dogmatics tended to follow this general pattern. Perhaps the most notable exception was Benjamin Warfield, who wrote a stimulating article in which he demonstrated that Calvin's doctrine of the Trinity represented a considerable advance on that of Augustine; but the promise that this held out for a new departure in evangelical theology never seems to have gone any farther than that. Even today, it has to be said that theologians in the Reformed tradition have scarcely managed to take Warfield's arguments on board, let alone develop them in any serious way. Evangelicals who are not in the Reformed tradition are even less well off; as far as one can see, most of them have hardly given the subject a moment's thought. Certainly there is no literature on the Trinity emanating from these circles that could even begin to compare with the vast tomes on dispensationalism, for instance, or on spiritual gifts.

All this stands in sharp contrast to what has been happening elsewhere in the Christian world. In continental Europe, the Reformed tradition was shaken to its foundations by the writings of Karl Barth (1886-1968), which made their initial impact in the years between the two world wars. Barth almost single-handedly rescued the doctrine of the Trinity from the neglect it had suffered since the time of Friedrich Schleiermacher (1768-1834), who had reduced it to an appendix of his dogmatics, and this rehabilitation set the tone for a new generation. Today we have the many trinitarian writings of Jürgen Moltmann, to name the most prominent German theologian in this field, as well as those of British theologians such as Colin Gunton, Thomas Torrance, and his nephew Alan Torrance, all of whom have made important contributions to the subject in recent years.

When we move beyond the confines of Reformed theology, we find that Roman Catholics have been scarcely less active. Slightly later in time than Barth, but to some extent following his lead, we have the thought of Hans Urs von Balthasar, Karl Rahner, and Bernard Lonergan, all of whom have produced major works on the Trinity. More recently, the writings of Yves Congar and Jean Galot have explored new avenues in trinitarian thought, though their writings remain largely ignored in the English-speaking world. Further afield still, there has been the remarkable revival of Eastern Orthodoxy, represented by theologians such as Vladimir Lossky, Dumitru Staniloae, and John Zizioulas. The last of these has produced a seminal work called *Being in Communion*, which develops a complete trinitarian ecclesiology from an Orthodox point of view and which has had considerable impact on the work of Colin Gunton and the Torrances.

The Present Evangelical Crisis

THE TRINITY IN THE EVANGELICAL WORLD

With all this going on, it is surprising that the evangelical world has been so little affected. Partly, of course, this is because we have few major theologians in our midst, and theology is given a low priority in most of our churches. The decline of the old Princeton tradition into arid scholasticism, and the tendency that some evangelicals have to sniff out "heresy" every time somebody comes up with a new idea, must be at least partly responsible for this attitude, because nobody is going to risk his career at an evangelical institution by advancing theories that may be incomprehensible to the self-appointed watchdogs on the board of trustees and/or in the local church. This is unfortunate, but it is understandable, particularly when we consider that some of the few evangelicals who have dared to do this have revealed their own lack of theological sophistication in the process by falling into the crassest forms of liberalism, producing results that can only justify the behavior of the watchdogs concerned.

But alongside the decline of theology as a serious discipline among evangelicals, there is also the extraordinary rise of several other phenomena that together have conspired to remove the doctrine of the Trinity from our midst. First of all, there is the great weight that is now placed on biblical studies, including so-called "Biblical theology," to the exclusion of traditional systematics. In contrast to the latter, biblical theology tries to remain within the parameters of the biblical writers, and because the word *Trinity* is nowhere to be found in the sacred text, that doctrine cannot receive the kind of treatment that one would expect it to be given in a systematic approach. It may not be "unbiblical" exactly, but there is no extended discussion of it in the New Testament in the way that there are expositions of the covenant, for instance, or of justification by faith. As a result, those kinds of doctrines claim center stage, and the Trinity is regarded as a doctrine that evolved in the early church as an attempt to make sense of Scripture rather than a teaching that is clearly stated in the New Testament itself.

Second, there has been an enormous concentration among evangelicals on evangelism. This has produced striking results, as the remarkable growth of evangelical churches can attest, but often this has been at the price of theological oversimplification. The message is that it is so easy to

Evangelicals Losing Their Way: The Doctrine of the Trinity

become a Christian: all you have to do is respond to the altar call and give your life to Jesus. Once that happens, you are enrolled in the club, and nothing else really matters. Doctrine appears to be a diversion for intellectuals and is potentially dangerous, because people who discuss ideas tend to fall out with one another over things that nobody else can understand. If you are trying to raise hundreds of thousands of dollars for a project and organize a dozen evangelistic enterprises at the same time, the last thing you need is a split over metaphysics. So the best thing to do is to avoid it and get on with what "really matters."

Third, there has been a great increase of what can broadly be called "charismatic" worship and practice in evangelical circles, which has tended to dull people's interest in intellectual matters, including anything to do with Christian doctrine. The charismatic movement is hard to pin down precisely, and it means different things to different people, but there is no mistaking a charismatic when you meet one. Evangelicals who have been nurtured on a religion of emotion and experience are particularly susceptible to this way of thinking, because the charismatic impulse offers a semipermanent spiritual high that takes them back to the moment when they were first saved. It can even claim to be profoundly trinitarian, in the sense that it emphasizes the work of the Holy Spirit, whose divinity and active work in the world must be its most fundamental teachings. Nevertheless, the overall effect is to stress practice over principles, with the result that in some circles "being filled with the Spirit" may now mean barking uncontrollably like a dog (as in the so-called "Toronto blessing") and has little, if anything, to do with any kind of biblical faith.

In this atmosphere, proponents of a renewed trinitarian theology are likely to be seriously misunderstood, if not completely ignored. For example, to say to a charismatic that being filled with the Spirit means becoming more like Jesus might lead him to conclude that God wants him to walk on water or to begin a faith healing ministry. After all, is not that what Jesus did, and did it not glorify the Father? The entire emphasis will be on acquiring some new experience or "gift," regardless of what this has to do with the rest of the Christian life. This complete absence of any theological framework is the main difficulty we have to face. The doctrine of the Trinity is nothing if it is not a structure of belief that is designed to make sense of our spiritual experience; if there is no felt need for such a structure, the doctrine will probably go by the board.

What If We had No Doctrine of the Trinity?

It may be easier to understand how important a trinitarian structure is for a well-rounded Christian faith if we try to think what it would look like if there were no doctrine of the Trinity at all. What would happen, for example, if we had only God the Father? Such a doctrine might bring us closer to Judaism and even to Islam, though it should be noted that neither of those monotheistic religions is accustomed to using the word *Father* with reference to God. In Christian terms it would make us neo-Arians, at least to the extent that we would not have a divine Savior. Jesus, however wonderful He might be in other respects, would not be God, and He would therefore be unable to pay the price for our sins. Even if He were somehow sinless Himself (as a mere human being), He would have no authority or power to take your sins and mine upon Him. In the Christian scheme of things, Christ's divinity is not an added extra that complicates matters unnecessarily; it is an essential ingredient of His saving work.

Similarly, without a divine Holy Spirit, God would not be dwelling in our hearts, and we would have no direct access to the Father. This would probably produce a religion in which God was a remote Judge with little rapport or relationship with His people. This tendency can be observed in certain strands of eighteenth-century Calvinism, which appear to have developed the notion of a distant God along what were almost deistic lines. In the end, this gave rise to such heresies as Christian Science and the Jehovah's Witnesses, who perhaps give us some idea of what a non-trinitarian evangelicalism would look like.

On the other hand, if all we had was the Son, our faith would be a Jesus cult without any supernatural dimension. Christianity would become a kind of Buddhism, in which we would follow the teachings of an enlightened leader and hope that these might eventually lead us to peace of mind in some eternal state of nonbeing. Without the Father or the Holy Spirit, a Jesus religion could hardly be anything more than an ethical code. This may sound unattractive to believers, but in fact it is what large numbers of people think Christianity is. "My religion is the Sermon on the Mount," they say, by which they mean that they do what they can, they keep themselves out of trouble, and they hope for the best, but they do not really believe anything beyond that. Such a religion has widespread popular appeal, but true Christians are the first to recognize that it is not the real thing.

Finally, if all we had was the Holy Spirit, our faith would be reduced to mystical experience. This is already evident in certain forms of the charismatic movement, where it is difficult to tell what connection there is with the gospel message of sin, righteousness, and judgment. If nothing outside the self really matters, if it is what I feel and experience that gives me the assurance I am on the right track, then no objective criteria will be allowed to interfere with my judgment. This attitude is common in certain charismatic circles, and it is the result of ignoring the trinitarian context of the Spirit's promises and work. Its inadequacy can be seen in its fundamental self-centeredness and its tendency to reduce the knowledge of God to a series of unusual human experiences that have no obvious purpose beyond themselves.

THE NEED FOR TRINITARIANISM

The truth is that we need a trinitarian framework if we are to make sense of our experience as Christians and if we are to grow deeper in our knowledge of God. One of the biggest criticisms one must make of some charismatics is that it often appears they use the Bible mainly to support what they have already felt, not to learn what new experiences await them. Having no structure outside their own emotions, they cannot imagine there is a whole spiritual world beyond their experience that is still waiting to be explored. Of course, they do have new experiences, but these seem to be acquired by contagion from other believers rather than from studying the Scriptures and being convicted by them, and so the value of those experiences must be regarded as suspect. Certainly nobody ever seems to ask whether the experiences in question have brought those who have had them closer to God the Father or have given them a deeper understanding of the cross of Christ. The experience itself is all the justification required.

Of course it is easy to be critical of the current evangelical scene, particularly when we are dealing with trends that may not affect every church or body of believers in the same way or to the same extent. Undoubtedly there are many deeply trinitarian people in the churches who find it hard to articulate their faith but who nevertheless seek to preserve a balance in their life and practice. These people need to be helped and encouraged to develop a more articulate understanding of what they believe, not only so that they will be able to resist unhealthy trends, but also (and ultimately more importantly) so that they will be equipped to witness more effectively to others. What practical steps can and should we take to make this happen?

How to Respond

First of all, it must be obvious that a more serious study of theology is essential, though great care must be taken to ensure that this is not divorced from the life of the church. After all, it was at least partly because an earlier generation found dogmatics boring and irrelevant that they abandoned it, and we must not go back to that situation again. A true theology must be a preachable theology, and it must speak to the hearts and minds of believers, even if they do not have an earned doctorate in the field. Academics must not be divorced from spirituality or practical matters that affect us as ordinary church members. If we cannot speak to them, we cannot speak to anybody, and our theological pretensions are worthless. These observations have a particular relevance where the doctrine of the Trinity is concerned, because many people find it abstract, incomprehensible, and basically irrelevant to everyday life. If that is the position we are starting from, anything that encourages such tendencies any further can only be resisted.

Similarly, we must take great care to remain as biblical as possible. If we really believe in *sola Scriptura*, then we must practice it, not in an overly analytical way that ignores the overall cohesion of the Bible, but with a synthetic spirit that does justice to the underlying unity of biblical thought. If we start from the principle of "the whole counsel of God," we shall soon find that the doctrine of the Trinity is indispensable, since that counsel cannot be understood without constantly referring to the work of the three Persons, both individually and in tandem. There can be no better illustration of this than to look at some New Testament passages that proclaim the doctrine of the Trinity. Take, for example, Galatians 4:6: "Because you are sons, God sent the Spirit of his Son into our hearts, the Spirit who calls out, '*Abba*, Father.'" Here we have a neat summary of Christian experience in a clearly trinitarian framework, and

Evangelicals Losing Their Way: The Doctrine of the Trinity

it could almost be said that the whole of our trinitarian doctrine, or at least its basic essentials, can be found in a careful exposition of it. Let us look carefully at what it says.

Note the context, first of all. It is *because we are sons* that the rest follows. The doctrine of the Trinity is not a mathematical abstraction cooked up by some clever theologians who wanted to confuse simple believers. On the contrary, it was revealed to us by God once we had been adopted by Him as His "sons." To live in that relationship and develop it to its full potential, we have to understand God's trinitarian being, since only that can make sense of the new life we have been called to live. The first ingredient is plainly experiential. "God sent the Spirit of His Son into our hearts." In other words, the Holy Spirit is our contact point with God, the means by whom we enter into a deeper knowledge of Him. There can be no Christian life without the indwelling presence of the Holy Spirit in our hearts (which in biblical language includes our minds as well as our feelings). In this respect the charismatic emphasis is absolutely right and must be rescued from the distortions it has too often suffered. To be filled with the Spirit is the essential precondition of a healthy Christian life; but as Paul reminds us in this verse, such an experience is profoundly trinitarian in nature.

Paul tells us that the Spirit who dwells in our hearts is the Spirit *of the Son*. He is not an unattached spiritual force who has come to give us uplifts of various kinds, but a messenger from God whose main purpose is to bring us closer to the Son in every possible way. From other parts of Scripture we know that this means it is the Spirit's task to change us spiritually so that we have the mind of Christ within us, with all that implies for practical decision-making in the rough-and-tumble of everyday life. It is the Spirit's task to apply Christ's saving work of atonement within us, so that it is far more than a belief to which we assent intellectually. It is the touchstone to which we are constantly being referred, the sin-killing medicine that turns us (by God's grace) into something we could never be on the strength of our own merits.

Most important of all, it is the Spirit's task to instruct us in the nature of our new relationship with God the Father. The apostle Paul tells us that the Spirit makes us cry "Father" in our prayers, an act that forms in us a true sense of the relationship we now have with God. But note that Paul uses the Aramaic word *Abba* when he says this. His hearers would imme-

The Present Evangelical Crisis

diately have known that this is how Jesus addressed His Father. Indeed, so characteristic of Jesus was this that *Abba* may be said to stand for the whole spiritual revolution His preaching and teaching introduced. When Jesus cried *Abba*, He was denounced by the Jewish leaders of His day for "making himself equal with God" (John 5:18). That was bad enough in their eyes, but a Christian would argue that at least Jesus was right to make such a claim. For a Christian to follow suit, however, is quite another matter because we have no claim to be considered divine. What Paul is saying here is that *even though we are not God and cannot ever be anything like Him in terms of our created human nature, we are nevertheless able to engage with Him on a level of intimacy that parallels that of Jesus.*

This is the astonishing privilege that is given to us as believers, and it forms the basis of our Christian life. Intercessory prayer, for example, makes sense because I have been accepted within the fellowship of the Triune God. I am no longer a supplicant forced to stand outside the gates of the heavenly palace, hoping that somehow my pleas might reach His ears. Thanks to Christ, and in the power of the Holy Spirit, I have access to the Father (Eph. 2:18). I am seated with Christ in the heavenly places, at the right hand of God (Eph. 2:6). This is the basis of my assurance that He will hear my prayers and answer them, perhaps not in the terms in which I have conceived them, because my understanding is limited, but in ways that I shall one day recognize as fulfilling both His will and mine.

THE TRINITY: THE SACRAMENTS

This trinitarian context also makes sense of my baptism. Evangelicals are often ready to fall out over baptism because they concentrate on the mechanics of it—who should be baptized, when they should be baptized, and how they should be baptized. These are important questions, of course, but they should not be allowed to deflect us from the central theological affirmation of baptism, which is that we are born again into a relationship with the Holy Trinity. Jesus commanded His disciples to baptize disciples in all nations in the name of the Father, the Son, and the Holy Spirit, without specifying any of these other matters that claim so much of our attention. Should we not respect the biblical emphasis in our exposition of this great theme? It might not solve every problem that the

Evangelicals Losing Their Way: The Doctrine of the Trinity

practice of baptism raises, but at least we would find a solid basis for agreement in principle and a positive message to which we could bear a common witness.

However we look at it, baptism is the rite of initiation into the life of the church. It is not that we cannot be saved without it—arguments of that kind are silly and miss the point—but in the normal course of events it is meant to be the beginning of a life of worship and of personal consecration to the service of God in Christ. Worship that presupposes baptism must by definition be trinitarian, and here we meet what for many evangelicals will surely be the greatest challenge of all. In most evangelical churches, "traditional worship" means the hymn-sandwich: hymn, prayer, hymn, reading, hymn, etc. The high point, indeed usually the only point, of all this is the sermon, which could presumably be delivered just as well without all the preliminaries. Of course, it is important to remember that this style of worship is in large measure a reaction to the opposite extreme, which characterized the medieval church and can still be found in many strands of Catholicism today. That put so much emphasis on various devotional practices, particularly the celebration of Holy Communion, that preaching was often left out altogether. As a result, people were not taught the Word of God or challenged to follow it. The result was an ignorant church that turned the gifts of God into superstition, even if that was never official church doctrine, and it is not surprising that the Reformers turned away from that as vehemently as they did.

We certainly do not want to lose the great emphasis we have traditionally placed on the ministry of the Word, but perhaps it is time to recognize that this needs to be supported by a doctrinal context if it is to be fully effective. The fact of the matter is that it is not possible to preach every doctrine in every sermon. Often it is not possible even to explore the doctrines that are in the sermon in the depth they deserve. Lack of time and the weakness of the flesh conspire to ensure that relatively little will be communicated effectively on any one occasion. For this reason, it is necessary to supplement the preaching with a form of worship that teaches people the basic ingredients of the faith. This is the main purpose of liturgy. Sadly, some so-called "liturgical renewal" has obscured this by practicing its own peculiar kind of fundamentalism. In modern liturgiology, it often seems that what matters most is antiquity. Curious practices that can be found in some ancient text are revived, whether they have any

The Present Evangelical Crisis

real purpose or not. The form of the service is turned around to reflect a theological position that gives more weight to the sacraments than to the preaching of the Word, a development that many evangelicals rightly see as a betrayal of their Reformation heritage.

THE TRINITY: LITURGY

The word *liturgy* evokes very mixed feelings in our ranks, but the principle it enshrines (at its best) is surely one that we need to take with the utmost seriousness. Anyone who finds it hard to believe that a liturgy can be consonant with the teaching of Scripture should look at the Anglican *Book of Common Prayer*—not the modern jazzed-up versions of it, but the classical texts, and preferably the one produced in 1662, which is still the official liturgy of the Church of England. There you will find a model of biblical worship. The *Book of Common Prayer* is literally dripping with Scripture—not simply isolated proof-texts, but a carefully constructed, systematic presentation of Christian doctrine, using the very words of the Bible itself. It takes time to get used to this, of course, but the daily repetition of the offices of Morning and Evening Prayer, far from being vain rote worship, can (if used in the right spirit) provide a resource for spiritual growth the real strength of which is most obviously seen in times of crisis.

If the sermon is good and the spirit of the congregation is right, a fixed liturgy may appear to be an irrelevance, even a constraint on the freedom of the Spirit. This is evidently what many of the Puritans felt, and they objected to being pushed into what they saw as a spiritual straitjacket. They clearly had a point, and nobody would want to quench the Spirit by a form of words. But when the times of dryness come, when we reach a plateau in our spiritual growth, then the structure of a liturgy that keeps both the biblical depth and the biblical balance can provide us with fresh inspiration and keep us from falling into the many different errors caused by our natural proclivity toward omission and distortion. A person who is well trained in biblical liturgy will have a feel for what is orthodox, because it will be embedded in his consciousness. Furthermore, he will have a sense of the right kind of trinitarian balance, because whatever the sermon may be like, there will be a doctrinal framework to restore his spiritual equilibrium and keep him from going off the deep end.

Evangelicals Losing Their Way: The Doctrine of the Trinity

We are not required to go back to the pattern of the seventeenth century, though that provides us with the classical example of what we are looking for; but we ought to be challenged to think toward producing modern equivalents that will unite us in a profoundly doctrinal sense, which will feed our spirits and set us apart as men and women called to proclaim the Gospel of Christ's salvation to a world that is perishing. Without such a framework, we will almost certainly fall into some distortion or other, even if only because we cannot say everything all at once. With such a framework, we will have a way of conveying complex theological ideas to ordinary people in a way that they can absorb naturally.

THE TRINITY: PRAYER

Prayer is obviously at the heart of all worship and forms the backbone of all good liturgy. When we pray, we ought to pray to the Father, through the Son, in the Spirit. This is the essential framework that should form the basis of all of our praying, particularly our public praying. No doubt in a perfect world there would be no gap between our public and our private prayers; but the reality is that in private we are often eccentric in the way we pray, either because we lack the time to be structured or because trying to dot every theological *i* and cross every *t* is a distraction that, if we pursued it at any length, would take us away from what we are meant to be doing. But public prayer is also a form of teaching, and we ought not to lose sight of that dimension of it. In public prayer we cannot indulge our own private eccentricities but are forced to speak in a way that can be shared by every believer present. Such prayer does not have to be long, but it must have real content, and a trinitarian structure is the best guarantee of that.

CONCLUSION

Carefully chosen words with the right theological content have a way of penetrating the consciousness. This can be seen, for example, in the Lord's Prayer, which is one of the few things that all Christians (and indeed many non-Christians who have had a religious upbringing) share. To preach on the Lord's Prayer is an exhilarating experience because people recognize what is being talked about, even if they have never thought

The Present Evangelical Crisis

much about it before. Good theological liturgy can and does have the same effect. It is not (or should not be) a substitute for preaching, or a way of stifling spiritual fervor, but a framework in which to place biblical teaching and an encouragement to explore areas of it that we might otherwise neglect. One again, words like *structure* and *framework* provide the key. Start disciplining your faith into a structure, and you will inevitably come to the doctrine of the Trinity, which is the most basic and universal structure of all.

No one can predict the future, but if the evangelical churches are to fulfill the potential that a generation of growth has given them, they must find this self-discipline. If they do not, they will lose the next generation to more hierarchical and structured forms of Christianity, just as the second generation of evangelicals in the early nineteenth century was decimated by the rise of ritualism and Anglo-Catholicism. The signs are already there—charismatics becoming Orthodox, Protestant intellectuals turning to what they see as the more satisfying framework of high church Episcopalianism or Roman Catholicism. There is no need for this. A healthy, robust Reformed faith has as much to offer as any other form of Christianity, and more. Our ancestors abandoned their Catholic heritage not merely because the church was corrupt, but because they had found a deeper peace with God. They lived the trinitarian faith and, as Warfield demonstrated in his study of Calvin, explored its dimensions more fully than had thitherto been done. We who follow after have the same challenge given to us. May God grant that we shall not be found wanting in our day!

3

Church-O-Rama
or Corporate Worship

Monte E. Wilson

Evangelical worship is becoming an oxymoron. Our songs are either belted out in the same mindless intensity with which we sing our football team's fight song, or we are crooning romantic ditties that would be more at home in an old 1930s B movie. Irreverence has become so rampant in our worship services that one would not be shocked to hear of deacons walking up and down the aisles yelling, "Popcorn, peanuts, sacraments!"

There are many reasons for the denigration of worship in modern evangelical churchville. There's the dumbing-down effect of public education, 150 years of revivalism that—armed with songs geared to working up the masses—approaches church solely as an evangelistic crusade, and the drive to compete with MTV and be "relevant" (i.e., more like the world), thereby pleasing the tastes of the congregation. Each of these dynamics perverts our ability to appreciate any music that is not simplistic and emotionally intense. All of this together erects almost insurmountable barriers we must overcome if we are to truly worship the Lord.

WORSHIP: ACT OR EXPERIENCE?

For the modern evangelical, worship is defined *exclusively* in terms of the individual's experience. Worship, then, is not about adoring God but about being nourished with religious feelings, so much so that the worshiper has become the object of worship.[1] When we study the ancient approach to worship, however, we see that the church did not overly concern itself with feelings of devotion, but rather with heartfelt and biblically informed obedience. Moreover, believers had a firm grasp on the fact that when they gathered "as a church" (1 Cor. 11:18), their worship was to be a *corporate expression.* Church worship was not a gathering of individuals but of the body of Christ.

Christopher J. Cocksworth notes that the two underlying elements of the evangelical consciousness are existential and theological. In other words, there is a wedding between piety and theology, an apprehension of the Gospel and a communication of that Gospel.[2] Tragically, much of evangelical worship today has chosen to divorce what must remain married if there is to be God-glorifying worship. Some have abandoned any quest for piety, preferring a pharisaical doctrinal purity. Their "worship" services may be correct in every fashion, but they are void of any sense of true devotion or of the life of the Holy Spirit. Others—probably the majority in modern American evangelicalism—have utterly neglected any commitment to the content of the Word and have ended with narcissistic "worship" services where everyone drowns in a sea of subjectivism and calls it "being bathed in the presence of the Holy Spirit." These people come to church exclusively to "feel" God.

I am not discounting the worth of the conscious presence of the Holy Spirit. I am saying that although the apostolic and primitive church emphasized worship as an act of obedience, we see it solely as an experience. Why? Because "church is for me. Sunday worship is to be centered on *my* needs and desires. Never mind what the Father desires and commands. I am at the center. My needs are paramount. Meet them or I'll go to church elsewhere." The ego reigns supreme.

Where did we go wrong? Historically, as I have noted, evangelicals have been defined by engaging and experiencing the truth of the Gospel. Now, however, we are defined solely by experiences, the validity of which is "proven" by the word of the believer. Subjectivism and existentialism are redefining biblical worship. When did we evangelicals trade our rich inheritance for the poverty of revivalistic or MTV-style worship?

FINNEYISM

Up until the 1800s, the evangelical church approached church worship from the same perspective. It was seen as a command performance before the King, Jesus Christ; He was the audience, and we were "the

The Present Evangelical Crisis

performers." All action, all content, was God-centered and God-directed.

During the 1800s, the United States witnessed the Second Great Awakening, which transformed not only our ideas concerning church worship but those concerning the Gospel itself. Modern evangelicalism bears little resemblance to the faith of our fathers. Our aim is to make people feel better; theirs was to teach the people how to worship God. We hear of how God enables people to save themselves; they spoke of the God who saves. Our aim is to evenly distribute honor and praise between God and man; their chief aim was to see that God received all glory. The average modern evangelical believes that revivals come via techniques; our Puritan and Pilgrim fathers believed revivals were sovereign acts of God. Today the local church is held in low esteem and evaluated not by the fruit of obedience and changed lives but by the standard of numbers: how many buildings, how much money, how many converts. Today the mind is seen as a hindrance to true spirituality. Jonathan Edwards and the average minister of his day believed the training of the intellect to be of paramount importance.

This transformation of mind-sets did not happen overnight and cannot be solely attributed to one event or one person. However, it can be said that one man, more than any other, acted as a catalyst and prototype; that man was Charles Grandison Finney (1792-1875). While practicing law in New York, Finney attended church services conducted by a friend, George Gale. In 1821 he became a Christian and almost immediately declared that he had been retained by God to "plead His cause." For the next eight years he held revival meetings in the eastern states and for a short while was pastor of Second Presbyterian Church in New York City. Eventually, however, he withdrew from the presbytery, rejecting the Presbyterian disciplinary system.

When Finney began itinerating as a frontier evangelist, his meetings were almost immediately attended with large numbers of conversions, as well as great controversy.[3] The controversy centered upon Finney's methodology and his belief that techniques were the means to attaining revival. Up to that time the majority of ministers attributed revivals to the sovereign act of a merciful God. With the coming of Finney, such beliefs were supplanted.

Finney believed that revivals could be planned, promoted, and prop-

agated by man. Such a redefinition of revival required a revamping of
one's appraisal of human nature. If humans are dead in sin, as the apostle Paul had written, then regeneration depended upon the sovereign act
of the Holy Spirit. However, if regeneration was a matter of a will not
enslaved to unrighteousness but free to choose between sin and righteousness, then the individual needed to be argued or persuaded into the
Kingdom of God.

One obvious consequence of this reappraisal of human nature was
the placing of technique at the forefront of evangelism and revivals.
Before Finney, prayer and preaching the Word of God were generally
believed to be the means of grace God would use, in His sovereign tim-
ing, to bring revival. Now it was a matter of changing people's minds.
Therefore, most anything that could accomplish this end became "holy,"
and anything that was seen to hinder the individual's decision-making
process was either foolish or evil. Did teaching "mouldy orthodoxy"
(Henry Ward Beecher) bore people? Then it must be replaced with emotionally challenging storytelling that would move the masses. Did the
singing of the Psalms excite the masses? If not, write simple (simplistic?)
choruses and put them to popular tunes. Everything the church did had
to be evaluated by one thing—results.

The church as revival center replaced the church as *Mater* and
Schola. What was all-important to the leaders of the Second Great
Awakening was one's "personal salvation." Every other concern was secondary, if of any importance at all. Subsequently, only those denominations that "exploited innovative revival techniques to carry the gospel to
the people, flourished."[4]

Before Finney, the church identified its purpose as the worship of the
Triune God. Now it was the attainment of "revival" or the engendering
of experiences. With the Second Great Awakening, the church's mission
changed from making disciples to getting people to "make a decision for
Jesus." In the mid-nineteenth century, the ministry team of Dwight
Moody and musician/composer Ira Sankey solidified this transformation
(the first beginnings of what would eventually become the "crusade
rally"). Their model would be copied by vast numbers of new churches
that sprang into existence in the wake of these crusades.

The focus of church worship changed from God to man. The chief
aim was no longer to glorify God, but to please and excite the masses—

The Present Evangelical Crisis

especially those who were showing *some* interest in Christianity ("seekers"). This required not only that the church change its focus from the Creator to the created, but that the church cease gathering as the church. Instead, it was to gather around the purpose of reaching the lost.

WORSHIP: FORM AND CONTENT

Worship means to ascribe to God supreme worth (*worth-ship*). "Ascribe to the LORD the glory due his name" (Ps. 96:8). It is God's worthiness that makes worship possible. As J. I. Packer brings out in his definition of worship, it is a "due response" in the face of His holy nature and His gracious gifts.

> Worship in the Bible is the due response of rational creatures to the self-revelation of their Creator. It is an honoring and glorifying of God by gratefully offering back to Him all the good gifts, and all the knowledge of His greatness and graciousness, that He has given. It involves praising Him for what He is, thanking Him for what He has done, desiring Him to get Himself more glory by further acts of mercy, judgment, and power, and trusting Him with our concern for our own and others' future well-being.[5]

In the Old Testament, when the people of God worshiped corporately, they had a very specific liturgy to follow. There were specific sacrifices and offerings to be given in a specific fashion by a specific group of men—the priests. They were not free to worship, corporately, in any manner that suited them. Of course, if they were simply worshiping as individuals while watching over the flocks and herds, they could sing, dance, and exult with spontaneous zeal. But this was not so in the temple. There one had to follow the prescribed order.

Because there are multiple regulations concerning Old Testament worship, there is a common misunderstanding that all that mattered to God was the form: walk through the steps, perform properly, and all was well. However, this was not the case. Just as one was not a Jew unless he was circumcised in the heart, worship was not "true" unless it flowed from a heart of faith.

Form and substance were *both* critical to true worship. The form

Church-o-Rama or Corporate Worship

pointed the worshiper in the right direction; it ensured that all spoke with one heart, one mind, and one voice. However, God was not satisfied with mere outward observance. Time and time again the prophets were sent to rebuke Israel for such heartless service, thinking that God could be satisfied with outward observance alone. As Calvin wrote:

> God did not command sacrifices in order to busy His worshipers with earthly sacrifices. Rather He did so that He might lift their minds higher. This can be clearly discerned from His own nature: for, as it is spiritual, only spiritual worship delights Him. Many statements of the prophets attest to this and charge the Jews with stupidity; for they think some sacrifice or other has value in God's sight. Is that because they intended to detract something from the law? Not at all. But, since they were true interpreters of it, they desired in this way to direct man's eyes to the objective from which the common people were straying.[6]

The external rituals were to be a manifestation of faith and love (Deut. 6:5-6). When used merely as a disguise for a cold and distant heart, they became an abomination. The outward signs were to be manifestations of an inward reality. When they were not, God rejected the sign as having any real worth (1 Sam. 15:22; Ps. 51:14-19; Isa. 1:11-18; Jer. 6:20; Mal. 1).

When Jesus tells the woman at the well that God is to be worshiped "in spirit and in truth" (John 4:24), He is not condemning forms, as such, but the idea that they can have a significance separate from the inner reality they are to embody. The externals were never to be a substitute for the inner reality.

We are humans. Not being wholly spirit, we need external aids to lead and support us in our quest for obedient, spiritual worship. (Certainly man cannot live by "bread alone." But he also cannot live by "Word alone.") We are also sinful humans, however, and we must be careful that our rituals never detract from the necessary substance to which they point or become an end in themselves, rather than the means to the end.

More importantly, of course, Jesus was noting the impending abolishment of Old Covenant forms and regulations concerning worship. Soon the Kingdom of God would no longer be bound to the temple in

The Present Evangelical Crisis

Jerusalem and to fellowship with the nation of Israel. The ceremonies and rituals had all pointed to Jesus Christ, the Messiah. Now that He had come, there was no more need for the signs. This was not rejection of the old, but the fulfillment and perfection of the one true faith.

> "The old had passed away, now all things are new." This meant that in the light of the coming of the Messiah, as a result of His saving work, everything "old" had acquired a new meaning, had been renewed and transformed in its significance.[7]

Any theology of worship, any study of Christian liturgy, will be deficient if it ignores the influence of the temple and synagogue upon the apostolic church. Christian worship was not created in a vacuum. Certainly there was discontinuity, but there was also continuity. Early Christian worship adopted the pattern provided by the temple ritual and synagogue liturgy.[8] We see continuity—Peter and John go up to the temple "at the time of prayer" (Acts 3:1)—and discontinuity—they do *not* offer up a slain animal as a sacrifice. Continuity—Paul returns to Jerusalem to celebrate Pentecost (Acts 20:16); discontinuity—the Feast now takes on added meaning for the Christian.

Given this mind-set, the post-apostolic church studied apostolic doctrine and examples, as well as Old Testament doctrines and practices, and developed a full-blown pattern of worship. Sadly, many today restrict their patterns of worship to the direct commands of the New Testament. It's as if the Old Testament is utterly irrelevant when it comes to defining biblical worship.

How many of us evangelicals were lured by the ideal of "primitive Christianity"? How many of us rejected the historical outworking and maturing of Christian faith and practice, thinking that we would be more pure, more spiritual, and more biblical? How many of us awoke to the realization that we had a very truncated and impoverished Christianity?

DEFINING "BIBLICAL" WORSHIP

Not long after the passing of the apostles, the church had crafted four principal liturgical forms, attributed to various early leaders (James, Mark, Peter, and John). While there was diversity, there was also a common struc-

Church-o-Rama or Corporate Worship

ture.[9] Commands, patterns, and expressions of worship found in Scripture regulated all of them. Tragically, the church began to add to these forms in ways that were contrary to the express commands of Scripture.

The Reformation was fueled by a commitment to reform the church's worship and message of salvation. With regard to her worship, the *Regulative Principle* was put forth, stating that "Nothing should be introduced or performed in the churches of Christ for which no probable reason can be given from the Word of God" (Bucer). However, as James Jordan brings out in his book *The Sociology of the Church*,[10] we must not apply this dispensationally, as if the Word of God no longer includes the Old Testament. He also rightly comments that we must recognize that this original definition is quite different from the more narrow "whatever is not commanded is forbidden."

The Puritans made the mistake of not being consistent with their view of covenant theology when it came to their ideas concerning worship. As Ray Sutton has written, in every other area of theological concern they held to the hermeneutical principle that "Unless the New Testament changes it, do what the Old Testament commands." However, when it came to worship, they became dispensationalists and said, basically, "If the New Testament does not command it, we cannot do it."[11] The present-day consequences of this narrowing of the *Regulative Principle* are asthmatic worship services that only have the one lung of the New Testament to breathe life into its services, rather than the two lungs of Old and New Testaments.

One cannot help but wonder if the typical evangelical fear of "forms"—of rituals, ceremonies, art—is due more to a reaction to all things Roman Catholic than to a desire to obey God. "If the Roman Catholics do it, then it is evil" quite often appears to be the working definition of the *Regulative Principle*! Do they use art? It must be a sin. Do they utilize ceremony? Ceremonies are evil. Do they light candles? Candles are of the devil.

When your daughter is married, will there be "pomp and circumstance"? Will there be the beauty of flowers and music? Will everyone run down the aisle in shorts and sandals or walk in a manner appropriate to the occasion? When you baptize (or dedicate) an infant, do you just run through the motions or is there a sense of the weightiness of the moment? On all of these occasions, we act in certain ways because we know there

The Present Evangelical Crisis

is something going on that demands a reverent demeanor appropriate to the event. Is church worship any less significant?

The forms, of course, are not for God. They are for us. The ceremonies do not impress God, but they can impress upon us the significance of what we are doing. Certainly they can also obscure the *focus* of our worship and distract us from reality, but that does not make them evil. The beauty of music can distract us from the content of the psalms and hymns we sing. Does that make music sinful?

Early in my ministry as a Baptist evangelist, the word *liturgy* conjured up pictures of robes, incense, prayers by rote, and death by carbon monoxide; it was a game of smoke and mirrors to hide the fact that the Holy Spirit was nowhere to be found. It had never occurred to me, however, that *all churches* have a liturgy.

In the Baptist, Lutheran, and Presbyterian churches, the liturgy typically begins with a call to worship and proceeds with three or four hymns. The offering is then taken, there is a presentation of special music, the sermon, and finally the benediction. The Baptist, of course, will be called to respond to the message (the "invitation") before the pastoral benediction. The Pentecostal liturgy mirrors the Baptist's, except that during the worship the songs are salted with a few "prophecies" and "exhortations" given by laypeople. In some charismatic worship services, the songs of praises will reach an apex with the congregation "singing in tongues" for a few moments. There will then be another prophecy and then pastoral prayer or special music.

Many neo-Pentecostals (charismatics) and all classical Pentecostals insist they have no liturgy. The reality, however, is that while they may have rejected the idea of a written liturgy, they have an unwritten, oral tradition. This liturgy may be more flexible than, say, the liturgy found in the *Book of Common Prayer*, but there *is* an overall structure.

The idea of liturgy is patently biblical. In Old Testament worship there was a prescribed step-by-step order one had to follow or there were grave consequences. In the New Testament Paul gives an overall view of the early church's liturgy in 1 Corinthians 12—14, emphasizing its exquisite integration of order and spontaneity, and we see this liturgy mature and take on more form in the latter epistles. We have seen the apostles and church keeping certain feasts, as well as hours of prayer. The book of Revelation also gives us a beautiful glimpse of heavenly liturgy.

Church-o-Rama or Corporate Worship

THE VALUE OF LITURGY

Purposeful liturgies help us experience an orderly and meaningful worship service. The more we consciously "act out our faith," which consists of the life, death, resurrection, ascension, and glorification of Christ and the subsequent outpouring of the Holy Spirit, the more we fulfill our calling to be the church.

One value of a thoughtfully considered liturgy is that it enforces the idea that we are worshiping *as the church*, not as individuals or home groups. We are the Ship of Orthodoxy, not 350 separate rafts in a lagoon. In many evangelical circles this is a great temptation. An individual may soar into the heavenlies and, oblivious to everything and everyone around him, dance and shout to his heart's content. However, when we gather as the church, we can never be oblivious to those around us (1 Cor. 14). A home group may sing, testify, confess, sing some more, laugh, break for coffee, and come back together for teaching; but when we gather as the church, we must remember we are in God's Throne Room, not our living room. This is not coffee with our buddies but a royal audience with the King of the Universe. This is of particular relevance because so many Christians today approach church worship as an extension of their prayer closets.

A liturgy also has the priceless value of keeping us rooted in the primary realities of the faith. In listening to various (written) liturgies, we hear what the congregation recites each week. Even a cursory reading will reveal the emphasis upon the death, burial, and resurrection of Jesus Christ; praying for the needs of others; the giving and receiving of forgiveness; and the believer's response to all these spiritual realities. No matter how "dead" the singing is, no matter how "boring" the sermon is (God forbid!), a biblical liturgy sees to it that we are confronted with the basic elements of the faith every week.

As a Protestant, my "model" of worship has the pulpit at the center of the service. Everything serves the sermon. Even the music and ministry at the altar are evaluated by how they support or detract from the pulpit. Interestingly enough, as one tours the great seventeenth-century Protestant churches in Western Europe, he or she immediately notices that the pulpit is off to one side with the Lord's Table at the center.

Now, before we accuse the Reformers of holding on to vestiges of

The Present Evangelical Crisis

Roman Catholicism, think about the liturgy as a journey with each step being significant. It's not that the pulpit is insignificant or that the Lord's Supper is meaningful without the spoken word. Both are critical. The Reformers saw the worship service as a whole. All too often we, on the other hand, see only the pulpit. Consequently our liturgies as well as our architecture has man (the minister and his pulpit) at the center. (Is it any wonder we have produced so many spiritual celebrities who allow themselves to be set up as idols?)

A biblical liturgy will model the faith. This is a benefit of a liturgy consciously fashioned in a biblical manner. It is an auxiliary teaching tool. Concretes—times, places, forms, symbols—help us to see, hear, and remember the message of God's redemption in Christ. While such forms can become more important than the life and the Spirit of Christ, to ridicule forms is to fall into the error of dualism.

When the worship service is completed, the congregation has seen, heard, and tasted the King and His Kingdom. They have offered up praise, thanked Him for His creation and for redemption in Christ, received and given forgiveness, and are now empowered to go out into the world, seeking all things summed up (i.e., finding their meaning) in Christ.

BIBLICAL PATTERNS AND FORMS

Old Testament worship was patterned after the worship that occurs in heaven (Heb. 8:5; 9:23-24). It was more than just a shadow. A specific order was to take place that followed the worship pattern of heaven. When the people of God worshiped, there was (and is) to be a "heavenly pattern" that expresses the worship of heaven.

In John's Revelation, we see heavenly worship. The Holy Spirit takes John up into heaven. Accordingly, all the earliest liturgies of the post-apostolic church began with the celebrant crying out, "Lift up your hearts!" The congregation would then respond, "We lift our hearts to you, O Lord!" (4:1, a.k.a. *Sursem corda*). In Revelation 4—6 we see the throne, as well as the elders and living creatures all crying out "Holy, Holy, Holy" (the *Sanctus*). The people of God approach His throne with praise, adoration, and thanksgiving. In chapter 8 we read of the prayers and praises of the saints on the earth below being added to those of the heavenly host, telling us that in some very real ways the church militant worships in heaven with the church triumphant and that our praise, adoration, and petitions are joined to those of the angels, archangels, and martyrs who all are standing before the throne of the Lamb. Here the earliest liturgies followed praise with prayers and petitions for the descent of the Holy Spirit, for those in need and all those in authority, as well as including a recitation of the Lord's Prayer (all interspersed with readings from the Scriptures).

Now, standing before the Lamb upon the throne, we see Him who was sacrificed and raised to Lordship over heaven and earth (Rev. 5:6). At this juncture of the church's worship, which was following the "heavenly pattern," the people would hear of their Redeemer's life, death, and resurrection from the "memoirs of the apostles." This should follow with more adoration of the Lamb (Rev. 8), which included the eating of the Lord's Supper—feeding upon the presence of the Lamb who had been slain.

Going back to Old Testament worship being a pattern that revealed the liturgy of heaven, the early church sought to celebrate the New Covenant, following in principle the pattern previously revealed. For example, just as there were daily sacrifices, there would be morning and evening prayers (Daily Offices). It is also significant that when we study the earliest liturgies, we see the church celebrating the Lord's Supper in ways that expressed the liturgy of the tabernacle, especially as practiced on the Day of Atonement.[12] The church's practice should not surprise us. God had given His people a liturgy that was to teach them how to worship; since this worship was following a heavenly pattern, the church would craft its worship accordingly.

I suggest that one way to view a liturgy is as a spiritual journey, an approach to the presence of the Triune God. We "enter his gates with thanksgiving and his courts with praise"; we offer up prayers and petitions; the Word is preached, cleansing and strengthening us; we then celebrate the memorial of Christ's redemption by eating the Lord's Supper; and finally we are sent back into the world, commissioned to be salt, light, and leaven.

In taking this liturgical journey, the church is reenacting the historical journey of God's people. We are acting out our history as we know it has been and will be: God called us out of the world, united us to His Son's body (the church), is making us into a people of worship and service, and will bring us to His wedding supper at the end of time. Again note the journey taken in Revelation.

Consider some of the basic steps or, if you prefer, ingredients of the liturgical journey:

Step one: *We have separated ourselves from the world.* God has called, and we have responded. The liturgy, then, actually begins when we leave our houses and travel to become "His house." We are reenacting our passing from death to life and are entering what has been called "the realm of grace."

Step two: *We come before Him with thanksgiving and praise.* Given the reality of our "coming into His courts" and celebrating His redemption, we should take care that our worship is marked with joy and beauty. The early Christians gathered to praise God for His creation and for the new creation (2 Cor. 5:17). It was not a funeral service but a celebration. This is why early on there was such an emphasis on artistic beauty in the liturgy. We give beautiful gifts to loved ones, so why not do the same for God? Even in the middle of great persecution, the early church's liturgies were almost utterly silent as to any reference to its suffering but, rather, was quite majestic and triumphal.[13]

Part of our thanksgiving, of course, is demonstrated in the giving of tithes and offerings. These are not things to be hidden by a choir's musical offering as if we are embarrassed to obey God, nor are they so "unspiritual" that they should be wrapped around the announcements. The giving of our finances represents the giving of our lives to Him who gave His life for us.

Step three: *The reading of Scripture and prayer.* It is important to remember that this service is different from other fellowship—group meetings, house groups, prayer meetings, evangelistic services, etc. We have gathered *as the church* (1 Cor. 11:18); so we are now subject to standards of order and demeanor that are different from those of Christian fellowship over a dinner table.

Scripture is replete with passages concerning what and for whom we should pray. The church took seriously such commands as praying for all those in authority, the needy, and the sick and remembering those imprisoned for their faith. Historically, the church has also assigned certain passages (Old Testament, Gospel, Epistle) to be read each Lord's Day, so that over a period of a few years the congregation would have heard the major events of God's redemptive work on their behalf.

Step four: *The teaching of the Word.* God is now bringing His message to us. By receiving this Word, our minds are renewed and our souls strengthened for service. Here Christ washes us with the water of His Spirit and Word (Eph. 5:25-27).

Church is for believers. In fact, in the early days of the church when confessing Christ could get one thrown into prison or executed, the meetings were closed to visitors. (And the church still grew numerically! Imagine that!) The exhortation and instruction that is given in the Sunday worship should be to build up the believer. Now is not the time to get into heavy theological discussions or political harangues. The Great Shepherd of the sheep wills for His covenant people to be fed.

Actually, the entire worship service is a sermon that speaks to us of Christ and His redemption. The service is a dialogue (*liturgy* means "the work of the people") in which God speaks to us and we respond. This is why it is so important that our special worship be seen as more than just an opportunity to hear the minister teach. In biblical worship, there will be congregational participation. For example, God calls us to worship, and we respond with praise and adoration. We hear God's law in the reading of the Decalogue and, consequently, publicly repent of our falling short of His standard. We then hear the Lord, through one of His representatives, forgive us our sins.

Step five: *The Lord's Supper.* We have now arrived, symbolically, at the throne of Christ. By faith we experience the Kingdom of God—His righteousness, peace, and joy in the Holy Spirit. Whether this step in the journey should take place every week or not cannot be considered here. However, it is interesting to note Edersheim's comment that "the apostolic practice of partaking of the Lord's Supper every Lord's Day may have been in imitation of the priests eating the shewbread every Sabbath."[14]

Historically, part of the church's weekly prayer life always included the Lord's Prayer. Here we are confessing our sins, forgiving those who have sinned against us, asking the Lord to make earth like heaven, and renewing our covenant with Him. It is with this latter understanding (covenant renewal) that, throughout the church's history, some liturgies

The Present Evangelical Crisis

have included this prayer with the giving of the elements (distribution) of the Lord's Supper.

Now we have not only followed a heavenly pattern, but have reenacted the rhythm of history that is moving toward all things being summed up in Christ (the culmination of history) and the beginning of eternity with the wedding supper of the Lamb. It is here that we see Christ as the center of life and eternity, here that we see the source of all life and blessing.

Step six: *In the benediction we are blessed* and sent out to make disciples of all nations. The church is not a place for escape. It is the realm of spirit and of truth, the place where we gather to be empowered to become what we are called to be before God and the world: the people of God, the church of Jesus Christ, stewards, servants, kings under the King of kings. In fact, when the church fully realizes herself in worship of the Triune God, she is manifested before the world as a witness to the Kingdom of God.

The point of this excursion through what I believe to be some of the more necessary elements of a worship service is not to assert any specific order (either oral or written) as being the *only* biblical one. It is simply to help evaluate what we are doing in our worship services and to provoke dialogue and reflection in each local congregation concerning how it may become more biblical in its worship.

Again, the question is not whether or not we have a liturgy, but what is our liturgy telling us about our theology? And is it congruent with the theology we confess? Do our forms of worship place Christ at the center, or man? Does the Bible govern our special worship, or does the surrounding religious culture dictate what we do? Those who love Jesus Christ, the Head of the church, must seriously consider all these questions.

It is not always easy to find the delicate balance between spontaneity and order. Today much of what passes for spontaneity is irreverent showmanship spawned by a desire to be "unique" and "relevant" rather than obedient and biblical. On the other hand, we must also be concerned not to mistake antiquity and orderliness for authentic New Testament worship in the twenty-first century. After all, cemeteries are both ancient and orderly.

Church-o-Rama or Corporate Worship

PRIORITIES

It must seem strange to the average Christian of our day to read in history
where, in the midst of poverty, religious persecution, social upheaval of
every sort, war, and plagues, some of the sixteenth-century church's greatest leaders (Luther, Zwingli, *et al*) gathered at the Colloquy of Marburg
to argue about the nature of the Eucharist. What were they thinking?
Shouldn't they have been out evangelizing Roman Catholics or picketing
the local brothels or preaching sermons on the great social issues of the
day? But if we look back to the time when Luther was shown that justification was by faith alone and consider the effects of this single theological insight upon all of western civilization, we can see that theological
issues have greater societal ramifications than we have heretofore thought
possible. Furthermore, we may be challenged to change our priorities.

The cultural mandate (Gen. 1:26-28) declares that we are to cultivate the world for God's glory. As Ray Sutton has written:

> What is "culture"? "Culture" comes from "cultus," meaning
> worship. Thus, the task of dominion was to transform the world
> into a place of worship and thereby create true culture. . . . In
> Adam's case, he was to take the raw materials on the ground and
> fashion a society, not just a cathedral, in concert with God's pres-
> ence. In our case, it consists of transforming the unethical debris
> of society into the glorious praise of God.[15]

How does this happen? How do we seek to make all of life a praise
to the Creator-Savior? How do we work toward influencing the world
for Christ and His Kingdom (Matt. 5:13, 16; 13:31-33)? I assert that it
all begins in church worship.

As we have already noted, many well-meaning, serious-minded, conservative evangelicals have turned the Sunday service into a revival or,
worse, a political rally. What they do not realize is that by changing their
priorities from worship to evangelism and political action, they are actually weakening their effectiveness in these endeavors. If the people do not
focus on Christ, worship Christ, feed on Christ, ascend into the heavenlies
with Christ in worship as a church, all of life suffers due to a perverted perspective, not to mention suffering a depletion of spiritual empowerment.

If we are not straight about the nature of worship or the nature of

The Present Evangelical Crisis

the God we worship, what and whom will we be taking to the world? If our understanding of the bread and the wine of the Lord's Table is defective, won't this pervert how we view the world and, more importantly, Christ Himself? And if we are wrong here, what sort of gospel are we taking to the world? Worship is critical not only to our spiritual welfare but to our mission to the world as well.

> The world will never be as radiant with the glory of God as is the church. In itself, indeed, the world is darkness, uncomprehending of the Light. But with the coming of the Sunrise from on high (Luke 1:78), and the shining of His light through His city, the world is lighted and is transformed into an image of the heavenly kingdom. Though the world cannot be God's kingdom in the same way that the church is, the world can, however dimly, reflect the glory of the kingdom that shines through the church.[16]

If we wish to see God glorified in the world, He must first be glorified in the church. Toward that end, we must completely rethink our paradigms of worship. The secular culture has far more influence upon how a vast number of evangelical churches conduct their worship services than does the Bible or church history. Consequently, when the world looks to the church, all it sees is its own face with a religious veneer.

Theology, biblically-based liturgy, and spirituality must all take their place at the heart of our worship. It is not enough to just *speak* appropriately of God; we must also *perform* our worship in a way worthy of Him, with hearts on fire with love for Him in whom we live and move and have our being.

NOTES

1. Alexander Schmemann, *Introduction of Liturgical Theology* (New York: St. Vladimir's Seminary Press, 1986), p. 30.

2. "Gospel," in Christopher J. Cockworth, *Evangelical Eucharistic Thought in the Church of England* (Cambridge, England: University Press, 1993), pp. 3, 5.

3. Iain H. Murray, *Revival and Revivalism: The Making and Marring of American Evangelicalism 1750-1858* (Edinburgh: Banner of Truth, 1994).

4. Mark Noll, *The Scandal of the Evangelical Mind* (Grand Rapids, MI: Eerdmans, 1994), p. 62.

Church-o-Rama or Corporate Worship

5. J. I. Packer, *Concise Theology: A Guide to Historic Christian Beliefs* (Wheaton, IL: Tyndale, 1993), p. 98.

6. John Calvin, *Institutes of the Christian Religion* (Philadelphia: Westminster), Book II, ch. VII, p. 349.

7. Schmemann, *Introduction of Liturgical Theology*, p. 100.

8. Cf. Ralph Martin, *Worship in the Early Church* (Grand Rapids, MI: Eerdmans, 1995), p. 19.

9. Cf. Royal Grote's monograph, *Calling on the Name of the Lord* (The Reformed Episcopal Church, 211 Byrne, Houston, TX 77009), where he gives an excellent overview of J. H. Blunt's, *The Annotated Prayer Book of 1868* and the history of the church's liturgical forms. Also note Alexander Schmemann's *Introduction of Liturgical Theology*.

10. James Jordan, *The Sociology of the Church* (Tyler, TX: Geneva Ministries, 1986), pp. 208-210.

11. Ray Sutton, *That You May Prosper* (Tyler, TX: ICE, 1987), p. 4n.

12. Alfred Edersheim, *The Temple: Its Ministry and Services As They Were at the Time of Jesus* (Grand Rapids, MI: Kregel, 1997 repr.), pp. 176-196.

13. Schmemman, *Introduction of Liturgical Theology*, p. 96.

14. Edersheim, *The Temple*, p. 126.

15. Sutton, *That You May Prosper*, p. 125.

16. Peter Liethart, *The Kingdom and the Power: Rediscovering the Centrality of the Church* (Phillipsburg, NJ: Presbyterian & Reformed, 1993), p. 167ff.

4

THE PRIESTHOOD OF ALL BELIEVERS:
RECONSIDERING
EVERY-MEMBER MINISTRY

Mark E. Dever

THE ISSUE STATED

Is every member of the church to be a minister? If so, in what sense is each member to be a minister? And what implications does that have for those traditionally regarded as ministers?

The last few decades have seen these questions come to the fore in hundreds, if not thousands, of congregations around the world. For many it has been a herald of a renewal of the ministry of the congregation. For others, "every-member ministry" has been one more passing spiritual slogan. And for still other congregations, what has been called "every-member ministry" has been a part of a degenerative disease that has resulted in the decline and even the death of some churches.

What is the idea called "every-member ministry"? Where does it come from? What does it mean? Is it good or bad? These are the questions considered in this chapter.

THE BIBLICAL BACKGROUND

In order to understand this discussion we must first understand what has been meant by two words—*clergy* and *laity*. *Clergy* has meant those ordained in the church for special service—the priests, pastors, and ministers. The word *laity* has referred to everyone else. Both these words come from the Greek of the New Testament. The word *clergy* is derived

The Priesthood of All Believers

from the word *kleros*, meaning a "part, lot, or inheritance." In the New Testament *kleros* refers to all of God's people as being His special portion, as, for example, in Ephesians 1:11 or 1 Peter 5:3. The word *laity* is derived from the Greek word *laos*, meaning simply "people."

Building on the image of God's choosing people for special ends, we see even in the Old Testament God's expansive grace. In Exodus 18 God causes Moses, through the advice of his father-in-law, to delegate. In the prophecy of Joel, the prophet foresees a time when God's Spirit will be poured out ever more widely.

The reality of this is seen in the New Testament as well. The ministry of Christ and the outpouring of the Holy Spirit heralded a new age. Among many other passages, the parable of the wineskins, the rending of the veil at the crucifixion, the outpouring of the Holy Spirit, and Paul's use of the body image and his language in Ephesians 4 were all used in the Reformation to recover the idea of the priesthood of all believers; and they have all given impetus to the every-member ministry movement.

The New Testament church was born into a world of small communities.[1] "With the exception of Ignatius of Antioch, who applies the notion of *kleros* to the martyr, we have to wait until the beginning of the third century before encountering the term *kleros* used to describe a limited group within the Christian community."[2] While the synagogue and the *ecclesia* were not egalitarian organizations, they were voluntary associations. It was into such organizations—actual gatherings of people in regularly constituted meetings—that Christians were spiritually born. The church in the New Testament was clearly understood to be neither a physical building, nor an abstract concept, but an actual gathering of people, a context of committed relationships, gifted by God with life in order to live and serve. As such, the church was like a family, with a combination of defined roles, and yet suffused with a mutual, self-giving love. It was like a body, with a cohesion of the distinct parts for the benefit of the whole. There was an order of the whole to the benefit of all.

While the New Testament outlines several distinct roles within the body, one looks in vain for individuals in the community who are called "priests" distinct from the other members of the church.[3] In the New Testament, all believers were priests; the whole community was priestly. Priestly offerings (*prosphora*), sacrifices (*thusia*), and firstfruits (*aparche*) are offered not by a particular priestly class of Christians, but by

Christians in general.[4] According to the New Testament picture, every member is a minister, a servant, a priest. Every member is consecrated to this end. We are all made holy. We all congregate. We are all baptized. We all commit ourselves to one another. We all give attention to God's Word and join in singing His praises. We all bear witness to the truth of the Gospel, and we all give ourselves in service. We all pay the bills of the church, and we all join together around the Lord's Table. Together we love, we pray, we learn, and we study. None of these tasks are the special preserve of a priestly caste. It is precisely this biblical emphasis on the role of all Christians that many today are claiming to have even more faithfully grasped in their understanding of every-member ministry.

EVERY-MEMBER MINISTRY

The Beginnings (The Reformation to the 1960s)

The current popularity of the idea of every-member ministry is in many ways an echo of the Reformation. One of the chief changes in churches that occurred in the European Reformation of the sixteenth century was the reemergence of the laity. It may seem strange to suggest that people could ever have been submerged or obscured in the church, being composed, as it is, of people. But such was the case. For a thousand years those who called themselves Christians intended to relate to God through a church that they conceived to be something other than themselves. There they went. There they had God's grace given to them (or withheld from them). By the action of the church they understood themselves to be admitted to God's Kingdom, and by the action of the church they obtained their final earthly cleansing before being sent on to have their purging completed beyond the grave. The church was a structure, a living organism composed of those specially ordained to dispense God's grace and shepherd His flock.

It is not that the pre-Reformation church had no appreciation for the importance of the unordained, but there were some unbiblical constraints on the laity in traditional Roman Catholicism. The Reformation recovered the biblical truth of every member being a priest. This belief in the priesthood of all believers, "far from being anti-ministerial . . . sets the ministerial priesthood within the context of the universal priesthood."[5]

The Priesthood of All Believers

Along with stressing the priesthood of all believers, most of Protestantism (excluding a few movements like the Quakers and the Plymouth Brethren) also had its own traditions about an elevated role for the pastor and allowed a clergy-centered conception of the church to dominate once again.[6]

Some, however, did not. Some children of the Reformation had always stressed the priesthood of all believers and the consequently high responsibility of all church members.[7] In the twentieth century, the discussion about the role of the laity reemerged as a central discussion of theologians, pastors, and other Christians throughout Christendom. With the rise of the ecumenical movement early in the century, discussion of Christian commonalities was encouraged, and the role of the laity was one obvious similarity between denominations; yet little substantive change was affected. The 1940s saw America at large witnessing what could be done through every-citizen mobilization, as even women were encouraged to leave their homes to take wartime jobs in order to help the war effort. Americans learned what could be done through mobilizing all of one's resources.

By the 1960s the church seemed to much of the youth culture hidebound and increasingly irrelevant. In 1968 a Gallup poll indicated that 72 percent of Americans thought religion was losing its influence on American life, over five times more than Gallup had reported holding that opinion just ten years earlier. Insisting on change, one young writer wrote a fictional piece called "Mr. Clergyman, Listen." Part of it was as follows:

> The Christian church is without hope unless you, Mr. Clergyman, are willing to change. Many of us still have faith in the institutional Christian church. We haven't given up, but we want a new church, a church that is not centered around you but only coordinated by your guiding hand. A church that is layman-centered instead of clergy-centered. A church that will listen to our gripes and our suggestions and discuss them with us. We want desperately to have a dialogue with you. Will you listen to us? We've listened to you for years.[8]

The changing 1960s saw several streams of "renewal" that would contribute to the every-member ministry mind-set shift in the 1970s away from traditional pastor- or priest-centered conceptions of the church. Old structures were questioned, and new structures were advocated. In Roman Catholicism there was a renewed appreciation for the role of the laity at Vatican II. Mass is now said in the vernacular, and the laity communicate in both elements (i.e., they receive both bread and wine at Communion).[9] It seems that everyone from the Quaker Elton Trueblood to the Baptist Findley Edge was writing about recovering the ministry of the average church member.[10] From the mainline Protestant denominations, the older ecumenical stream of reconsidering the place of the laity was coming into evangelical circles through the work of Trueblood, Edge, Keith Miller, Donald Bloesch, and others. In 1960 Joseph Bayly published his modern parable *The Gospel Blimp* in which he lampooned the lame ministries that hindered true ministry, which is relational, extramural, and fruitful.

In 1961 a number of more popular books were published independently of one another that called for renewal of church life *via* a recovery of lay ministry.[11] Trueblood called for the company to be committed and for the fellowship to be incendiary. Lay members of churches had no right to expect reduced terms of service, he insisted.[12] "There can be no renewal without the glad acceptance of universal ministry."[13] Until the early 1970s, this idea seemed to be far more advanced among the more liberal denominations than among the more evangelical churches.

In the 1960s another headwater of the move toward every-member ministry gained prominence. Since the late 1940s the Church of the Saviour, an innovative church in Washington, D.C., had been growing up under the leadership of Gordon Cosby. Trained as a Southern Baptist, Cosby had served as a chaplain in World War II. There, on the field with the soldiers in his care, he had tried out some new ideas about the nature of the church. He focused on the church not being a building, but rather being wherever the people of the church were. Upon his return to the States, Cosby founded the Church of the Saviour as a church based on ministry-oriented small groups and high member commitment. The church gained increasing prominence in the 1960s through the writings of one member, Elizabeth O'Connor.[14] In 1975 Cosby published his *Handbook for Mission Groups* as both a theoretical and practical guide to the more small-group and ministry-focused form of church that he had pioneered.[15] Cosby stressed the importance of "discovering and calling

The Priesthood of All Believers

forth the gifts of each group member." In fact, "the discovering and nurturing of the gifts of its members remains the primary work of the mission group."[16]

Cosby began one sermon by saying, "Every person called by Jesus Christ into his Body is given a gift, and he is to employ it on behalf of the whole Body, thus making it to function smoothly and know richness and power."[17] Cosby stressed 1 Corinthians 12 and the gifts that God gives to shape His body in service. By the 1970s Cosby's work was becoming more well known among American evangelicals.

Elton Trueblood wrote in 1972, "Up to now, there has been less interest among strong evangelicals in the development of small groups and in the cultivation of the universal ministry than there has been among those of liberal tendencies."[18] But in the late 1960s and early 1970s this stream increasingly poured into evangelical circles. There it was met not only by a culture shifting toward anti-institutionalism, but by an existing anti-clericalism among evangelicals, and by some groundbreaking work by Robert Coleman (in part recovering and packaging A. B. Bruce and reinforcing what was happening in many of the major parachurch youth and college movements).

The anti-clericalism is well-represented by the works of Watchman Nee. Though much of his teaching was simple, searching, and scriptural, still more of it could be described as an eclectic combination of Plymouth Brethren anti-clericalism with Keswick higher-life teaching informed by a nearly gnostic distrust of the physical world.[19] In the 1960s and 1970s several of Nee's works that dealt with church life were translated into English and published.[20] Nee's understanding of the individual Christian life was that the Holy Spirit was to become his spirit. So, too, Nee believed that the church was to be a continuation of the incarnation of Christ, so much so that the church was to become ever more an extension of Christ. The local church was to depend not on a minister, but on the elders. Nee taught that "the ideal meeting-place of the saints is their own private homes" and that "church meetings are not the responsibility of the workers. Local believers should learn to use the spiritual gifts with which God has entrusted them to minister to their fellow-believers. The principle on which all church meetings are conducted is that of the 'round-table,' not of the 'pulpit-and-pew.'"[21] Nee's conclusions, spoken originally in China in the 1930s, but not published in English in America

The Present Evangelical Crisis

until the early 1960s, seemed like prophesies about much of the "renewal" teaching that was to come in the next decades.

Certainly another key proponent in the 1960s' reconsidering the face of the church and of ministry was Robert Coleman. First published in January 1963, Coleman's book *The Master Plan of Evangelism* has gone through more than sixty printings and has sold more than a million copies, making it one of evangelicalism's best-selling books. In this book, Coleman reminded evangelicals that Jesus is not only our Savior, but He is also our example in ministry. Along with reenergizing the historic Christian model of discipleship, Coleman's book certainly did have the effect of challenging Christians more broadly to be involved in ministry. Evangelism and discipleship were not simply to be left to the pastors; indeed, they were ministries in which all Christians could and should participate. One did not need to be able to preach to crowds on Sunday mornings in order to follow the Master's plan of evangelism.

Coleman's ideas were not novel, of course. Antecedents ranged from Roman "spiritual directors" to the writings of A. B. Bruce to the ministry of E. J. Nash and his boys' camps in Britain. What was new, however, were the responsive fields Coleman's message of lay ministry found in the campus parachurch ministries. For example, while working with the Navigators in the 1970s, LeRoy Eims applied the same principles to training disciples that Coleman advocated for evangelism. In 1978 Eims published a "how-to" book that was to be a manual of practice for such discipleship training—*The Lost Art of Disciple Making.*[22] In the foreword to it, Robert Coleman warmly commended the volume. "Jesus came to save the world, and to that end He died, but on His way to the cross He concentrated His life on making a few disciples. These men were taught to do the same, until through the process of reproduction, the gospel of the kingdom would reach to the ends of the earth."[23]

Eims's account begins portentously with the story of a busy and successful pastor "willing to fly anywhere in the United States to meet me and discuss his problem for half a day or so." For the first few chapters of his book, Eims laid out for the reader a step-by-step process similar to that which Coleman had encouraged as the pattern of Jesus. Eims picked up where Coleman left off and traced the continuing pattern of discipling until the disciple reproduces. Again, in Eims's work the ministry was something that was expressly not for ministers only (indeed, as his open-

The Priesthood of All Believers

ing illustration showed, recognized ministers often don't know how to
minister); rather, the ministry was open to all those with the spiritual
maturity and ability to win and build others. To the late 1960s and early
1970s, office seemed irrelevant; function alone was clearly to be the concern of sincere Christians.

The Change (1970s)

The 1970s were the time when every-member ministry seemed to win the
day in evangelical circles. At the beginning of the 1970s, the idea seemed
novel; by the end, it seemed standard. Three key factors in gaining this
dominance were the writing of Larry Richards, the ministry of Ray
Stedman, and the spiritual gifts movement (which would eventually be
brought to many evangelicals as a part of the church growth movement).

Larry Richards. In many ways Larry Richards has been the model-
builder for the recovery of every-member ministry. Through his popular
writings, and perhaps even more through his books used as seminary
textbooks for more than two decades, Richards has fed and shaped the
way pastors and other church leaders have thought of ministry. In 1970
Richards wrote that "there must be openness in all our meetings to per-
mit the participation of any and every member. This is a principle which
is basic, significant, and crucial in the renewal of the church. Each
believer does have a special ability from God to contribute to the common good. The life, and the meetings, of the church *must* recognize the
existence of these gifts, and make provision for their exercise."[24] Richards
went on to provide many practical tools for those involved in church
renewal. In 1973 he published a book with a study guide on church unity
and a book on starting and running small groups.[25] In 1974 Richards
published a popular book on Christian growth and in 1975 *A Theology
of Christian Education.*[26] Then in 1980 Richards coauthored a textbook
on church leadership, and in 1982 a book on personal ministry, subtitled
Spiritual Giftedness in the Local Church.[27] These last three became
widely used textbooks in American evangelical seminaries throughout the
1980s.

Richards seemed effectively, if unintentionally, to translate cultural
trends of self-expression and egalitarianism into popular evangelical
idiom. "There is no . . . distinction in the body between 'clergy' and 'laity.'

The work of the Spirit is in all and through all. Every believer, as a member of the laos of God, is a minister. Leaders in the church, as servants of the servants of God, are to guide others into the exercise of their gifts so that the whole body might grow. The 'superstar' approach to ministry is clearly rejected, for each member's function is vital to the growth of the body, and thus indispensable."[28]

Ray Stedman. What Coleman, Eims, and others did for particular aspects of the pastor's role, Ray Stedman did for much of the thinking about the ministry of the church as a whole. "For the *ministry's* sake," said Coleman and Eims; "for the *church's* sake," said Stedman and Richards, "the laity must reassume the ministry." In light of the need and of the ability of the laity and of the gifted nature of the whole congregation, the ministry must no longer be left to one qualified person. The first group said that ministry *could* be done by others, and the second that it *must* be.

If just one book could be said to be the father of the every-member ministry movement, it would probably be Ray Stedman's 1972 book *Body Life.*[29] In it, said Billy Graham in a foreword, Stedman "has given us a 'how-to' book which shows us how the church can relate to community life in a meaningful, satisfactory and redeeming manner."[30] In this book Stedman, pastor of the Peninsula Bible Church in Palo Alto, California, advocated the rediscovery of the church as fellowship, a group of Christians living in close, loving, caring community with each other. Especially emphasizing Ephesians 4, Stedman laid out the biblical purpose of the church. Much of the power will be recovered in the church, he suggested, when Christians discover and use their spiritual gifts.

Pivoting his understanding on the word "began" in Acts 1:1, Stedman insisted that the church was the continuing incarnation of Jesus.[31] Stedman decried the pastor's being exclusively responsible for the church's ministry: "Surely, if a pope over the whole church is bad, a pope in every church is no better!"[32] He called for a return to the New Testament practice of having the ministry carried on not simply by the few pastor-teachers, but by the priesthood of all believers, each one gifted by the Holy Spirit.

Spiritual Gifts. "God continues to say to the Church worldwide that the ministry of the Church must be placed in the hands of the laypeople. And He continues to steer the Church toward the biblical teaching on spiritual gifts as the essential foundation for the ministry of the laity." So wrote C. Peter Wagner, guru of church growth, in 1994.[33] The charismatic renewal in the Roman Catholic Church and the mainline Protestant groups helped to propel the idea of spiritual gifts onto the front burner of attention, even in non-charismatic renewal circles. Gordon Cosby actually tied together lay ministry, small groups, and spiritual gifts in his teaching:

> . . . the gift conferred by the Holy Spirit upon the new person in Christ is not a vague, general propensity, but a specific power or capacity peculiar to an individual, to be exercised for the good of the group. The failure to take this teaching of Paul seriously is the cause of the apathy and ineffectiveness in the Christian church of our time. These specific spiritual gifts are received only when the church is the church as Christ intended it to be, that is to say, when it is made up of relatively small groups of people characterized by intimate, close relationships, and committed to a specific mission directed toward winning some small corner or segment of the world for Christ.[34]

But it was neither charismatics nor Cosby who finally opened up the evangelical heartland to spiritual gifts. While there were certainly hundreds and thousands of Christians who had a part in this, Ray Stedman's call for a rediscovery of spiritual gifts was particularly significant. As a well-known non-charismatic pastor (Dallas-trained, no less!), Stedman's call drew the attention of many who otherwise might well have remained skeptical of the whole movement. Indeed, "No other book did so much in opening the way for an awareness of the value of spiritual gifts in the non-Pentecostal denominations. . . ."[35]

So widespread and basic have instructions to Christians to find their spiritual gift or gifts become that one finds sections on this in introductory books on the Christian life. For example, in the basic discipling guide by Navigator staff-worker Walter Henrichsen, *Disciples Are Made—Not Born*—he writes:

> Another problem we face today regarding the gifts is the tremendous feeling of inadequacy that many Christians have simply because they are not sure what their gifts are. They know that

they are supposed to have gifts—at least this is what they have been taught from the Bible—but if you were to ask them what their gifts are, they would be unable to answer. As we train young Christians to become disciples, one of our primary objectives should be to help them discover and develop their gifts, since every believer has gifts which God holds him accountable for developing and using for the sake of the body.[36]

In K. C. Hinckley's helpful *Compact Guide to the Christian Life* (NavPress, 1989), the section on the Holy Spirit is largely taken up with the question of discovering our spiritual gifts.[37] One third of Darrell Robinson's *Total Church Life* has to do with spiritual gifts and their use for a church's growth.[38] Discovery of one's gift or gifts is to take place through reflection, action, and evaluation.[39] A number of "inventories" have been published for the use of Christians looking for their spiritual gifts.[40]

Probably the most influential book on discovering spiritual gifts has, at this writing, gone through two editions. C. Peter Wagner originally published his book *Your Spiritual Gifts Can Help Your Church Grow* in 1979. After being widely used for fifteen years, Wagner updated and expanded the book, adding a questionnaire and altering his understanding of some of the more extraordinary gifts, based in part upon his experience with John Wimber and the Anaheim Vineyard Christian Fellowship. Wagner wrote from a belief in the primary authority of Scripture, but with his own experience as admittedly another "source . . . equally essential for my conclusion."[41] His book is both better researched and more balanced than many other books on the topic.

Wagner, like those who wrote before him, presented spiritual gifts as pivotal for the spiritual health of the individual and the church. "Ignorance of spiritual gifts may be a chief cause of retarded church growth today. It also may be at the root of much of the discouragement, insecurity, frustration and guilt that plagues many Christians and curtails their total effectiveness for God."[42] He used much of the same subjective language as other writers, referring to discovering one's spiritual gift as a "liberating, invigorating and uplifting" experience.[43] He referred to Christians' "spiritual personalities," with our "gift-mixes" being their most fundamental component.[44] Wagner defended using the word "dis-

The Priesthood of All Believers

cover" in reference to finding our spiritual gifts because "spiritual gifts are received, not achieved."[45]

Wagner openly discussed the dangers of focusing on spiritual gifts: that believers will be confused by the teaching, that they will use the discovery of a gift to release themselves from obedience in areas where they are not gifted, that people will deceive themselves about what gifts they have. Good teaching and honest conversations, Wagner suggested, should remedy these problems. This should be a fundamental role of the pastor. It is his role, after all, Wagner suggested, to ensure every-member ministry. "The best pastor is not one who relieves members of their ministries, but one who makes sure each member has a ministry and is working hard at it."[46] This understanding has now become the received wisdom among American evangelicals.

The Development (1970s Through the Present)

From the 1970s until now, two broad streams have developed from the earlier excitement for every-member ministry. The first stream we will call the "open church" stream. These are those who think that the church must be largely redefined and dissolved into the ministry of the laity. The second stream we will call the "active church" stream. These are those who feel that the ministry of the laity can be accomplished within more traditional structures.

THE OPEN CHURCH. Early in the move to every-member ministry, there came to the fore a more pure, radical school of every-member ministry in which the work of the people came very much to submerge and sometimes even to eliminate any distinct work for the traditional pastor. This more radical stream has found some expression in many denominational traditions. Among Wesleyans, it was represented by Larry Richards himself and Robert C. Girard (Richards's pastor) and found its most notable champion in Howard Snyder.

One place where the call to body life seemed to be radically heeded was at Our Heritage Wesleyan Church in Scottsdale, Arizona. The pastor, Girard, wrote about this congregational renewal and some of the principles that he saw it embodying in two books in the 1970s. First he wrote *Brethren, Hang Loose* (1972) and then *Brethren, Hang Together*

(1979). Girard had gone to Scottsdale sponsored by the Wesleyan Methodist Church in order to pioneer a new work there. He was a successful evangelical church planter, having been encouraged in his evangelistic strategies by reading Coleman's *Master Plan of Evangelism*. After a few years at it, though, Girard began to wonder what he had actually accomplished despite numerical growth.

At this time, discouraged in his own church planting, Girard was influenced by Watchman Nee's book, *What Shall This Man Do?* (Christian Literature Crusade, 1967), in which Nee stressed the importance of every-member ministry. Girard also heard Major W. Ian Thomas speak on resting in Christ, and he embraced Thomas's idea of quitting and letting Christ live through you. During this time he also read some of Larry Richards's ideas about reforming the church and reported being deeply influenced by them.[47]

One of the practical results of these influences was Girard's church rejecting traditional Sunday evening and midweek meetings and moving to a cell group structure that, by its very nature, could not have leadership from the senior pastor alone. The very structure of this refashioned church would necessitate a shift of both authority and responsibility from the pulpit to the pew, from the preacher to the people. Girard enunciated seven principles of New Testament church life, including "Recognize the priesthood of all believers" and "Release church life from the confines of the church building."[48] Girard told his congregation:

> We must come to realize that this church has more than one minister. You have depended too long on the ministry of one man. I've helped to teach you to do that. But now I see that God has given *every* believer in Christ a ministry to the other members of the Body. Until each of us begins to find his ministry, the church will never really be healthy. As long as the congregation looks only to its pastor for life and ministry, we will never experience the kind of fellowship the New Testament Church experienced, and our life together will never be full and abundant as God intended it to be.[49]

Instead of more traditional patterns, Girard led his church into practical expressions of the theology of the priesthood of all believers. These expressions included small groups, a time for informal conversation

The Priesthood of All Believers

between members during the Sunday morning service, a completely unstructured evening meeting, and the use of laymen for more of the church's teaching. His own role diminished in significance. In fact, Girard even had a service of ordination in which he led his church in ordaining to ministry all the members of the church.[50] All of this was naturally accompanied by refocusing from the ministry done in the church building to ministry done outside its walls.

The church Girard built increasingly became a network of relationships. Inside the building, first the pews were unbolted and changed into a semicircular arrangement, and then eventually, in 1979, the congregation returned the building to the sponsoring denomination as the church itself moved solely to meeting in homes and rented spaces.[51] As Girard said to a reporter for the *Scottsdale Press* in January 1979, "One of our strong emphases in the past ten years has been to get away from the whole idea that only professionals can do something. Every believer is a priest; it is a matter of personal talents and gifts and sensitivity; it has nothing to do with training."[52]

Another influential writer in advancing the cause of every-member ministry in evangelical circles was Howard Snyder, a Free Methodist pastor, missionary, and seminary professor. The author of a number of books published by InterVarsity Press, three in particular helped shape the evangelical mind on this matter in the late 1970s and early 1980s. Snyder's *The Problem of Wine Skins*, *The Community of the King*, and *Liberating the Church* each had the kind of radical message that appealed to the student and staff-worker audience of InterVarsity Press's books.[53]

The first of these three books was *The Problem of Wine Skins*. In it, surveying the life of the church in the mid-1970s and utilizing his cross-cultural experience, having lived in Brazil, Snyder asserted the importance of understanding the church: "the church is an essential part of the gospel, and ecclesiology is inseparable from soteriology."[54] Other than Scripture, Snyder attributes the insights of his critique of the church to four movements: the personal evangelism movement, the church renewal movement, the church growth movement, and the charismatic movement. From these came insights about the ministry of the laity, small groups, sensitivity to needs, and spiritual gifts, which Snyder developed throughout his writings.

Snyder acknowledged his indebtedness to Coleman's *The Master*

Plan of Evangelism and to Stedman's *Body Life*. He also cited Larry Richards and Gene Getz. But he said such books didn't go far enough. Seeing the Old Testament temple and king as parallel to the modern-day church building and pastor, Snyder suggested that we needed to recon- sider the likelihood that God preferred the movable tabernacle to the fixed temple, and the charismatic judges to the worldly kings. He there- fore suggested that we need to get rid of our "edifice complex" and our love of superstar pastors. The church's structures are the negotiable wine- skins, and the Gospel itself the wine. Form, therefore, must follow func- tion. (Wesleyanism was always more open to experience as an authoritative source for Christian practice.)

Small groups, he argued, are the basic structure for experiencing New Testament *koinonia*. (Wesley was of course a pioneer in this.)[55] The laity are the church, and spiritual gifts are essential for our spiritual health. In his 1983 book *Liberating the Church*, Snyder maintained that "the three foundation stones for the ministry of God's people are the priesthood of believers, the gifts of the Spirit and the servanthood example of Jesus."[56] Snyder cautioned that the priesthood of the believer must not degenerate into a kind of rugged individualism, nor a concentration on spiritual gifts into self-gratification. "All are priests; all are gifted. . . . Believers carry out their ministries differently, according . . . to the gifts they receive from God."[57]

Among Baptists, the open church stream was represented by David Haney and Ralph Neighbour.[58] Among those Baptists who are more the- ologically conservative, it continues to be represented by Neighbour and by Gene Edwards.[59] Among more liberal Baptists, the priesthood of all believers is a doctrine of special significance for another set of reasons.[60] Among Presbyterians, Greg Ogden has called for a new reformation, writing that the sixteenth-century Reformation had succeeded in return- ing the Word of God to the people of God, but that now a second refor- mation was needed in order to return the ministry of God to the people of God.[61]

Typical of this more radical strain is James Rutz's book, *The Open Church*. Indebted to Gene Edwards and Watchman Nee, endorsed by Ray Stedman and other notable evangelicals, Rutz called the church back to its earlier openness. The openness that he intended in particular is the open worship of praising God, the open sharing in which Christians build

The Priesthood of All Believers

each other up, and the open ministry in which we serve others. According to Rutz, the church simply handed all this over to professionals in the fourth century. The sixteenth-century Reformation recovered some lost ground, but churches still remained too closed to laymen.[62]

Rutz held up Gordon Cosby's Church of the Saviour in Washington, D.C. as an example of a more "open" church. Larry Richards was cited as having written "the" book on leadership.[63] Gene Edwards contributed a few chapters to the book. The reader was told that nearly all parts of today's institutional churches are post-Constantinian and therefore pagan, from choirs to pulpits. The answer, he suggested, was to return to the early church pattern of a lay-centered "living room" church with needs and ministries shared by all.

THE ACTIVE CHURCH. At the same time, alongside this more radical stream of every-member ministry, there arose a more moderate stream. These pastors and authors advocate melding every-member ministry into traditional structures. They are represented among the mainline denominations by the work of Melvin Steinbron (Presbyterian Church—USA), Patricia Page (Lutheran), and Anne Rowthorn (Roman Catholic). Such lay ministry has been encouraged for years across denominations by the Stephen Ministries and the Alban Institute and through the church consulting work of Lyle Schaller.[64]

Melvin Steinbron is one of the best examples of a mainline evangelical pastor who has been active in championing lay ministry both in life and in writing. From his ministry at College Hill Presbyterian Church, Cincinnati and Hope Presbyterian Church, Minneapolis, Steinbron has developed Lay Pastors Ministry. In two books—*Can the Pastor Do it Alone?* and *The Lay Driven Church*—Steinbron lays out his challenge to pastors and lay-leaders alike to share the ministry.[65] The pastoring that Steinbron calls all Christians to be a part of is the practice of praying, being available, and exemplifying the Christian life to others during good and bad times. Steinbron's conviction is that "it takes all the people of God to do all the work of God."[66] He suggests deliberate relationships and commitments, training, discovery of spiritual gifts, use of small groups (though in his later book he acknowledges that their use may now be declining in churches), and the commitment of the leadership of the church to lay ministry.

The Present Evangelical Crisis

Among evangelicals, this active church stream has been well-represented among pastors across denominational traditions. Gene Getz's work stands out as a particularly balanced appreciation of special gifts being exercised in the context of every-member ministry.[67] Getz influenced the lay ministry movement among evangelicals not only through his teaching at Dallas and by pastoring churches, but through his many writings. In 1981 he published a series of three books called the "One Another Series."[68] Here Getz was particularly careful in his exhortation about the importance of every member's responsibility for his or her gifts. He wrote that the Bible does "not emphasize that we as individuals are to look for and to try to discover our gifts so we can function as members of Christ's body. Rather, we're simply to use the gifts and abilities God has given us to build up the body of Christ with a proper attitude."[69]

In a footnote, Getz corrected the way some had taken 1 Corinthians 14:1 as an exhortation to individuals to seek spiritual gifts, suggesting that instead Paul's audience there, as throughout that section, was the Corinthian congregation as a whole. Getz warned against introspection and instead encouraged focusing on serving others.[70] Getz stressed the fact that the New Testament corporate nature of the Christian life is to be reproduced in churches today in everything from evangelism to discipling.

Many other evangelical pastors have incorporated combinations of small group structure and the utilization of spiritual gifts into somewhat traditional church structures and have written about it. Among them are Baptists Frank Tillapaugh, Leith Anderson, Eric Wright, and Darrell Robinson, non-denominational pastors Daniel Brown, Earl Comfort, Wayne Mack, and David Swavely, and Nazarenes Eddy Hall and Gary Morsch.[71]

Baptist pastor Rick Warren and Evangelical Free Church pastor Bill Hull have each written particularly carefully about every-member ministry. If other pastors have written with confidence because of the success of their own congregations, none could exceed the confidence with which Rick Warren writes. Warren, pastor of Saddleback Valley Community Church in Orange County, California, has seen thousands come into his church, and many of those have been equipped for lay ministry. He included a chapter called "Turning Members into Ministers" in his 1995 book *The Purpose-Driven Church*. Warren wrote that "Every church needs an intentional, well-planned system for uncovering, mobilizing and supporting the giftedness of its members."[72] Warren teaches in his church that every believer is a minister and that every ministry is important. Furthermore, Christians are dependent on each other, and a believer's ministry is an expression of his or her spiritual gifts, heart, abilities, personality, and experience (or "SHAPE"). In his book Warren cautioned against an overemphasis on spiritual gifts to the neglect of these other factors that he mentioned. He suggested that Christians not try to reason so much from their gifts to their ministry, but from their ministry to their gifts. According to Warren, giving the ministry to the people is crucial for growth.

Bill Hull, an Evangelical Free Church pastor, has followed in the line of Coleman and Eims, writing of the centrality of disciplemaking for the Christian church, and particularly for the pastor's ministry. Most notable in this regard are his books *Jesus Christ, Disciplemaker* (NavPress, 1984), in which he (like Coleman before him) looked to the model of Jesus' own ministry, *The Disciple Making Pastor* (Revell, 1988), in which Hull presents such disciplemaking as the heart of pastoral ministry, *The Disciple Making Church* (Revell, 1990), in which he advocates "churchocentric evangelism," and *7 Steps to Transform Your Church* (Revell, 1993), practical congregational distillations from his earlier work.

Throughout all of these Hull, like Getz, represents a balance between an appreciation for the recovered New Testament necessity of every-member ministry while retaining a fine appreciation for the crucial nature of the leaders within the congregation, especially the pastor. The second of these books, *The Disciple Making Pastor*, has a foreword by Robert Coleman commending the work, and well it should, for in this work Coleman's initial contribution of twenty-five years earlier found its way back to the heart of the pastoral ministry of the church. Coleman's work, which wittingly or unwittingly encouraged the laicizing of ministry in the evangelical church, was now being presented as the fundamental work of the church's full-time pastors.

Bill Hull has well summarized the conclusion of the previous quarter-century's thinking about the role of the pastor: his "top priority as teacher/equipper is to get the work of ministry done through others. Doing it right means multiplication of ministry through every member." This emphasis has been endemic to American evangelicalism for the last few decades. From college inductive Bible studies to Evangelism

Explosion, from Bear Valley Baptist Church in Denver to College Hill Presbyterian in Cincinnati, the received wisdom has been that if the work of the ministry is to be done, every member must be seen as a minister.

CONTRIBUTIONS OF EVERY-MEMBER MINISTRY AT ITS BEST

At its best, the ideas that are propagated in the name of every-member ministry can contribute substantially to the health of evangelical churches. Here are suggestions of what some of those blessings might be.

The Blessing of Perspective

For the pastor in particular, the recovery of some more biblical shape to his role can be immensely helpful. While Scripture leaves us in no doubt that he is in a role of particular responsibility, it is wholesome to remind the pastor that it's not all up to him.

The Blessing of Fellowship

This movement has often encouraged small groups, which can make important contributions to the life of the body by the fellowship they can foster and the pastoral needs they can help meet. Small groups can be an important vehicle for helping people to grow spiritually. Sociologist Robert Wuthnow has suggested that "the desire for community appears to be less significant as a factor driving the small-group movement than the desire for spiritual growth."[73]

For the individual believer, there may be important contributions made.

The Blessing of Gifts

There is no doubt that one of the central emphases of this movement has been to recognize the importance of the gifts in the church and to recognize that all these gifts are important, as is every member of the body. The members exercising these gifts can foster both gratitude to God and a

The Priesthood of All Believers

heightened sense of accountability for them. It can also encourage us in our responsibility for each other.

The Blessing of Growth

Serving God and others as we are called to may well lead to more completeness for the individual believer in many ways. Our self-centeredness may be countered and our complaining curbed. (People involved in ministry tend to spend less time complaining because their priorities are clarified by close involvement in ministry.) Biblical knowledge may be encouraged. The serving believer may be more fulfilled and satisfied within himself, and even more understanding and supportive of those in leadership.

The Blessing of Relationships

There is no doubt that giving oneself in ministry with others could encourage real relationships to form, relationships that would go beyond the shallow substitutes that may pass for spirituality as pleasantries are exchanged after church meetings.

The Blessing of Seriousness

Every-member ministry may well help the believer take church and the Christian life more seriously.

The Blessing of Obedience

For many Christians, an emphasis on every-member ministry may well be tantamount to a recovery of obedience in many areas of the Christian life, from evangelism to discipleship, from giving to loving.

The Blessing of Service

One specific area of obedience that may flourish through this emphasis is a renewed recognition that to be a Christian is to be a minister. The call

The Present Evangelical Crisis

to Christ is the call to service. In that sense, it may emphasize the deeply Christian and profoundly countercultural ethic of service as we are changed from being a taker to being a giver.

The Blessing of Priesthood

Obviously, this emphasis may be part and parcel of a recovery of the biblical teaching of the priesthood of all believers, both in our dependence upon and service to God, and in our dependence upon and service to others.

The Blessing of Maturity

Such an emphasis may lead to more completeness and wholeness in the body, and in its witness and work. As each Christian does what we are gifted and called to do, the body is built up, and God's character is displayed. Doing what we're made to do should help everybody and should glorify God.

The Blessing of Resources

Stressing the biblical responsibilities of all Christians can help to mobilize the entire church for God's ends. It can quite simply mean more resources for God's work.

The Blessing of Efficiency

Lay ministry is often the most efficient and economical way to meet needs, in terms of time and money, effort and resources.

The Blessing of Corporate Responsibility

Every-member ministry may encourage a recognition of the responsibility of the whole body. In Matthew 18 Jesus tells the one sinned against to bring the unrepentant sinner not to the clergy, but to the whole assembly. And in 2 Timothy 4:3-4, Paul held accountable not simply the false teach-

The Priesthood of All Believers

ers, but those who gathered the teachers to say what they wanted to hear. In Acts 6 it was the whole congregation who chose the early deacons.

The Blessing of Witness

Each member being involved in Christian service may be a good witness to outsiders, showing them more of the humanity that God created us to bear as we serve others. The image of God is displayed as we give our lives in service.

The Blessing of Perseverance

Recovering the ministry that every member is to perform may make the church better suited for an openly hostile age like ours. It may be our best protection against a devouring secularism. Loren Mead, in his 1991 study *The Once and Future Church*, wrote that "Clericalism—like sin—is carrying a good thing too far."[74] In his insightful treatment, Mead suggested that the situation in which the church has found itself has changed from its mission being at "the edge of the empire" to being at "the front door of the local church." Among its many other implications, this change will mean the laity necessarily becoming much more active in fulfilling the ministry of the church.

CAUTIONS ABOUT EVERY-MEMBER MINISTRY AT ITS WORST

At its worst, some versions of every-member ministry can damage or even destroy individual congregations, as even some of those congregations mentioned in this chapter found. Here are suggestions of what some of the dangers of every-member ministry might be.

The Danger of Misunderstanding the Bible

Biblically, the proponents of every-member ministry seem to misunderstand Scripture sometimes. The most notable example of this is in the treatment of Ephesians 4:11-12. There the three phrases translated as parallel by the AV as "for the perfecting of the saints, for the work of the min-

The Present Evangelical Crisis

istry, for the edifying of the body of Christ" are taken by some proponents of the every-member ministry movement as better translated, "to prepare God's people for works of service, so that the body of Christ may be built up." Grammatically the former translation is preferable.[75] Is it simply coincidence that the latter translation (the NIV) was done in the early 1970s?

The Danger of Misunderstanding the Church

Theologically, those in the every-member ministry movement often speak of the church as the continuing incarnation of Christ (parallel to the idea of Watchman Nee and others that the Holy Spirit replaces the fallen human spirit at regeneration). This idea can lend itself to a misunderstanding of the incarnation of Christ and to an overidentification of the church with God.

The Danger of Misunderstanding History

Historically, several of these authors simplify history to the point of making the church before Constantine seem near perfection and the church after Constantine completely without redeeming merit. More than simply bad history, this is distortion and can result in wrongly justifying our own ideas and hiding our own errors from ourselves.

The Danger of Anarchy

As a whole, every-member ministry can simply be difficult to manage, even tending to produce anarchy if people desert the care of the body as a whole for concern with the parts.

The Danger of Divisiveness

There are, of course, drawbacks to small groups. They can foster a parochialism and a narrowness of interest and outlook that leads to divisiveness. Could it be that some parts of the lay ministry movement are wrongly wedded to small groups, taking them to be an essential expression of the church rather than simply a cultural expression for our own time?

The Priesthood of All Believers

George Barna suggests that the popularity of small groups among evangelicals is already waning. Too, small groups can be a substitute for an even better level of regular relationships in a church. Such relationships can be even more natural, flexible, evangelistically useful, and personal than all but the best small groups. Lutheran theologian Carl Braaten has warned:

> Neopaganism is spiritual religion attuned to the "Zeitgeist." It has no use for the concrete historical element of the biblical gospel. It has no need of the church and the external word (*verbum externum*), turning instead to pure immediacy and inwardness in which each individual personality acquires knowledge of God out of the depths of his or her own experience. People of this type care solely for their own spiritual journeys through life, and while they believe in an emerging universal fellowship in the spirit of love, the reality of the church as an elect communion of saints and sacred things is alien to their thinking. They do not understand the doctrines of the gospel to be true statements about events that have happened once for all, but see them as symbols of eternal truths reflecting ever-recurrent processes of life in the presence of God. History itself is nothing but a resource of symbols to stimulate certain moods and feelings according to each person's private fancy. Worship means getting together in small groups of kindred spirits to hear one another's stories.[76]

For the individual believer, there are a number of further dangers.

The Danger of Reductionism

The Christian life could be misunderstood to be composed entirely of ministry.

The Danger of Busyness

An active every-member ministry program could encourage a believer to lose himself wrongly in the church, forfeiting natural time with family or friends as a result of busyness.

The Present Evangelical Crisis

The Danger of Mismatching

An emphasis on every-member ministry can unwittingly encourage people with not a lot of maturity to be put in places where they either feel, or in fact are, out of their depth spiritually.

The Danger of Narcissism

Ironically, the every-member ministry movement can encourage a hypersubjectivity, a wrong individualism and narcissism, with the needs of the church being subverted by the needs of the individual. Changes in culture make a certain biblical truth more open to our view than it had been previously, as when, for example, trials make us open to understanding the sovereignty of God. But changes in culture—apparent or more subtle—can have more ambiguous effects. How much of the recent discussion of spiritual gifts and lay ministry has been motivated by concern for the edification of the body and for good stewardship of God's gifts, and how much is simply the religious expression of a growing narcissism or a concern to maximize one's individual human happiness or potential regardless of others?

The Danger of Strength

The stress on strengths and giftedness, rather than weakness and willingness, is potentially a dangerous one for Christians. Certainly we are to be stewards of the gifts God gives to us, but there is no doubt that as Christians we are often called to acts of obedience that seem both strange and difficult at the time, obedience for which we might not readily say we were "gifted." Did Jeremiah or Ezekiel enjoy their work for God? Did Moses serve in an area of his particular giftedness? The emphasis on serving God according to what we perceive to be our spiritual gifts could lead us to be blind to the profoundly Christian calling to serve in areas where we are weak.

The Danger of Rebelliousness

It may be that some of the positive response to the call for lay ministry is fed by an antipathy to authority, so that we Christians could be in the

The Priesthood of All Believers

position of unwittingly aiding and abetting an anti-authoritarianism and a wrong radical secular individualism. While always dangerous, such aid would be particularly perilous for us today. Eugene Kennedy and Sara Charles have recently observed that "Americans do not distinguish authority, which is something good, from authoritarianism, which is something bad. . . . The stabilizing character of healthy authority is what has been missing. Its return is what will make us more confident and less anxious in managing our lives."[77]

The basic point in all of this for the church today is to recognize, in contradistinction from our culture, the goodness of authority. Humanity first fell by wrongfully distrusting good authority. While much authority in our world (and even in our churches) is twisted and self-serving, authority itself is not and should not therefore be despised. As evangelical Christians, we must beware of conducting our church life in ways that (intentionally or not) exploit the fear of authority in a fallen world. God is a God of order, and He has made us in His image. The very word *authority* reminds us of the relation between directing and creating. In our fallen, grasping, distrustful world, the church has been given the special task of showing that God's leadership, His kingship, His authority is non-abusive and good; that it is, in fact, that for which we were created. Distinction is not inherently unjust; authority is not inherently oppressive.

In a world at best full of insightful descriptions of the problem, the church has been entrusted with the solution. We are called to live out together a picture of the renewed relationship between us and God. That picture is our relationships with each other in the church. And one vital component of that is godly leadership.

The Danger of Poverty

Finally, there is within the every-member ministry movement a danger of the church impoverishing herself. Championing a lack of leadership can be a temptation for the minister to give in to laziness, and a temptation for the laity to engage in anti-clericalism. This may give rise to a confusion that causes us to ignore gifts (Eph. 4:11) that Christ intends to give to His church.

The Present Evangelical Crisis

CONCLUSION

This chapter has only scratched the surface of the wide world of contemporary evangelical thought and practice, which could stretch from the epic theme of the democratization of American Christianity to the longstanding ministry of Bill Gothard or the current influence of the Willow Creek model of networking.

The basic question before us remains: is every member of the church to be a minister? We are all to serve; we all bear some responsibility for the ministry of the Word in our midst. But we are not all responsible for it in the same way as the elders of a congregation are. Pastors and teachers are gifts of Christ to the body. Not all Christians are pastors and teachers, but we can all benefit by them if we do not ignore or abuse them, but rather receive them as Christ's good gifts to His church. If so, every member can be "built up until we all reach unity in the faith and in the knowledge of the Son of God and become mature, attaining to the whole measure of the fullness of Christ" (Eph. 4:12-13).

To conclude that members of the body are differently gifted, and that some functions are denied some persons is not to relegate the church to clericalism. The 1917 Code of Canon Law of the Roman Catholic Church treated all laity as minors. We need not go to that extreme simply in order to recognize legitimate offices in the church. God in His goodness has called all Christians to be priests, and He has called some among us to be pastors and teachers to mature God's people, to minister God's Word, and to build Christ's body. The way to do this lies between tyranny and anarchy; it is the way of sound service and healthy authority.

On the west front of Lincoln Cathedral in England, atop one pinnacle is a statue of Hugh, saintly bishop of Lincoln from 1188 to 1200. Opposite it, on another pinnacle, stands a statue of the Swineherd of Stow. According to legend, this man wondered what he could do to help the bishop build the cathedral. He decided to live a life of self-denial and save as much as he could for that cause. After years of such self-imposed sacrifice, he took the coins that had filled his horn and gave it all to the bishop. In gratitude, a statue of the swineherd was commissioned and placed atop the building for which he had so selflessly sacrificed.

The Priesthood of All Believers

The Swineherd gave his silver, the Bishop gave his might
Of heart and energy and brain, all precious in God's sight.
So in the Heavenly fabric, the Church of God Most High,
Each Christian has his part to do, and dare not pass it by.
The lowliest and the poorest in this may take his share,
For God has need of workmen to help him everywhere.
Blow, blow thine horn, good Swineherd, the sound shall echoes wake,
And laymen rise to do their part as thou, for Christ's dear sake.
And good St. Hugh shall bid us read and take it for our own,
A lesson from your statues twain, a sermon carved in stone.[78]

NOTES

1. See Robert Banks, *Paul's Idea of Community* (Grand Rapids, MI: Eerdmans, 1980), pp. 16-17.

2. Alexandre Faivre, *The Emergence of the Laity*, trans. David Smith (New York: Paulist, 1990) , p. 23.

3. See ibid., *passim*.

4. Romans 15:16; cf. Ephesians 5:2. Romans 12:1; Philippians 2:17; 4:18; cf. Ephesians 5:2; 2 Thessalonians 2:13; 1 Corinthians 16:15; Romans 16:5; 5:2; Ephesians 2:18; 3:12.

5. Cyril Eastwood, *The Priesthood of All Believers* (London: Epworth, 1960), p. 171.

6. See Richard Baxter, *The Reformed Pastor, passim*; John Gill, *A Complete Body of Doctrinal and Practical Divinity*, pp. 859-881.

7. See, for example the First London Confession (Baptist, 1646), Articles XXXVI-XLVII. A classic study of the priesthood of all believers is a study by that name, written by Cyril Eastwood (London: Epworth, 1960). For a collection about this topic in modern American Baptist life, see Walter B. Shurden, ed., *Proclaiming the Baptist Vision: The Priesthood of All Believers* (Macon, GA: Smith & Helwys, 1993), though this is largely a collection of poor work, excepting the pieces by the editor of the volume.

8. Rich Weaver, *Let This Church Die* (Plainfield, NJ: Logos, 1971), p. 89.

9. It is certainly true that many Roman Catholics are not satisfied with the amount of recognition that their church gives to the ministry of the laity. Lay presidency at the Eucharist is still a goal that eludes the laity in the Roman church. See, for example, Anne Rowthorn, *The Liberation of the Laity* (Harrisburg, PA: Morehouse, 1986).

10. Elton Trueblood, *The Incendiary Fellowship* (New York: Harper & Row, 1967); Findley B. Edge, *The Greening of the Church* (n.p., 1971).

11. E.g., Francis O. Ayres, *The Ministry of the Laity* (Philadelphia: Westminster,

The Present Evangelical Crisis

1961); Robert Raines, *New Life in the Church* (New York: Harper & Row, 1961); Elton Trueblood, *The Company of the Committed* (New York: Harper & Row, 1961).

12. Trueblood, *The Company of the Committed*, p. 49.

13. Elton Trueblood, "Foreword," in David Haney, *Renew My Church* (Grand Rapids, MI: Zondervan, 1972), p. 12. It is interesting throughout the annotations in the chapter to notice how many, particularly of the renewal/spiritual gift/every-member ministry books from the mid-1960s to the mid-1980s, were published by Zondervan Publishing House.

14. Elizabeth O'Connor, *Call to Commitment* (New York: Harper & Row, 1963); *Journey Inward, Journey Outward* (New York: Harper & Row, 1968).

15. Gordon Cosby, *Handbook for Mission Groups* (Waco, TX: Word, 1975).

16. Ibid., p. 60.

17. Ibid., p. 70.

18. Trueblood, "Foreword," in Haney, *Renew My Church*, p. 12.

19. Contemporary popularizations of the stream of thought that Nee represents can be found in the works of Major Ian Thomas, Bob George, and Gene Edwards, among others.

20. Watchman Nee, *What Shall This Man Do?* (Fort Washington, PA: Christian Literature Crusade, 1961); *The Normal Christian Church Life* (Washington, D.C.: International Students Press, 1962); *Assembling Together* (New York: Christian Fellowship Publishers, 1973); *Love One Another* (New York: Christian Fellowship Publishers, 1975).

21. Nee, *The Normal Christian Church Life*, pp. 117, 124.

22. LeRoy Eims, *The Lost Art of Disciple Making* (Grand Rapids, MI/Colorado Springs: Zondervan/NavPress, 1978), p. 17.

23. Robert Coleman, "Foreword," in ibid., p. 9.

24. Lawrence O. Richards, *A New Face for the Church* (Grand Rapids, MI: Zondervan, 1970), p. 108.

25. Lawrence O. Richards, *Becoming One in the Spirit* (Wheaton, IL: Victor, 1973); *69 Ways To Start a Study Group and Keep It Growing* (Grand Rapids, MI: Zondervan, 1973).

26. Lawrence O. Richards, *Born to Grow* (Wheaton, IL: Victor, 1974); *A Theology of Christian Education* (Grand Rapids, MI: Zondervan, 1975).

27. Lawrence O. Richards and Gib Martin, *A Theology of Personal Ministry: Spiritual Giftedness in the Local Church* (Grand Rapids, MI: Zondervan, 1981).

28. Ibid., p. 122.

29. Ray Stedman, *Body Life* (Ventura, CA: Regal, 1972). For more on Peninsula Bible Church during Stedman's years, see James Hefley, *Unique Evangelical Churches* (Waco, TX: Word, 1977), pp. 29-49.

The Priesthood of All Believers

30. Billy Graham, "Foreword," in Stedman, *Body Life* (1972; revised and expanded 1995), p. 8.

31. Stedman, ibid., pp. 57-58.

32. Ibid., p. 106.

33. C. Peter Wagner, *Your Spiritual Gifts Can Help Your Church Grow*, rev. ed. (Ventura, CA: Regal, 1994), p. 11.

34. Cosby, *Handbook*, p. 91.

35. Wagner, *Your Spiritual Gifts Can Help Your Church Grow*, p. 29.

36. Walter Henrichsen, *Disciples Are Made—Not Born* (Wheaton, IL: Victor, 1974), p. 132.

37. K. C. Hinckley, *A Compact Guide to the Christian Life* (Colorado Springs: NavPress, 1989), pp. 19-21.

38. Darrell W. Robinson, *Total Church Life* (Nashville: Broadman & Holman, 1997), pp. 81-144.

39. Cf. Rick Yohn, *Discover Your Spiritual Gift and Use It* (Wheaton, IL: Tyndale, 1974); Wagner, *Your Spiritual Gifts Can Help Your Church Grow*, rev. ed., pp. 109-124; Robert Logan, *Beyond Church Growth* (Old Tappan, NJ: Revell, 1989), p. 168; Eric Wright, *Church—No Spectator Sport* (Welwyn, England: Evangelical Press), pp. 120-129; Wayne A. Mack and David Swavely, *Life in the Father's House: A Member's Guide to the Local Church* (Phillipsburg, NJ: Presbyterian & Reformed, 1996), pp. 128-129.

40. Richard F. Houts, *Houts Inventory of Spiritual Gifts* (Pasadena, CA: Fuller Evangelistic Association, 1985); C. Peter Wagner, *Wagner-Modified Houts Questionnaire* (C. Peter Wagner, 1995).

41. Wagner, *Your Spiritual Gifts Can Help Your Church Grow*, rev. ed., p. 25. See too his books *Effective Body Building* (San Bernardino, CA: Here's Life, 1982); *Leading Your Church to Growth* (Ventura, CA: Regal, 1984); *The Healthy Church* (Ventura, CA: Regal, 1996).

42. C. Peter Wagner, *Your Spiritual Gifts Can Help Your Church Grow*, rev. ed., p. 24; cf. *The Healthy Church*, p. 16.

43. Ibid., p. 24.

44. Ibid., p. 32.

45. Ibid., p. 36.

46 Ibid., p. 133.

47. These ideas were published in Richards, *A New Face for the Church*.

48. Robert Girard, *Brethren, Hang Loose* (Grand Rapids, MI: Zondervan, 1972), p. 68.

49. Ibid., pp. 85-86.

50. Ibid., p. 135.

51. For some more interesting ideas of what renewed church life might look like,

see Girard, *Brethren, Hang Together* (Grand Rapids, MI: Zondervan, 1979), p. 91. In the appendix, Girard discusses his church's move out of its building. For more information on this move, see Lawrence O. Richards and Clyde Hoeldtke, *A Theology of Church Leadership* (Grand Rapids, MI: Zondervan, 1980), pp. 358-367.

52. Quoted in Richards and Hoeldtke, *A Theology of Church Leadership*, p. 360.

53. Howard A. Snyder, *The Problem of Wine Skins* (Downers Grove, IL: InterVarsity Press, 1975); *The Community of the King* (Downers Grove, IL: InterVarsity Press, 1977); *Liberating the Church* (Downers Grove, IL: InterVarsity Press, 1983).

54. Snyder, *Wine Skins*, p. 18.

55. See Howard A. Snyder, *The Radical Wesley and Patterns for Church Renewal* (Downers Grove, IL: InterVarsity Press, 1980).

56. Snyder, *Liberating the Church*, p. 170.

57. Ibid., p. 178.

58. Haney, *Renew My Church*; *The Idea of the Laity* (Grand Rapids, MI: Zondervan, 1973); Ralph Neighbour, *The Seven Last Words of the Church or We Never Tried It That Way Before* (Grand Rapids, MI: Zondervan, 1973).

59. Gene Edwards, *How to Meet* (Auburn, ME: Seed Sowers, n.d.); *The Revolution. Volume One: The Story of the Early Church* (Auburn, ME: Seed Sowers, n.d.).

60. E.g., Walter Shurden, ed., *The Priesthood of All Believers* (Macon, GA: Smyth & Helwys, 1993).

61. Greg Ogden, *The New Reformation: Returning the Ministry to the People of God* (Grand Rapids, MI: Zondervan, 1990).

62. James H. Rutz, *The Open Church* (Auburn, ME: SeedSowers, 1992).

63. Ibid., p. 40.

64. Patricia N. Page, *All God's People Are Ministers: Equipping Church Members for Ministry* (Minneapolis: Augsburg, 1993); Anne Rowthorn, *The Liberation of the Laity* (Ridgefield, CT: Morehouse, 1986); Lyle Schaller, *Activating the Passive Church: Diagnosis and Treatment* (Nashville: Abingdon, 1981).

65. Melvin J. Steinbron, *Can the Pastor Do It Alone?* (Ventura, CA: Regal, 1987); *The Lay Driven Church* (Ventura, CA: Regal, 1997).

66. Steinbron, *Lay Driven Church*, p. 87.

67. Gene Getz, *Sharpening the Focus of the Church* (Chicago: Moody, 1974); *Building Up One Another* (Colorado Springs: Chariot Victor, 1981); *Encouraging One Another* (Colorado Springs: Chariot Victor, 1981); *Loving One Another* (Colorado Springs: Chariot Victor, 1981).

The Priesthood of All Believers

68. Getz, *Building Up One Another; Encouraging One Another; Loving One Another.*

69. Getz, *Building Up One Another,* p. 23.

70. Ibid., p. 25.

71. Frank R. Tillapaugh, *The Church Unleashed* (Ventura, CA: Regal, 1982); Leith Anderson, *Dying for Change* (Minneapolis: Bethany House, 1990); Daniel A. Brown with Brian Larson, *The Other Side of Pastoral Ministry* (Grand Rapids, MI: Zondervan, 1996); Earl V. Comfort, *Living Stones: Involving Every Member in Ministry* (Cincinnati: Standard, 1988). Many other books have been published that recount specific attempts at implementing a lay ministry. E.g., Eddy Hall and Gary Morsch, *The Lay Ministry Revolution: How You Can Join* (Grand Rapids, MI: Baker, 1995).

72. Rick Warren, *The Purpose Driven Church* (Grand Rapids, MI: Zondervan, 1995), p. 367.

73. Robert Wuthnow, ed., *"I Come Away Stronger": How Small Groups are Shaping American Religion* (Grand Rapids, MI: Eerdmans, 1994), p. 386.

74. Loren Mead, *The Once and Future Church* (Washington, D.C.: Alban Institute; 1991), p. 33.

75. See T. David Gordon's well-argued article, "'Equipping' Ministry in Ephesians 4?" *Journal of the Evangelical Theological Society,* 37:1 (March 1994), pp. 69-78.

76. Carl Braaten, "The Gospel for a Neopagan Culture," in *Either/Or,* eds. Braaten and Jenson (Grand Rapids, MI: Eerdmans, 1993), pp. 19-20. See also Robert Wuthnow, *Sharing the Journey* (New York: Free Press, 1994); ed., *"I Come Away Stronger."*

77. Eugene Kennedy and Sara Charles, *Authority: The Most Misunderstood Idea in America* (New York: Free Press, 1997), pp. 1-2.

78. Mary Shipley, *An English Church History for Children* (London, England: Methuen & Co., 1909), p. 151.

5

Prophets, Priests, and Kings: Biblical Offices

Derke P. Bergsma

There are many areas of doctrinal disagreement encountered in the Christian tradition. But there is one article of faith virtually universally accepted: the belief in the headship of Christ over the church. It is not surprising that there is such unanimity of belief affirming Christ as the head of the church. It is a truth taught transparently in Scripture. The apostle Paul's testimony is especially clear. "He is the head of the body, the church" (Col. 1:18); "Christ is the head of the church" (Eph. 5:23b). The apostle Peter emphasizes the authority of Christ with reference to the church by using the figure of a building. Believers, says he, are "like living stones . . . being built into a spiritual house to be a holy priesthood, offering spiritual sacrifices acceptable to God through Jesus Christ" (1 Pet. 2:5). Of this spiritual household, Jesus Christ is the cornerstone (v. 6), the stone that serves as the point of reference for everything in that spiritual structure. The church is not a private club with rules determined by those who are dues-paying members, but a community of faith ruled by Christ through His Word.

Agreement quickly evaporates, however, when attention is focused upon the manner in which Jesus Christ exercises His authority. How does the head of the church rule His church in the existential reality of a local congregation? Through whom does He exercise His Lordship? Are there identifiable agents who serve as undershepherds of the divine Shepherd of the sheep? Does the Bible support the need in the church for "officials" who are charged with the responsibility of speaking, teaching, and ruling on behalf of Christ Himself? If it

Prophets, Priests, and Kings: Biblical Offices

does, how many offices are there, and what are their distinguishing responsibilities?

It is important to have a biblical understanding of the place of office in the life of the church in order to understand how leadership must be exercised in the name of Christ. Much confusion exists on the issue of who is in charge in a particular fellowship of believers, to the detriment of the spiritual life of the congregation and its witness in the world. Tensions mount as groups rally behind self-appointed leaders. Sometimes dictatorial pastors push their own agendas as though they are accountable to no one. Fickle church boards are often guilty of making decisions with tactless disregard for the consequences in the life of the church. Members of churches organized in a "democratic" manner sometimes act like stockholders who only need a simple majority vote to dump a pastor or other leader. Poor or ill-defined leadership often precipitates the trauma of church splits.

Contemporary literature on the subject of leadership in the church focuses attention almost exclusively on the qualifications and gifts of the pastor. We are told that a pastor must be creative, energetic, farsighted, and charismatic and must especially be a people motivator if he is to have a successful, growing church. The pastor should operate like the head of a corporation, it is said. Further, if a board of elders or deacons fails to promote the program recommended by the chief executive officer, they must be replaced.[1]

The Bible offers much evidence for a high view of the office of pastor. But the scriptural pattern requires a plurality of offices that precisely avoids the danger of vesting authority in a single office or person. Each of these offices has a defined area of primary responsibility exercised in the name of Christ for the welfare of the church. Failure to rightly understand or apply the relevant passages of Holy Scripture have led the evangelical church today into confusion and compromise.

ECCLESIASTICAL OFFICE ROOTED IN CREATION

God created human beings, Adam and Eve, as divine image-bearers. Unique among the creatures in God's perfect world order, they lived in the reality of a conscious relationship to God. They, unlike the rest of creation, knew they were God-related beings. They communicated with God and therefore enjoyed communion with Him. While the rest of creation reflected the glory of the divine Artist, it did so passively, unconsciously, and robot-like, just as a mirror reflects a person's image or a painting reflects an artist's skill. Neither mirrors nor paintings are conscious of what they are doing. Human beings, by contrast, are.

Adam and Eve could respond to the divine initiative actively, deliberately, consciously, and, as it turned out, disobediently. They were "responsible," that is, response-able to the God who addressed them in personal encounters as well as through the creation of which they were a part.[2] The evidence of God's presence was everywhere. Everywhere the message was clear. "You are God's image-bearers. You are accountable to Him. Your special relation to Him makes you unique in the created order."

As divine image-bearers, Adam and Eve were appointed by God to be stewards of creation and accountable to God. They and their descendants were assigned as caretakers of God's creation. "The LORD God took the man and put him in the garden of Eden to work it and take care of it" (Gen. 2:15). Furthermore, Adam was charged to "name" the animals, which was not simply to provide labels of identification. Rather, "naming" meant to recognize the unique role each animal was to play in the perfect order of God's world (Gen. 2:19-20).

The honor of serving as steward of the creation required Adam to be obedient to every word from God. Both God's positive commands as well as His prohibitive commands circumscribed and structured the life of obedience that would provide the perfect sense of fulfillment and purpose for human life. Adam and Eve and their descendants were responsible to live by every word that proceeded from the mouth of God.

Further, as God's image-bearing steward, Adam was required to honor the Lord as God alone. God was to be the supreme object of praise and delight. This we identify as the worship dimension of life as an obedient steward.

What we observe emerging from this understanding of man's God-relatedness as divine image-bearer is a threefold role. This threefold role or calling is best identified as prophetic, priestly, and kingly in nature. Man was created to live by the Word of God (prophetic calling), to worship God alone (priestly calling), and to be the responsible head or ruler of the created order on behalf of its Owner (kingly role). To be human,

Prophets, Priests, and Kings: Biblical Offices

that is, a divine image-bearer, meant to be a prophet, living by and declaring the Word of God, a priest bringing praise and adoration to God on behalf of the whole created order, and a king, managing every resource so that its God-determined use and potential would be realized to the glory of its Maker.

Then came the Fall.

THE DIVINE IMAGE DISTORTED IN THE FALL

The Fall, in its essence, was man's declaration of independence from God. The devil's lie was designed to distract man from his true relationship of God-dependency and to substitute for it a brokenness of supposed self-sufficiency apart from God. The lure of autonomy was attractive. The worship of the creature in place of the Creator was desirable, infatuating, and self-glorifying.

As a consequence, all three roles or callings that flowed from the nature of man as divine image-bearer were distorted beyond recognition. Man no longer lived by the Word of God, no longer worshiped God alone, and no longer served as administrative steward of the creation. His image-bearing roles as prophet, priest, and king were so corrupted as to have been wholly unfilled were it not for God's gracious intervention. God determined to right the wrong of human rebellion by means of the plan of salvation. God would one day crush the head of the serpent, destroy the works of the devil, and redeem a people for Himself. These new creatures in Christ Jesus would have the divine image restored in principle during their earthly existence and would be fully restored as eternal fact in glory at the end of the age.

The Bible records the emergence of a community of faith after the Fall. It details the history of a people called into covenant fellowship with God. This community of faith was characterized as an expectant people anticipating the fulfillment of the promise of a Messiah. They lived and died in the assurance that the Seed of the woman would crush the head of the serpent. By faith in the promise of a Deliverer, though dimly seen, they enjoyed a reconciled relationship with the Lord that anticipated better things to come.

With the emergence of a community of faith there came also the recognition of leadership within that community. These early patriarchal

The Present Evangelical Crisis

leaders were models of faithfulness to God and examples of what each member of the community should be. They also served in "official" capacities. As prophets they were sensitive to and lived by the Word of God and instructed the faith community in the divine Word. As priests they were the worship leaders who brought sacrificial offerings to the Lord on behalf of the community. They were also the kingly figures who ruled in the name of the Lord, and by bringing tithes, they testified that God is really King of all that is possessed.

Noah provides a model of one who exhibits a threefold pattern of leadership. As a prophet he was obedient to the Word of God and declared that Word faithfully to his contemporaries. He also brought priestly sacrifices by way of worship, specifically thank-offerings by which he acknowledged God alone as his deliverer. Noah also served as a kingly administrator in charge of the people and livestock preserved in the Ark from watery annihilation. Ideally, Noah was to represent what all people should have been.

Abraham may be an even clearer example. He received, was obedient to, and declared the Word of the Lord to his extended family. As such he filled the role of a prophet. Wherever he relocated, he built an altar for the purpose of priestly worship. And his kingly authority within his believing household extended to both biologically related members as well as to servants, those "bought with [his] money" (Gen. 17:13). The sacrament of circumcision given to infant and adult males alike served as a mark identifying the special privilege enjoyed by those who live in an environment where God is honored and His Word obeyed.

THE OFFICES OF PROPHETS, PRIESTS, AND KINGS DIFFERENTIATED

Throughout the patriarchal period, right up to and including Moses' time, the official leadership of the covenant community was vested in one person. Gradually, after the time of Moses, the three official capacities in which the leadership of God's people was administered became differentiated. That is, each office was administered by a separate person, and no one person was allowed to function in more than one office. Moses was the last to serve in all three capacities, prophetically declaring God's Word and will, ruling and judging the people in a kingly manner, and leading the worship life of the community by way of priestly sacrifices.

Prophets, Priests, and Kings: Biblical Offices

The priestly office was the first to have a separate identity. Aaron was consecrated High Priest, and his sons and male descendants were designated as the ones who were to occupy this office. Succeeding generations of Israel's people would look to the tribe of Levi for candidates to serve as priests (Lev. 8). From among these priests the High Priest was appointed.[3]

But it was also during the Mosaic period that the kingly office began to emerge as an office occupied by persons who held no other offices. They were called "judges," and the revelational period from Joshua to King Saul is identified as the period of judges. They functioned in a ruling capacity, adjudicating civil matters and mobilizing the nation to defend itself in time of war. When kings, beginning with Saul, were investitured, they each served as the supreme judge of the covenant nation, the one to whom the most complex or difficult cases were referred and who rallied the nation in time of war. Other judges in subordinate positions met "at the gate" to settle most cases.[4]

The prophetic office does not come into widespread prominence in the life of the Old Testament covenant community until the time of Samuel. But prophets were present during the time between Moses and Samuel. There were prophets in Israel from the very beginning of her residence in the promised land (Judg. 4:4; 6:8). The fact that Manoah, Samson's father, at first thought a prophet had appeared to his wife suggests that the prophetic office was not unknown or unexpected at that time (Judg. 13:8). A prophet rebuked Eli (1 Sam. 2:27), and Samuel became the bearer of God's message to Israel at a time in which "the word of the LORD was rare; there were not many visions" (1 Sam. 3:1).

This perspective on the biblical idea of office recognizes the emergence of three distinct "official" representatives of the Lord among His people. The differentiation of these offices is complete by the time of the kings shortly before 1000 B.C. So important was it to keep each office unique and separate that serious consequences followed when one person attempted to function in more than one office. Saul, a king, officiated in a priestly role at Gilgal prior to battling the Philistines. He was reprimanded by Samuel and told that his act disqualified his biological successors from occupying the kingly throne (1 Sam. 13:8-15). Azariah the priest clearly identified the burning of incense on the altar as a priestly prerogative: "It is not right for you, Uzziah, to burn incense to the LORD. That is for the priests, the descendants of Aaron, who have been conse-

The Present Evangelical Crisis

crated to burn incense" (2 Chron. 26:17-18). Uzziah's punishment for blurring office prerogatives was to be a leper for the rest of his life.

The period of the Exile in the experience of Judah is instructive in regard to the importance of three offices within the believing community. Once Jerusalem was destroyed by Nebuchadnezzar's army (587 B.C.), the kingly office within the covenant community was interrupted. Without a temple, destroyed as it was with the rest of the city, the regular priestly functions related to altar and festival ceased. Indeed, prophets, priests, and kings alike were made captives and marched off to Babylon.

But unlike the kings and priests, the prophetic office continued to function during the Exile. Daniel and Ezekiel are the most prominent examples. They continued to declare the Word of the Lord, both the word of warning and the word of promise. This points to the indispensable place the proclamation of the Word of God plays in the life of the believing community. With neither king nor priest, the covenant community continued so long as the Word of the Lord was not completely silenced. In their most vulnerable condition, the hope of survival and renewal depended on obedience to the Word of the Lord proclaimed by God's prophetic agents.

Following the defeat of the Chaldeans (Babylonians) by the Medo-Persians, the victorious emperor Cyrus decreed that those exiles who so desired could return to their ancestral homeland. Upon their return, the restoration of Judea and Jerusalem required reestablishing the official positions of leadership within the community. Haggai and Zechariah occupied the prophetic office, and Zerrubbabel, as a descendent of King David, the kingly office. Under their leadership the temple was rebuilt. But the threefold leadership circle was not complete until Joshua, son of Jehozadak, was officially installed as High Priest to function in the newly rebuilt temple. With his ordination, as well as that of the whole company of regular priests, the restoration from exile was complete (Zech. 3). The threefold office pattern was once again in place, and leadership roles were reestablished within the community of believers.

JESUS CHRIST: OUR CHIEF PROPHET, ONLY HIGH PRIEST, ETERNAL KING

We observed earlier that the official representatives of God in the midst of His people, office-bearers, served as reminders of what all humans should be as divine image-bearers. All were created to live by the Word of God, to worship God alone, and to administer all their talents and possessions as stewards of the Divine Monarch. These human officials were, of course, imperfect reminders of the true calling of every divine image-bearer. Their very presence therefore was an anticipation of the perfect image-bearer who was to come—He who is the perfect image of the invisible God, He who is the radiance of God's glory "and the exact representation of his being" (Heb. 1:3).

In this regard it is quite easy to understand why some post-Reformation creeds testify of Jesus that He is our chief Prophet, our only High Priest, and our eternal King. This designation of our Lord appears in the Westminster Shorter Catechism in Question 23, and each "office" is specifically elaborated in the three questions that follow. Similarly the Heidelberg Catechism (1563) asks: "Why is He called Christ, that is, anointed one?" The answer?

> Because He is ordained by God the Father and anointed with the Holy Spirit to be our chief Prophet and teacher, fully revealing to us the secret purpose and will of God concerning our redemption; to be our only High Priest, having redeemed us by the one sacrifice of His body and ever interceding for us with the Father; and our eternal King governing us by his Word and Spirit and defending and sustaining us in the redemption He has won for us.[5]

Indeed. How appropriate for our Lord to be identified as prophet, priest, and king. He is the only begotten of the Father. He is the incarnate Son come to live in perfect obedience to the Father, as mankind was originally intended to do. As prophet, He lived and proclaimed the Word of God, for He was the Word become flesh. As priest, He was both sacrifice and sacrificer in His atoning work on behalf of His own. In His person the Kingdom has come. The rule of God over every challenge to that authority is assured because of King Jesus. The divine image is in principle restored for all who are in Christ and will in fact be realized for all believers in glory.

ECCLESIASTICAL OFFICES IN THE NEW TESTAMENT

We observed early in this essay that God created image-bearers whose calling was to live by every word of God (prophetic calling), to worship

The Present Evangelical Crisis

God alone (priestly calling), and to exercise a dominion of stewardship over all the natural and spiritual resources that God has provided (kingly calling). The Fall distorted human life in all of these God-ordained callings. But God graciously intervened with the promise of a Seed of a woman who would crush the head of the serpent. By way of fulfilling His redemptive intentions, God chose a people to serve as the agency through whom the promised Savior would come. These "chosen people" were served by leaders or office-bearers who were imperfect reminders of what human beings were originally intended to be.

Let us suppose that the threefold office pattern is granted for the Old Testament leadership provision within the community of faith. We must still ask whether there is biblical warrant for a threefold leadership structure for congregational life in the New Testament church. Certainly there are differences between the household of faith in the Old Testament and the New. The two revelational epochs present some rather strong contrasts. The Old was geographically and ethnically restricted; the New is for the nations and all people groups. Believers in Old Testament times anticipated the coming of a promised Savior; New Testament believers are commissioned to proclaim the good news that He has come and that all nations must now be challenged to repent and believe. We could go on to mention many other contrasts.

But the necessity for leadership within the community of faith is clearly demanded in the New Testament as well as in the Old. And since the church, like the Old Testament covenant people, is comprised of divine image-bearers called to be God's faithful people, is it too much to expect that leadership positions within the church would be similar to Old Testament patterns? That a prophetic office with primary responsibility for declaring God's Word would be required? That a kingly office would be identified to exercise spiritual oversight? That a priestly office would be charged with the responsibility of receiving the offerings (no less) from God's people to be dedicated as pleasing sacrifices to the Lord to advance His Kingdom and to aid the sick and destitute? Let us look at the New Testament evidence of such a pattern.

Jesus is our chief prophet, only High Priest, and eternal king. He appointed apostles who, like the patriarchs of old, constituted a unique fraternity and functioned in a threefold official role as representatives of Jesus, the Lord. They proclaimed the Gospel, they adjudicated issues

Prophets, Priests, and Kings: Biblical Offices

related to the teaching and practice of the churches, and they collected offerings and tended to the needs of widows and the poor, even to the point of serving tables. They served in roles that we have identified as those of prophet, priest, and king.

Before the death of the apostles, provision was made for the differentiation of distinctive offices in the church. The first was the office of deacon. Acts 6 records the election of deacons whose ministry of compassion to the needy defined the character of their responsibility. Like the priests of the Old Covenant, the deacons were required to receive gifts and offerings from the Lord's people to support the ministry of mercy. Widows were their special concern because, given the lack of provision for them in that culture, they represented the most needy. Like the priests of the Old Covenant who isolated the sick, such as lepers, from the larger believing community and guaranteed their restoration when healed, so deacons were to be responsible for the material and physical provision for the sick and needy. Theirs is a ministry of compassion in the name of Christ, the head of the church.

Next the prophetic office appears to emerge in the New Testament record. Acts 13 records the ordination of Barnabas to the task of gospel proclamation. Paul, called to be an apostle by direct revelation, served in a unique role. But Barnabas was "set apart" by the church as a minister of the Word. Later Timothy was challenged by Paul to be "a good minister of Christ Jesus" (1 Tim. 4:6), sound in doctrine, faithfully engaged in the public reading and teaching of the Scriptures, and godly in his personal life. It is interesting to note that Timothy is never referred to as an elder. It appears that administrative oversight, which is the primary responsibility of elders, should not interfere with the prophetic calling to declare the Word of the Lord. In the case of Timothy a prophetic message qualified him for his ministry (1 Tim. 4:14), which suggests the close connection between the prophetic proclamation and the pastoral office.

Elders are required as soon as a believing community emerges in response to the preaching of the Gospel. Examples include the elders of the church of Ephesus to whom Paul gave a moving farewell address (Acts 20:17-35). Also, Paul reminds both Timothy and Titus of the importance of elders in every congregation (1 Tim. 3:1-7; Titus 1:5-9). The listing of their responsibilities in these two passages emphasizes the task of general oversight over the affairs that define the believing com-

The Present Evangelical Crisis

munity of faith, a role similar to that of elders of the Old Testament people of God.[6]

QUALIFICATIONS FOR OFFICE-HOLDERS

Careful attention to the listing of qualifications that Paul gives to Timothy for office-bearers supports a three office understanding. Careless attention leads to compromise and misdirection. First Timothy 3:1-7 sets forth the qualifications for elders who are entrusted to "take care of God's church." Then follows in verses 8-13 a careful description of qualifications for those ordained to the office of deacon. The apostle writes in the third person while enumerating the qualifications for both elders and deacons. But in chapter 4 the apostle addresses Timothy in the second person, calling him "a good minister of Christ Jesus" (1 Tim. 4:6-16). Timothy is then challenged to devote himself to the public reading of Scripture, to preaching and teaching. Paul, it seems, is distinguishing the unique role of Timothy, the pastor, from the primary duties of elders and deacons. In addition, as already mentioned, Timothy (and Titus as well) is never called an elder.

First Timothy 5:17 is often quoted in support of a view that pastors are "teaching elders." "The elders who direct the affairs of the church well are worthy of double honor, especially those whose work is preaching and teaching." The pastor, in this view, is a "double honor" elder, a cut above, presumably, a non-teaching elder. Since *elder* implies oversight or "ruling" authority, what we would have in the church then are "ruling rulers" and "teaching rulers," the latter of whom are worthy of greater honor than the former, perhaps implying a hierarchy among church offices.

A better way to understand this verse is to recognize that elders represent Jesus Christ in His kingly authority. Their primary responsibility is to exercise governance over the affairs of the church, including everything related to the faith and life of the congregation. If in addition to their primary work there are elders who can preach and teach, they are especially valuable to the church. As a matter of fact, preaching and teaching per se are not unique to any single office. Philip, a deacon, taught the Ethiopian eunuch to understand the Scriptures (Acts 8:26-40). Stephen, another deacon, publicly taught the Scriptures and suffered mar-

Prophets, Priests, and Kings: Biblical Offices

tyrdom for his work (Acts 6:8—7:60). We conclude from these examples that those ordained to the prophetic office—pastors, as specialists in the Word—must preach, while elders and deacons may preach and teach as their gifts allow.[7]

Understood in light of the foregoing, the offices in the church represent Jesus Christ in His threefold mediatorial office. Each office includes a unique primary area of responsibility, but also allows for service in additional capacities as God-given gifts allow. The pastoral office is held by the minister of the Word who, as a specialist in the Scriptures, not only proclaims the Word but expounds its teaching for doctrine and the requirements of piety and Christian witness. But, like the prophets before them, they exercise no ruling authority beyond that inherent in "thus says the Lord." The diaconal office provides for a ministry of mercy as deacons give priestly attention to mobilizing the church's sacrificial offerings for purposes of a compassionate ministry to the sick and needy. And the kingly office provides a ministry of oversight as the elders take responsibility for the supervision over all the affairs of the church, especially the soundness of the doctrine confessed by the church and the disciplined Christian lives that believers in Jesus should be living.[8]

THE HISTORY OF OFFICE IN SCRIPTURE

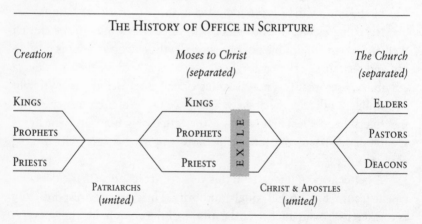

Creation	*Moses to Christ* *(separated)*	*The Church* *(separated)*
KINGS	KINGS	ELDERS
PROPHETS	PROPHETS	PASTORS
PRIESTS	PRIESTS	DEACONS
	PATRIARCHS *(united)*	CHRIST & APOSTLES *(united)*

THE SIGNIFICANCE OF OFFICE IN THE CONTEMPORARY CHURCH

One might be tempted to question whether this matter of office in the church is really so important in view of the church's commission to evangelize the world and edify believers. Certainly there have been examples

The Present Evangelical Crisis

of one-office and two-office leadership structures that have "worked." Or there have been three-office patterns where one office, usually the pastor, has served in a primary role while the other two functioned in subordinate roles.

The proper organization of every fellowship of believers is important to fulfill its God-given mission. This is particularly true if there is a discernible pattern to be observed in Scripture for congregational organization. It then becomes a matter of obedience to follow that pattern regardless of whether we fully understand the reasons why.

Further, the offices established within the redeemed community of believers serve as constant reminders of what each member was created to be. As image-bearers of God, our purpose for existence is to live by every word of God, to worship Him alone, and to be stewards of all we are and have in gratitude to God. Godly candidates who meet the biblical standards for service as office-bearers are then examples to the rest of the flock of Christian piety and service.

Also, lines of authority and decision-making are well defined. As rulers in the name of the church's ascended King and as undershepherds of the great Shepherd, the elders are overseers of the total life of the congregation. They are mutually accountable to each other for the discharge of their office and must promote the faithful discharge of the offices of pastor and deacon. While pastors and deacons will, of course, advise the elders in detail regarding their areas of ministry, the elders must assume final responsibility for whatever is approved if the church is to function well.[9]

Continuity in the ministry of a local congregation is one of the major benefits of faithful elder leadership. Too often the varied ministries of a local church are wholly dependent on the leadership and coordination of the pastor. Sometimes the pastor aggressively takes control, and perhaps just as often the board of elders shirks its oversight responsibility, forcing the pastor to take control by default. In such situations the loss of a pastor has devastating effects on the continued ministry of the congregation. However, when elders take their oversight responsibility seriously, pastors may come and go with far less negative consequences for the work of the church. Even while a pastor is present, faithful elder leadership will go far toward freeing the pastor of supervisory distractions so

Prophets, Priests, and Kings: Biblical Offices

that the primary task of proclaiming, teaching, and applying the Word will not be compromised.

Most importantly, the three-office leadership style we have been advocating reflects the mediatorial work of the great Shepherd of the sheep, Jesus Christ. He is the Living Word who serves as the theme of the preaching of every faithful minister of the Word. He is the One whose offering of Himself serves as payment in full for the sins of all who trust in Him. And He is the King of the church whose loving mastery is always exercised on behalf of the spiritual welfare of His own.

Divine image-bearers were created, and the church exists to live by the Word of God, to worship God alone, and to be thankful stewards of everything we have and are. The offices of the church serve as reminders of what we were created to be. Therefore, great care should be taken that those who are appointed to such positions meet the biblical qualifications. They should be sincerely conscious that, in the exercise of their offices, they represent the Lord whose will, and not their own, must be their sole motivation. The affairs of the church should not be committed to the spiritually immature.[10] The honor of the Lord and the welfare of souls is at stake.[11]

NOTES

1. At a leadership conference I attended, a prominent television minister emphasized the necessity of getting rid of church board members who failed to "get with the program."

2. The late Professor Troost of the Free University of Amsterdam described humans as "response structures" since they are the only beings in all creation who are able to respond to the Creator. By virtue of their image-bearing nature, humans must respond, whether positively or negatively, to the divine address. All other structures in creation are passive in relation to the Creator. Only humans are morally accountable.

3. The tendency is to identify the priestly office with the daily ministrations of altar and temple. But Leviticus 13—15 details the important role of the priests in regard to the sick in the community and the control of disease.

4. Deuteronomy 25:1-10 provides an example of the elders in a particular locale who served as judges in specific cases.

5. *The Book of Confessions* (New York: UPUSA, 1970), Paragraph 4.031.

6. Two Greek words are used in the New Testament to identify the ruling office in the church, *presbuteroi* and *episkopoi.* The former is usually translated "elder" and identifies the position such an office-bearer holds. The latter is

The Present Evangelical Crisis

often translated "bishop" and identifies the task such an office-bearer performs—namely, oversight.

7. In this regard, K. Dijk makes a helpful observation. He notes that teaching and evangelism are really important concerns of all three offices. He identifies them as the Ministry of the Word, teaching and evangelism, the Ministry of Mercy, teaching and evangelism, and the Ministry of Oversight, teaching and evangelism. *De Dienst Der Kerk* (Kok: Kampen, 1958, Chapter 4).

8. The parallel with the Old Testament setting seems so obvious. The faithful prophets communicated the Word of the Lord to the people but had no coercive authority to enforce obedience to it. They repeatedly appealed to the ruling kings to clear the land of idolatry and to use their kingly power to insist on obedience to the Word of the Lord. No matter how earnest the prophets were, without the cooperation of the king, reform was impossible.

9. It is significant that every reference to the office of elder in a specific location appears in the plural form. Each congregation needs a plurality of elders where mutual accountability can be practiced to avoid domination by any one person.

10. V. S. Poythress emphasizes the appropriateness of having both mature and less mature believers in the organized church. But he insists that Christian maturity is required for leadership roles, especially for elders. "Indifferentism and Rigorism in the Church," in *Westminster Theological Journal*, 59 (1997):13-19.

11. Our focus here is upon the essential nature of the offices in the church through which Christ's authority is exercised. For practical guides covering the duties of elders and deacons see G. Berghoef and L. DeKoster, *The Elders Handbook* (Grand Rapids, MI: Christian Library Press, 1979) and *The Deacons Handbook* (Grand Rapids, MI: Christian Library Press, 1980).

6

THE EVANGELICAL FALL FROM THE MEANS OF GRACE: THE LORD'S SUPPER

R. Scott Clark

The prayers had been offered, the promises read, and the psalm sung. Two princes stepped forward to receive Communion, but the deacon refused to give them the cup. The superintendent of the city's pastors ordered a second minister present to take the cup from the deacon and give it to the nobles, and a struggle for the cup ensued. Outraged by the deacon's insubordination, the superintendent excommunicated him on the spot. This nasty business occurred in 1559 in Heidelberg, Germany. The minister was the Lutheran theologian Tilemann Hesshus (1527-1588), and the deacon was a Zwinglian named Klebitz.[1]

As ugly and sub-Christian as it was, the story of the Communion combatants of 1559 reminds us of a time when men took seriously the means of grace, and it presents us with a sharp contrast to our own times. Few evangelical Christians or churches in our time are so devoted to the Supper as to be willing to argue about its proper use, let alone physically struggle for the cup. Why? It is because we have become practically anti-supernatural and simultaneously super-spiritual in our theology, so that we are, on the one hand, bored with God's ordinary means of grace (the sacraments) and on the other hand have stopped believing that God can and does use those means to accomplish His purposes. That is to say, we are guilty of a sort of unbelief.

We have replaced the sacraments with spiritual exercises of our own making. A survey of virtually any evangelical bookstore finds dozens of books on spirituality, self-denial, church growth, and recovery from various addictions. Some of these contain useful advice; so did some of the medieval handbooks of spiritual direction. But few of them contain the Gospel, and almost none of them make any reference to the use of the Lord's Supper as a means to Christian growth.[2] Even Reformed churches that confess the Supper to be one of the two divinely instituted means of grace (*media gratiae*) normally serve the Supper only quarterly.

This essay is something of a continuation of a nineteenth-century debate in Reformed theology. The various revival movements of the eighteenth and nineteenth centuries tended to push the Lord's Supper to margins of Reformed piety. For various other reasons some nineteenth-century Reformed theologians became suspicious of what they regarded as Calvin's overly mystical view of the Supper. In turn, the German Reformed theologian J. W. Nevin criticized the influence of revivalism and realism on Reformed theology and defended Calvin's views.[3]

THE HISTORY OF THE FALL FROM THE MEANS OF GRACE

Who should participate in the Lord's Supper and how they should do it were two of the most hotly contested questions of the sixteenth-century Reformation. For both Luther and Calvin, the Supper was of critical importance as a means of grace, as a testimony to Christ's finished work, and as a seal of His work for us. Furthermore, it was a means by which our union and fellowship with the risen Christ and with one another was strengthened and renewed. As much as the Lutherans and Reformed disagreed about the relations of Christ's humanity to His deity and thus the nature of His presence in the Supper, they agreed on one very important truth—in the Supper the living, Triune God meets His people and nourishes them. The question was not *whether*, but *how*.

The most immediate reason for our fall from the Protestant idea of the Supper as a means of grace is that we have become practical modernists. Modernism (or the Enlightenment) was a profoundly anti-Christian theology and worldview. Building upon the conclusions of the great German philosopher Immanuel Kant (1724-1804), theologians such as Friedrich Schleiermacher (1768-1834) and others began to remove the overtly supernatural elements from Christian theology in order to make it acceptable to the cultured despisers of religion.[4] The task and trajectory of modernist theology has been to find a way to do theology without actually believing (in the same way as Luther and Calvin)

The Present Evangelical Crisis

what it actually taught. (By *modernism* and *modernity* I mean to encompass the various Enlightenment movements of the late seventeenth and early eighteenth centuries. By *rationalism* I mean the use of human reason and sense experience as the fulcrum by which all authorities, including Scripture, the creeds, and confessions, are levered.)

Those theologians who accepted the basic rationalist belief of modernity (man is the measure of all things) worked to find ways to express their modernism in Christian terms. Where the Reformation theologians were convinced of God's present activity in history, modernist theologians were convinced of His present inactivity and hiddenness from us.

The modernist theology provoked a crisis and a reaction. Since we could no longer be certain of God's existence and care for us by the old-fashioned Protestant ways (preaching of the Word and the use of the sacraments), we abandoned them for more direct and immediate means of knowing and experiencing God. This flight to the immediate encounter with God is pietism or mysticism. Pietism is not to be confused with piety. The latter is that grateful devotion to God, His Word, and His people that is at the heart of Christianity. Pietism believes that what is truly important about Christianity is one's personal experience of Jesus; it is a retreat into the subjective experience of God apart from any concrete, historical factuality. Though pietism is usually said to have begun with Philipp Jakob Spener (1635-1705), its roots were much deeper in the history of Christianity. World flight and the interior turn were the stuff of early medieval asceticism.Withdrawal from the world was a major theme among both Greek and Latin writers in the early church. Augustine (354-430), Tertullian (ca. 160-225), Jerome (ca. 342-420) in the West, as well as Clement of Alexandria (ca. 150-215) and Origen (ca. 185-ca. 254) in the Greek-speaking church, saw world flight as a means to spiritual improvement.

The *via mystica* (the mystical way) was one of the most prominent theological influences in the later Middle Ages. Mystical theology preceded and succeeded the twelfth-century development of the technical academic theology known as scholasticism. The synthesis by Pseudo-Dionysius (ca. 500) of neo-Platonism with Christianity produced an important example of early Christian mysticism. Bernard of Clairvaux (1090-1153), Hugh and Richard of St. Victor, Francis of Assisi (1182-1226), and the *Theologia Germanica* (ca. fourteenth century) are some of the outstanding examples of medieval mysticism leading up to the Reformation. In the sixteenth century mystical pietism found expression in much of the preaching of the Anabaptist radicals and in the theology of the Silesian (German) Lutheran Jacob Boehme (1575-1624), who taught a theology of direct experience of, and even absorption into, the divine.

Thus when Spener began to organize a pietist reaction to what he perceived to be cold Lutheran orthodoxy, he was only gathering up threads of a movement that had long been active in the church. In fact, Spener's more radical counterpart George Fox (1624-1691) was even more consistent than Spener.[5] Fox was the father of Quakerism or the Society of Friends. He quite logically followed his concern about one's experience of the "inner Christ" by abandoning the visible church and her sacraments.

In fact, pietism and modernism were family, and those close relations are evident in the theology of Friedrich Schleiermacher (1768-1834). He received his earliest Christian training from Moravian pietists. As he reduced Christian theology to the experience of dependence upon God (*Gefuhl*), he declared that he was now a mature Moravian, and so he was.

Despite its internal differences, the modern evangelical movement is united in its quest for a higher and purer direct experience of the Christ of faith. It is not, however, engaged in a more profound search for a more biblical understanding of God's communion with His people through the signs and seals of the covenant.

Repentance and Restoration to the Means of Grace

American evangelicalism is a pietist, experiential religion that is too busy with cell-group meetings to be troubled with the Lord's Supper. At the same time, we have functionally excommunicated ourselves and, to borrow Calvin's language, robbed ourselves of Christ's benefits.[6] The remedy for the pietist transformation of sixteenth-century Protestant evangelical religion into a religion of private, personal experience is to repent of our unbelief that God does not or cannot use created means to strengthen or edify us as His people. Here is one of the central differences between the religion of the Protestants and pietist-mysticism: Protestantism believes in the use of divinely ordained means. It also seeks to recapture those divinely ordered gospel instruments.

The Present Evangelical Crisis

THE INSTITUTION OF THE SUPPER

The Scriptures teach that God establishes the Lord's Supper as the means by which He testifies to us and strengthens us in our salvation in Christ by sealing to His people Christ's twofold benefits—justification and sanctification.[7] According to the Synoptic Gospels, our Lord instituted the Supper in the midst of the celebration of the Feast of Passover.[8] The Passover was part of a pattern of important communal feasts (including the Feast of Weeks and the Feast of Tabernacles) in which the covenant assembly met to offer worship and in which God drew near to His people.[9] The Passover narrative is found in Exodus 12:1-36, the Feast of Weeks in Exodus 34:22 and Numbers 28:26-31, and the Feast of Tabernacles in Leviticus 23:34. The Scriptures make it clear that these covenant assemblies were eschatological events with the holy ones of heaven in attendance. (See also Ps. 68:7, 17; Heb. 2:2.) Paul assumes this in 1 Corinthians 11:10: "because of the angels." God's people sat at His feet, as it were, to hear the Word and to enjoy sacramental fellowship with Him. Certainly the structure of the liturgical calendar, filled with major and minor feasts, expressed that repeated desire of the Lord to commune with His people.

The Passover pictured this as a time of fulfillment. The very act of painting the doorposts with the blood of a lamb was symbolic of the necessity of the propitiation of God's holy wrath and the expiation of our sins. The Passover was an eschatological feast as they ate the roast lamb by whose blood they had been redeemed. Already in the Old Covenant believers were tasting the powers of the age to come through these sacramental elements. I am alluding here to Hebrews 6:4-5. Hebrews 11:13 adds that Old Covenant believers died not having received the fulfillment of the promises, but they anticipated the day of fulfillment in Christ. Jesus teaches the same thing in John 8:56. The Passover was also an act of covenant renewal as God's people ate the Gospel and were called again to a life of holiness in the Feast of Unleavened bread.[10]

It is against the Old Covenant background of circumcision as the sign of initiation into the covenant community and the feasts as covenant renewal that Calvin and Reformed theology with him distinguished between baptism as the sign and seal of entrance into the visible assembly and the Supper as the sign of confirmation.

The Means of Grace: The Lord's Supper

Jesus is the paschal lamb of God (John 1:29; 1 Cor. 5:7). It was against this backdrop that the disciples understood the words of institution: "This is My body . . . this cup is the new covenant in my blood" (Luke 22:19-20). They were familiar with a world that may be nearly lost to us, a world of bloody rituals and sworn oaths to God and neighbor, in which God Himself came to Abraham and swore an oath to "be your God and the God of your descendants after you" (Gen. 17:7). So seriously does the God of the covenant take His promise that He swore an oath against His own life; He sealed this pledge first in the sign of the firepot going between the slaughtered animals (Gen. 15:17) and later with the bloody sign of circumcision (Gen. 17:10).[11]

All the bloody signs of the Passover feast were fulfilled in the body and blood of Jesus. The day of types and shadows was gone; the reality had arrived. This was Jesus' teaching against the backdrop of the feasts of Passover and Tabernacles. Though in John 6 Jesus contrasted Himself with the manna, declaring Himself to be the true bread from heaven (John 6:31-35), the broader context (see v. 4) involved the Passover. This explains why He said, "Unless you eat the flesh of the Son of Man and drink his blood, you have no life in you" (v. 53). His vocabulary was drawn from the Passover feast. Had he intended only to refer to the manna, he would not have included the reference to His blood.

In the history of exegesis it has been nearly impossible for Christians not to link this passage to the Supper, if only figuratively and indirectly. Thus, for Calvin the institution of the Supper was Christ's *sigillum* or "seal" of this sermon.[12] Our spiritual union with Christ, which Jesus called eating His flesh and drinking His blood, leads the Christian naturally to think of the communal, formal, sacramental expression of that ongoing, daily eating of Christ that Calvin called our "mystical union" with Christ (*unio mystica*).[13]

Jesus' words in John 6:54, "Whoever eats my flesh and drinks my blood," are quite shocking to us super-spiritual evangelicals. But such sacramental use of the ordinary is the character of redemptive history. The Lord's Supper, like the Old Covenant feasts that preceded it, involved the sacred use of ordinary things because grace does not replace creation—it renews it. The man born blind was not given entirely new eyes; his old, blind eyes were opened. Note also that Jesus used saliva, clay, and water to accomplish His miracle (John 9.1-7).

The Present Evangelical Crisis

Our piety is quite different from Jesus' in other ways as well. We have come to think of the Christian life primarily as a private affair between God and us in our prayer closet. Jesus conducted His ministry and instituted the Supper in a corporate setting, at a feast; and the New Covenant feast was intended to be a communal act of worship as well, not a private spiritual exercise. (See Acts 2:42-46; 20:7-11; 1 Cor. 5:7-8; 10—11.) It is beyond question that there are strong individual elements to the Christian faith—one must himself apprehend and appropriate the Gospel. The Bible, however, "deals with man, not only as a solitary unit in his relation to God, but also as a member of a spiritual society, gathered together in the name of Jesus."[14] And God has ordained signs and seals of that society that we neglect to our great peril.

THE REFORMATION OF THE SUPPER

After 250 years of revivalism and Pietism, it is about time for us evangelicals to renew our appreciation of Calvin's theology of the Supper. His exposition of the Supper is in his theological handbook for future pastors, the *Institutes of the Christian Religion* (1559). The heading of the fourth book is: "On the external means or aids by which God invites into Christ's society and retains us in it."[15] Unlike much popular evangelical piety of our time, Calvin did not juxtapose the use of means in the Christian life with direct, unmediated access to God. In Calvin's day, as in ours, "many" were persuaded out of "pride or loathing or envy" that they could grow spiritually by "privately reading and meditating" on Scripture and thus did not need the ordained means of grace.[16]

More than once the church has needed a call back to the biblical means of grace. As we need to be called away from our disregard and shallow understanding of the Supper and called back to a full-orbed theology of the Supper, so too the sixteenth-century church needed a reformation and restoration of the Supper. From 1995-1997 I surveyed the theological opinions of about 200 undergraduate and graduate students at Wheaton College, which I take to be a representative cross section of American evangelicalism. Almost uniformly at the outset of their basic theology course they confessed that they had been taught that the Supper is one's declaration of faith in Christ. Most had never been taught a connection between the Supper and the Gospel. Even Zwingli, who has some-

The Means of Grace: The Lord's Supper

times been criticized for teaching that the Supper was a mere memorial of Christ's death, taught that Christ strengthens us through the Supper.

The spiritual, theological, and moral corruption of the late medieval church was evident in its abuse of the Lord's Supper. The Supper had stopped being a gospel feast of covenant renewal and had become partly legal obligation and partly magic.[17] The doctrine of transubstantiation as promulgated by the Fourth Lateran Council (1215) taught that at consecration, the substance of the eucharistic bread and wine, or that which makes them what they are, is replaced by Christ's substance—hence transubstantiation. This dogma was reiterated at the Council of Trent (1551) (sessio XIII, cap. IV). That the eucharistic elements continue to look, feel, and taste like bread and wine was said to be accidental—i.e., not a mistake but a nonessential property. Though the consecration of the host was not normally intended as magic, it certainly appeared to most medieval parishioners to be a kind of magic performed by the priest. Hence the archaic expression hocus pocus (to trick someone) derives from the Latin expression, "hoc est" (this is), from the Latin (Vulgate) text of Luke 22:19, used in the celebration of the Mass. Like baptism, the Mass became one of seven means by which some thought one could receive within himself divine righteousness.[18] It was this infusion of righteousness (iustitia infusa) that was said to create within the Christian a habitus or disposition toward obedience leading to eventual justification.[19]

Thus there is more at stake here than just spiritual growth. For Luther and Calvin, the reformation of the church was first of all a recovery of the gospel message itself: Jesus Christ, the Lamb of God, lived and died to justify helpless sinners, not to enable them to cooperate with God toward sanctification and eventual, final justification. I fear that our devotion to private exercises is, partly at least, a sort of idolatry in which we worship the "Christ of faith," i.e., a savior of our own making. In short, it may be that we are disinterested in the Lord's Supper because we are disinterested in the Lord Himself and His free gift of righteousness.

For Protestants, the sacraments are not about what one has or has not done; rather, they testify and seal to us what Christ has done for us and in our place. The Supper as instituted by Christ speaks to us of our union with Him, effected by the Spirit and the Word. What could be more intimate than "Take and eat; this is my body" (Matt. 26:26)? The purpose of the Supper is not to save us, but to help us grow in grace, to con-

The Present Evangelical Crisis

firm our faith, and to seal to us Christ's imputed righteousness. We must first, however, embrace that righteousness by faith alone.

It may be that we have rebelled from God's weak and beggarly things in favor of super-spirituality because we overestimate our own well-being. For Calvin, the very fact that God gave us the Supper testified to our weakness. For those who have eaten Christ by faith, it should be the natural desire to want to feast on Him in the Supper with His people.

This exaltation of the ordinary (after all, even after consecration, the elements remain only bread and wine) at God's command explains why Calvin was quite vociferous against those whom he called "fanatics" (*fanatici*), those who refuse to use God's ordinary methods. It is non-Christian pride, not Christian humility, to despise divinely ordained means of Christian growth in grace.

It not that Calvin thought that we should love the sacraments in themselves.[20] Rather, the sacrament of the Supper is valuable because it is an "appendix" to the preaching of God's Word that confirms and seals (*obsignet*) it to the elect.[21] Though we ought to believe the Word by itself, and it is certainly true as it stands, nevertheless the sacraments are God's kind "gifts" (*dotes*) to strengthen our trust in the Word. The Christ of the Supper is the same Christ offered to us in the gospel word. Since it was not meant to be a mute witness by itself, the Supper therefore can be effective only in the context of gospel preaching.

At the heart of Calvin's view is that the Eucharist is a supper, and even more intimately, a family meal.[22] Scripture calls it a supper because it was given to nourish us and feed us.[23] He called it a "spiritual feast" (*spirituale epulum*), a "high mystery," and "this mystical blessing" (*mystica haec benedictio*) of which Satan hopes to deprive us.[24]

How does the Supper feed us? In several ways. First, as a visible representation of the Gospel it symbolizes for us the "invisible nourishment" we receive from Christ's flesh and blood.[25] Just as it is Christ who is preached to us in the Gospel, so it is Christ we eat in the Supper. Not that the elements are transformed; no, they remain bread and wine.[26] Christ, however, uses the elements to share Himself with us by the power of His deity. He is the "only food of our soul."[27]

We are fed by the Supper as Christ uses it to strengthen His spiritual union with us. Just as water pours from a spring, so "Christ's flesh is like a rich and inexhaustible fountain."[28] Though we confess that, with respect to Christ's humanity, he "ascended to heaven and is seated at the right hand of God," nevertheless God the Spirit overcomes the spatiotemporal distance between us and the risen Christ and unites us to Him.[29] For this reason, one does not need to think of Christ as being physically present in the elements of the table. His flesh is present by the "secret operation of the Spirit" drawing us up to Himself, not bringing Christ down to us.[30] It is not necessary "to drag Him from heaven" for us to enjoy Him.[31]

We eat because God has entered into a covenant with us to be our God, and He has given signs and seals to this covenant union. Thus when He calls us to the Lord's Table, "as often as He pours out His sacred blood as our drink," it is for the "confirmation of our faith" in which "He renews or continues the covenant once ratified in His blood."[32] So the Supper does not initiate faith in us; that is the function of the Spirit working through the preached Gospel. As we "constantly" eat this bread (by trusting in Christ's imputed righteousness), so in the Supper "we are made to feel the power of the bread."[33] There is more to union with Christ than "mere knowledge" (*simplex cognitio*). Christ meant to teach something more "sublime" in John 6:53. Just as it is not "seeing" (*aspectus*) the bread, but "eating" (*esus*) it that feeds the body, it is not the mere intellectual apprehension of Christ that is saving faith, but "the soul must partake of Christ truly and deeply," entering into His promises.[34]

The prime benefit of this mystical Supper with earthy elements is that by it the Holy Spirit works assurance of our faith. Christ is the object of our faith. His promises are the sure foundation of our confidence. As we eat it, Christ again says to us, "You are Mine."[35] As we hear the promises set before us weekly in the preaching of the Gospel, so we also see them in the Supper. In this way "pious souls" can derive "great confidence and delight from the sacrament."[36]

Calvin spoke thus because he believed that in the Supper Christians have real fellowship with Christ, who is truly present with them. Christ has not abandoned us. In the Supper we receive the "true body and the blood of Christ."[37]

HOW SHALL WE THEN COMMUNE?

Calvin has three words of advice for us: simply, solemnly, and serially. One of the great faults of the medieval church was that it forgot how to preach. Contemporaneous accounts of late medieval preaching make it clear that most priests could not or did not preach. When they did, the sermons were often guilty of the most dreadful moralizing as to make them worse than no sermon at all. In their place a popular piety of pageants, passion plays, and feasts arose.

The descriptions might well be contemporary accounts of modern evangelical church life. We are increasingly known for our big buildings, fast-selling recordings, and our tacky dramatic productions more than we are known for our gracious, warm, and winning gospel preaching. To us as much as to his contemporaries Calvin says:

> I ask all who are in the least affected by a zeal for piety whether they do not clearly see both how much more brightly God's glory shines here, and how much richer sweetness of spiritual consolation comes to believers, than in these lifeless and theatrical trifles.[38]

In place of trifles, the Supper should be administered "at least weekly."[39] Services should begin with public prayers, followed by the sermon, which itself should be followed by the Supper.[40]

The proper administration of the Supper requires that when the elements have been placed on the Table, the minister should recite the promises attached to the Supper by Christ. He should also excommunicate (*excommunicaret*) those who by the Lord's "interdict" are prohibited from the Table.[41] (See 1 Corinthians 11:27-29.) In the Reformed tradition, this practice of warning unbelievers away from the Table is known as "fencing the table." After the warning, the minister should give thanks and pray God's blessing on the Supper, followed by a Psalm or an appropriate reading afterward, with the minister breaking the bread, of which "the faithful" (*fideles*) should partake in an orderly manner.[42]

CONCLUSION

Perhaps the idea of coming to the Table weekly is troubling, but why? The most common argument against weekly celebration of the Supper is that it might become routine. Doubtless this is a danger, but by this rationale all churches should hold only monthly worship services so that the sermons and singing will be truly meaningful. The absurdity of the argument is obvious. The possibility of abuse is no excuse for not making use of the divinely instituted means of grace.

Perhaps there is a more fundamental reason we are reluctant to observe the Supper more regularly. One fears that the simple gospel message of Christ offered for and to sinners is not really on the evangelical *agenda*—or *credenda* for that matter.(*Agenda* is Latin for "things to do," and *credenda* is Latin for "things to believe.") It might be that regular observance of the Supper would require a transformation of most evangelical worship services. It is difficult to imagine how a solemnly joyful service of the Supper would fit into some "seeker sensitive" services.

Weekly Communion would also affect the preaching by tending to orient the service around Christ's finished work and away from the constant diet of "how to" messages. The juxtaposition of "Ten Steps to a Happy Marriage" followed by a Communion service is too jarring to contemplate. Simply considering a weekly Communion a hypothetical possibility in our time seems to present radical challenges to evangelical piety.

Notes

1. J. I. Good, *The Origin of the Reformed Church in Germany* (Reading, PA: 1887), pp. 144-145.

2. In this regard, A. E. McGrath's call to recover a genuinely Protestant piety is an antidote. See *Spirituality in an Age of Change: Rediscovering the Spirituality of the Reformers* (Grand Rapids, MI: Eerdmans, 1994), pp. 165-173. See also M. S. Horton, *Putting Amazing Back into Grace* (Grand Rapids, MI: Baker, 1994), pp. 215-236.

3. See R. L. Dabney, *Lectures in Systematic Theology* (Richmond, VA: 1878; repr. Grand Rapids, MI: Zondervan, 1975), pp. 810-812; C. Hodge, *Systematic Theology*, Vol. 3 (Grand Rapids, MI: Eerdmans, repr. 1982), pp. 646-647; J. W. Nevin, *The Mystical Presence: A Vindication of the Reformed or Calvinistic Doctrine of the Holy Eucharist* (Philadelphia: 1867).

4. See B. A. Gerrish, *A Prince of the Church* (Philadelphia: Fortress, 1984). Harold O. J. Brown shows the connections between pietism, mysticism, and romanticism. See "Romanticism and the Bible," in *Challenges to Inerrancy: A Theological Response*, eds. G. Lewis and B. Demarest (Chicago: Moody, 1984), pp. 49-66.

5. The continuing influence of Quaker spirituality upon evangelicalism can be seen in the immense popularity of the books of R. J. Foster. For example, see *Celebration of Discipline: The Path to Spiritual Growth* (San Francisco: Harper & Row, rev. edition, 1988).

6. Ioannis Calvini, *Institutio Christianae Religionis*, in *Opera Selecta*, ed. P. Barth

The Present Evangelical Crisis

and W. Niesel, 5 vols., 3rd edition (Munich: Chr. Kaiser,1962-1974), 4.18.1, 6. For the English text see John Calvin, *Institutes of the Christian Religion*, trans. F. L. Battles, ed. J. T. McNeill (Philadelphia: Westminster, 1960).

7. The doctrine of the twofold benefit (*duplex beneficium*) is an important part of Reformed theology. It is found in Calvin. See *Institutio*, 3.11.1. It was the organizing principle of the Heidelberg theologian Caspar Olevian (1536-1587), who used it frequently. See, for example, *De substantia foederis gratuiti inter Deum et electos* (Geneva: 1585), 1.1.2; 2.69. On the relations between seals and the covenant theology of Scripture, see S. S. Smalley, s.v., "Seal, sealing," *The New Bible Dictionary* (Grand Rapids, MI: Zondervan, repr. 1975).

8. Matthew 26:26-30; Mark 14:22-26; Luke 22:14-23. Passover was the first feast of the new year, celebrating God's deliverance of Israel from slavery in Egypt. For a contemporary critical account see B. A. Bokser, s.v., "Passover," *Anchor Bible Dictionary*, 6 vols. (New York: Doubleday, 1992). For an evangelical account, see M. R. Wilson, s.v., "Passover," *International Standard Bible Encyclopedia*, 4 vols. (Grand Rapids, MI: Eerdmans, 1979-1988).

9. See E. P. Clowney, *The Doctrine of the Church* (Downers Grove, IL: InterVarsity, 1995).

10. *Institutio*, 4.16.30.

11. See Jeremiah 34:17-20; K. A. Kitchen, *The Ancient Orient and the Old Testament* (Downers Grove, IL: InterVarsity, 1966); M. G. Kline, *The Structure of Biblical Authority* (Grand Rapids, MI: Eerdmans, 1972); *Treaty of the Great King* (Grand Rapids, MI: Eerdmans, 1963); *By Oath Consigned* (Grand Rapids, MI: Eerdmans, 1968); George E. Mendenhall, *Law and Covenant in Israel and the Ancient Near East* (Pittsburgh: 1955).

12. Ioannis Calvini, *Opera Omnia*, Vol. XI/1: *In Evangelium secundum Johannem commentarius pars prior*, ed. H. Field (Geneva: 1997), pp. 216-217. The English text is in John Calvin, *The Gospel According to St. John*, trans. T. H. L. Parker, eds. D. W. Torrance *et al.* (Grand Rapids, MI: Eerdmans, 1969), 169ff. In his interpretation of John 6:53-54 Calvin was working with two parts of the fourfold medieval hermeneutical matrix, the *quadriga*. According to the *sensus literalis et historicus* Jesus' discourse was not properly about the Supper. Yet according to Calvin the passage does touch on the Supper, but only figuratively. Though he said "*figuretur*" he could just as well have used the traditional category *sensus allegoricus*, i.e., the doctrinal sense of the passage.

13. *Institutio*, 3.11.10. See also D. E. Tamburello, *Union with Christ: John Calvin and the Mysticism of St. Bernard* (Louisville: Westminster/John Knox Press, 1994), pp. 4-101.

14. James Bannerman, *The Church of Christ*, Vol. 1 (Edinburgh: 1848), p. 2.

15. "*De externis mediis vel adminiculis, quibus Deus in Christi societatem nos invitat, et in ea retinet.*"

16. *Institutio*, 4.1.5.

17. See *The Oxford English Dictionary* (Oxford: 1971), s.v., "hocus pocus."

The Means of Grace: The Lord's Supper

18. The seven sacraments were: baptism, Eucharist, confession, penance, marriage, extreme unction, and holy orders. Of course no one was eligible for all seven. For Calvin's critique of the medieval sacramental system, see *Institutio*, 4.19.

19. *Canones et decreta sacrosancti oecumenici concilii Tridentini* (Leipzig: 1890), VI, cap. X. The English text is in *Canons and Decrees of the Council of Trent*, trans. H. J. Schroeder (Rockford, IL: repr. 1978); *Catechism of the Catholic Church* (Collegeville, MD: 1994).

20. See *Institutio*, 4.17.5, 9.

21. Ibid., 4.14.3.

22. Ibid., 4.17.1.

23. Thus Reformed scholastic theologian Peter van Mastricht (1630-1706) distinguished between baptism as the "*sacramentum regenerationis*" and the Supper as the "*sacramentum nutritionis*." See *Theoretica-practica Theologia*, Vol. 2, new edition (Utrecht: repr. 1699), pp. 828-845.

24. "*Tanti mysterii*" (*Institutio*, 4.17.1).

25. "*Invisibile alimentum*" (*Institutio*, 4.17.1).

26. Calvin resolutely rejected the Roman doctrine of transubstantiation. See *Institutio*, 4.17.13-7, 39. Christ did not say that the bread would become His body at consecration, but that it already was His body. Calvin regarded the words of institution as a metonym, or a figure of speech (ibid., 4.17.21). The bread "is" Christ in the same way that circumcision "is" the covenant, etc. See also ibid., 4.18.

27. *Institutio*, 4.17.1.

28. Ibid., 4.17.9.

29. Ibid., 4.17.10, 18.

30. Ibid., 4.17.31. Hence he rejected the Lutheran doctrine of the "everywhereness" (*ubiquity*) of Christ's humanity (*Institutio*, 4.17.30). Consequently he also rejected the Lutheran doctrine of the *manducatio infidelium*, i.e., that unbelievers eat Christ's flesh in the Supper. See *Institutio*, 4.17.33-4.

31. *Institutio*, 4.17.31.

32. Ibid., 4.17.1.

33. Ibid., 4.17.5.

34. Ibid., 4.17.5.

35. Hence the language of Heidelberg Catechism (1563) Q/A.1: "That I with body and soul, both in life and in death, am not my own, but belong to my faithful saviour Jesus Christ." See P. Schaff, *The Creeds of Christendom*, Vol. 3, 6th edition (Grand Rapids, MI: Baker, repr. 1983), pp. 307-308.

36. John Calvin, *Institutes of the Christian Religion*, trans. H. Beveridge, 2 vols. (Grand Rapids, MI: Eerdmans, repr. 1979).

The Present Evangelical Crisis

37. *Belgic Confession*, art. 35 in Schaff, *Creeds*, Vol. 3, p. 429.

38. *Institutes* (Battles edition), 4.17.43.

39. *Institutio*, 4.17.43.

40. Calvin's "Form of Church Prayers" has been recently reprinted in T. L. Johnston, ed., *Leading in Worship* (Oak Ridge, TN: 1996). See also, Bard Thompson, ed., *Liturgies of the Western Church* (Philadelphia: Westminster, repr. 1980), pp. 185-210.

41. See Calvin, *Institutio*, 4.17.40.

42. *Institutio*, 4.17.43. The reason for the *fractio panis* or the breaking of the bread was twofold. First, to illustrate Christ's body broken for us, but also as a demonstration that despite all the benefits conferred in the Supper, the elements remain bread and wine.

7

THE MEANS OF GRACE:
BAPTISM

Stephen J. Wellum

Anyone who is familiar with the history of Christian thought knows that the question of baptism has raised and still does raise a lot of debates and disagreements, rooted not only in ecclesiastical tradition and theological systems,[1] but also in the vagaries of church history.[2] To think that a resolution of the baptismal debate is possible within the confines of this chapter is to expect the impossible. Instead, my goal in the following pages is much more modest; in fact, it is threefold.

First, in keeping with the theme and purpose of this book, I want to highlight a baptismal crisis that I see in many evangelical churches today, namely a low baptismal consciousness[3] among many Christians. Second, I want to contrast these present attitudes toward baptism with that of the New Testament by briefly reminding ourselves of the meaning and significance of Christian baptism. Finally, I want to give some concluding reflections regarding the urgent need to recover and embrace the importance of baptism for the life, health, and mission of the church.

LOW BAPTISMAL CONSCIOUSNESS WITHIN THE CHURCH

As heirs of the Reformation, evangelicals of various traditions have viewed baptism as vitally important for the life, health, and practice of the church. No doubt, after this basic agreement, there is a lot of disagreement and debate regarding the mode and the proper subjects of baptism. However, with that admitted, evangelicals for the most part have viewed baptism as extremely significant—indeed, a beautiful, visible dec-

The Means of Grace: Baptism

laration of the Gospel, bound up with the mission of the church.[4] The reason for this attitude is quite simple, yet one that must not be overlooked or ignored: baptism is one of the two ordinances or sacraments[5] that the Lord of the church has instituted and ordained for the life and health of the church, until the end of the age; and as such, it is to be practiced in our day in obedience to the Lord.

Of course, this divine institution of Christian baptism[6] is found at the end of Matthew's Gospel, in what has been called "The Great Commission" (Matt. 28:18-20). Here we are presented with the risen Lord, who not only has all authority by virtue of who He is (John 1:1-4; Phil. 2:6; Heb. 1:3), but now has been given all authority from the Father by virtue of what He has done in His triumphant cross-work at Calvary. At this major turning point in redemptive history, Jesus the Christ, who inaugurated His Kingdom in His coming, has now won victory over all of his enemies, and as a result He has been given all authority in heaven and on earth as God's sovereign, mediatorial King. And it is now from this posture of authority that He commands and impels His followers forward, to go and make disciples of all the nations, a task that must be characterized by nothing less than instruction in and the proclamation of God's Word and baptism into the name of the Father, Son, and Holy Spirit.[7]

This Great Commission is significant for at least two reasons. First, as many have noted, baptism "in" (NIV) or better, "into" (eis) the name of the Triune God strongly suggests "a coming-into-relationship-with or a coming-under-the-Lordship-of."[8] Thus, it would seem from our Lord's institution of baptism that it serves at least a twofold purpose: a sign of initiation and entrance into Messiah's community, and a graphic declaration of faith and surrender to the Lordship of Jesus Christ.[9] This certainly implies, among other things, that from the perspective of the New Testament, we "can scarcely conceive of a disciple who is not baptized or is not instructed."[10] Baptism, in other words, is not a "take it or leave it" issue for the church or a Christian disciple.

Second, and underscoring what has already been stated, the authority of baptism rests on the command of the risen Lord. As Beasley-Murray reminds us, "Such a charge is too imperious to be ignored or modified. It behooves us to adhere to it and conform to it as God gives grace."[11]

When we look at the book of Acts, it seems that the attitude and practice of the early church was just that—they obeyed the command of

The Present Evangelical Crisis

the risen Lord to His church. Thus, we read that on Pentecost all those who repented and believed were baptized, which numbered about 3,000 Jews (Acts 2:41). And as the church continued to proclaim the Gospel, we read that this same pattern continued. Consider the converts at Samaria (Acts 8:12-13), the Ethiopian eunuch (Acts 8:36-39), Saul (Acts 9:17-18), the household of Cornelius (Acts 10:47-48), the household of Lydia (Acts 16:14-15), the household of the Philippian jailer (Acts 16:31-33), the household of Crispus and many other Corinthians (Acts 18:8), and the disciples at Ephesus (Acts 19:5).

Now it is quite evident that when we compare this first-century situation to our own day, one must sadly conclude that, generally speaking, there is a low baptismal consciousness within the church today, no matter what side of the baptismal divide you find yourself on. David Wright, in a very candid article, laments this fact as he reflects upon the state of baptism in the evangelical church.

On the one hand, Wright admits that those in his tradition (paedobaptist) can come forward to be admitted to the Lord's Table without even being aware whether they have been baptized or not.[12] Even worse, he argues that the practice of indiscriminate infant baptism has done a terrible harm. In fact, that is one of the reasons why, he believes, so many treat baptism so lightly, since "where baptism is so easily given and received, with so little effect, it cannot—so many biblical Christians would reason—amount to very much."[13] On the other hand, Wright points out that the believers' baptism tradition does not escape a low baptismal consciousness either. Either conversion eclipses baptism as "the moment constitutive of Christian identity" or one finds as a result of mass evangelism that people can become Christians without being related to any specific church—a concept Wright correctly points out "would have been almost incomprehensible to the church of most earlier centuries."[14]

I think you can state the problem in even starker terms—terms that would have been unthinkable to New Testament Christianity: in today's evangelical church there are many who profess faith in and allegiance to the Lord Jesus Christ, but they have either not been baptized or they see no need to be baptized.

Why is there such a low baptismal consciousness in the church, especially given our Lord's command and New Testament practice? No doubt there are many reasons that could be given, and it is very difficult to reduce

The Means of Grace: Baptism

the problem to one or two factors. However, I am convinced that a large part of our problem is due to the pervasive loss of the Gospel and sound theology in the church, which is ultimately rooted in our capitulation to a culture that is becoming increasingly pluralistic. What do I mean by this? Here I am following D. A. Carson's analysis in his important work, *The Gagging of God.*[15] Carson rightly argues that the great battle we face at the end of the twentieth century is the battle for truth—a battle against what he calls "philosophical pluralism," i.e., the notion that a "particular ideological or religious claim is intrinsically superior to another is necessarily wrong. The only absolute creed is the creed of pluralism."[16]

Carson's analysis shows that philosophical pluralism has impacted not only society, but sadly, also the church.[17] For example, in the religious realm it has brought about at least two debilitating effects: a growing biblical and theological illiteracy (and along with it an increasing denial of biblical authority), as well as an inclusivist attitude toward world religions.[18] That is one of the reasons why the weekly exposition of Scripture has fallen on hard times, and with it the knowledge of God and His Word. In the area of culture, which has also impacted the church, a corollary of pluralism is that of secularization—a process, experts tell us, that does not necessarily lead to the abolition of God, but rather to His marginalization in all aspects of our lives. Thus, what is no longer central to us and what no longer drives us to our knees and out to the world is the glory of God and the Gospel. Theological issues that used to captivate us no longer do—so much so that one rarely hears preached the great watershed doctrines such as union with Christ, election, justification, and sanctification. In addition, pragmatism and individualism have brought about a generation of church consumers who remain indifferent to the local church and cavalier about their participation in it.[19]

Given our present situation, is it any wonder that there is a low baptismal consciousness among us? Indeed, when the burning realities of the Gospel are far from us, when the glorious work of our Triune God to save us does not move us, when biblical authority does not captivate our minds and hearts and lead us to obedience, is it any wonder that baptism, along with many other things, fades in its importance and significance? For, as we shall soon discover, Christian baptism marks boundaries.[20] It defines us, and it testifies to the Gospel. It speaks of a majestic Lord who has come to save us and our identification with Him and with His people, by sovereign grace. It speaks of a salvation and a Savior who is the only hope of the world, and it speaks of a believer who was once alienated and estranged from God but now, by grace through faith, has been brought nigh, and thus gladly acknowledges and confesses before the world that Jesus Christ is Lord.

Is this the only reason for the low baptismal consciousness in our day? For me to answer yes, I think would be reductionistic. But I do think it is an important one, and something we must seriously address. With that in mind, let us now briefly contrast these present attitudes toward baptism with that of the New Testament.

THE MEANING AND SIGNIFICANCE OF CHRISTIAN BAPTISM

There is certainly much that could be written regarding the meaning and significance of baptism; indeed, the literature on it is abundant. Moreover, it is at this point that major differences between baptismal positions begin to surface, and thus what one writes on these matters is never neutral. However, with that in mind, it is my goal briefly to unpack four propositions regarding baptism, which I believe are consistent and true to the biblical data as we find it in the New Testament and necessary to affirm, especially given the baptismal crisis of our day.

First, baptism is one of the primary means God has given us to publicly declare our faith in Jesus Christ as Lord and Savior. Is this not part of what was going on at Pentecost in Peter's exhortation to the people who cried from their hearts, "What shall we do?" (Acts 2:37)? Peter had just demonstrated that the coming of the Spirit in power was nothing less than evidence that redemption had been accomplished, that Jesus is "both Lord and Christ" (Acts 2:36), and that the new age that the Old Testament longed for and anticipated (Joel 2:28ff; cf. Ezek. 36:25-27; Jer. 31:29-34) had now finally arrived. Thus, Peter proclaimed that a response is necessary to these great, climactic, redemptive-historical events. And what should that response be? It is repentance and baptism, administered in the name of Jesus Christ, signifying a person's submission to Him as both Lord and Christ (Acts 2:38). Or as Beasley-Murray succinctly states it: "Baptism in the name of the Lord Jesus, whatever else it came to imply, was in the earliest time a baptism 'for the sake of' the Lord Jesus and therefore in submission to Him as Lord and King."[21]

The Means of Grace: Baptism

I think this basic point is important for us to remember in our day. In a time in which altar calls, confirmation, public rallies, and what not have taken the place of baptism in our confessing the Lordship of Jesus Christ, we need to be called back to the beauty and simplicity of this God-ordained rite. This "instrument of surrender"[22] graphically and wonderfully portrays our submission to the Lord Jesus; that we were once separate from Christ, without hope and without God in the world, but now in Christ we have been brought near, gladly acknowledging, by grace, Jesus as Lord. I think Beasley-Murray is right when he says, "Baptism is peculiarly appropriate to express such a meaning, especially when the Pauline depth of significance is added to it. No subsequent rite of the Church, such as confirmation, adequately replaces it. The loss of this element in baptism is grievous and it needs to be regained if baptism is to mean to the modern Church what it did to the earliest Church."[23]

Second, and probably the most fundamental meaning of baptism, is that it signifies a believer's union with Christ, by grace through faith, and all the benefits that are entailed by that union. It is for this reason that throughout the New Testament, baptism is regarded as an outward sign that a believer has entered into the realities of the New Covenant that Jesus sealed with His own blood on the cross.[24] J. I. Packer captures this point well when he writes:

> Christian baptism . . . is a sign from God that signifies inward cleansing and remission of sins (Acts 22:16; 1 Corinthians 6:11; Ephesians 5:25-27), Spirit-wrought regeneration and new life (Titus 3:5), and the abiding presence of the Holy Spirit as God's seal testifying and guaranteeing that one will be kept safe in Christ forever (1 Corinthians 12:13; Ephesians 1:13-14). Baptism carries these meanings because first and fundamentally it signifies union with Christ in his death, burial, and resurrection (Romans 6:3-7; Colossians 2:11-12); and this union with Christ is the source of every element in our salvation (1 John 5:11-12). Receiving the sign in faith assures the persons baptized that God's gift of new life in Christ is freely given to them.[25]

In fact, so close is the association between baptism and New Covenant blessings in Christ that many have argued that in the New

The Present Evangelical Crisis

Testament baptism "functions as shorthand for the conversion experience as a whole."[26] Evidence for this is quite apparent.

For example, in Galatians 3:26-27 Paul says: "You are all sons of God through faith in Christ Jesus, for all of you who were baptized into Christ have been clothed with Christ." The language of being "clothed" with Christ most certainly refers to the fact of our union with Him.[27] But what is interesting about Paul's statement is how Paul can ascribe union with Christ both to faith (v. 26) and to baptism (v. 27). How can Paul do this? Does he have in mind an *ex opere operato* view of baptism? Of course, the answer is no. Paul is not referring to those who have been baptized but who have not repented or believed. That would go against the clear statement of verse 26. Rather, he is referring to those who have been converted; all such have clothed themselves with Christ and have been united with Him through faith. Thus baptism, by metonymy, can stand for conversion and signify, as an outward sign, that a believer has entered into the realities of the New Covenant as a result of his union with Jesus Christ through faith.[28]

We find something similar in Romans 6:1-4, where Paul sees the initiation rite of baptism as uniting the believer to Jesus Christ in His redemptive acts—His death, burial, and resurrection. No doubt, in this text Paul is not primarily giving a theological explanation of the nature of baptism, but is rather unpacking its meaning for life. Paul is deeply concerned to rebut the charge that the believer can remain in sin in order to underscore grace. Accordingly he uses the language of "realm transfer"[29] to show how inconceivable this suggestion really is. We Christians, Paul affirms, have "died to sin" (v. 2b). We have been transferred from the realm of Adam (sin) to the realm of Christ (life, resurrection, grace); therefore, it is quite impossible for us to still live in sin; its power in us has been decisively broken due to our union with Christ in His death.

Now it is quite legitimate to ask: when did this realm transfer take place, this death to sin? It is interesting that in verses 3-4 Paul connects death to sin with our baptism—when we were "baptized into Christ Jesus" we were "baptized into his death" (v. 3). We have died to sin because we have become one with the Lord who died and rose for the conquest of sin and death. "We were therefore buried with him through baptism into death in order that, just as Christ was raised from the dead . . . we too may live a new life" (v. 4). In this sense, then, baptism serves

The Means of Grace: Baptism

as the instrument by which we are united with Christ in His death, burial, and resurrection.[30]

Once again, how are we to understand this? Does the very practice of the rite of baptism unite us to Christ automatically? Certainly that is not Paul's point. Rather, as in Galatians 3:26-27, baptism functions as shorthand for the whole conversion experience. Thus, Moo is right in concluding that "just as faith is always assumed to lead to baptism, so baptism always assumes faith for its validity. In verses 3-4, then, we can assume that baptism stands for the whole conversion-initiation experience, presupposing faith and the gift of the Spirit."[31] In truth, if we understand Paul's argument, it is not baptism that is the primary focus at all; rather, it is the redemptive events themselves that Paul is stressing. Baptism is only introduced to demonstrate that we were united with Christ in His redemptive work, and now all the New Covenant blessings that our Lord has secured for us are ours by virtue of our relationship with Him. Beasley-Murray states it this way: "Through the faith expressed in baptism, what was done outside of us (*extra nos*) becomes effective faith within us. In Christ we are the reconciled children of God."[32]

First Peter 3:21 is further evidence for the close relationship between baptism and New Covenant blessings in Christ. In fact, the relationship is so close that Peter can speak of "baptism that now saves you." What does Peter mean by this? It is quite evident that Peter is not presenting baptism as a magical rite. He immediately points out that it is not the outward, physical act of baptism that saves, but it serves as an appeal to God for a clear conscience. In other words, we are not saved as a result of a outward, physical act or because we promise to live an obedient life. We are saved when we call upon the Lord for a "good conscience." Yet, there is even more: "it [baptism] saves you by the resurrection of Jesus Christ" (v. 21b). Not even a request to God for a clean conscience actually provides the basis for our salvation. Peter is emphatic that salvation has ultimately been earned for us by Christ and Him alone. Thus, as Grudem correctly states:

> All that baptism represents comes to us not on the merits of any
> response from us, but through the resurrection of Jesus Christ.
> His resurrection marked his once-and-for-all exit from the realm

The Present Evangelical Crisis

of death and judgment on sin, and our union with him in his resurrection is the means by which God gives us new life. . . . Our
rising out of the waters of baptism is a picture of our being raised
with Christ; by being brought safely through "these waters of
judgment" through Christ's resurrection we are indeed given a
clear conscience by God.[33]

Why is this second point important to stress? For at least this reason:
in contrast with the attitudes and practice of many contemporary evangelicals, the New Testament is clear—we cannot stand aloof and indifferent to baptism. Not only is the practice of baptism mandated by our
Lord, but the rite is closely linked with the Gospel itself. Hence, in baptism God beautifully testifies in a outward, visible way that salvation is
by grace alone, through faith alone, and by Christ alone. In fact, since
baptism and conversion are so closely associated in Scripture, it is not
enough to say that baptism is a mere symbol or a declarative act. Instead,
in the words of Beasley-Murray, it is also a "divine-human event."[34]

Of course, one must be careful at this point not to move either in the
direction of *ex opere operato* or of the absolute necessity of baptism for
salvation. The New Testament is clear: the benefits that come to us in baptism are bound up with faith. In other words, faith and baptism do not
enjoy the same logical status of necessity. But with that said, it is significant that Scripture can link God's gracious giving of all the believer's benefits of being united to Christ to the context of water baptism. Surely, this
New Testament teaching doesn't make baptism a trivial matter! That so
many Christians can stand as loose to baptism as they do can only reflect
the current crisis of the loss of sound biblical theology in the church. That
is why it should not surprise us that in a day in which we are consumed
with so many secondary issues rather than the Gospel itself, we also find
ourselves in a baptismal crisis, for the Gospel and baptism go hand in
hand. And thus when the Gospel is recovered in all of its beauty and
depth, and people once again seek to know nothing but Jesus Christ and
Him crucified, baptism will once again take its unique role as the initiating rite of the church.

Third, baptism very graphically signifies a believer's entrance into the
body of Christ, the church. Beasley-Murray bluntly states this reality
when he writes: "Baptism to Christ is baptism to the Church; it cannot

The Means of Grace: Baptism

be otherwise, for the Church is *sōma Christou*, the Body of Christ."[35] So, for example, in Galatians 3:27-28 Paul can immediately move from "putting on" Christ in baptism to the body of Christ in which we are all one. Or in Ephesians 4:22-25, Paul can use the baptismal imagery of "putting on" and "putting off" to speak of the kind of behavior we should have both as individuals and because "we are all members of one body" (v. 25), certainly a reference to the church. In this sense, baptism is similar to an "adoption certificate into the family of God."[36] It is the defining mark of belonging, as well as a demarcation from the world (cf. Acts 2:40-41). Thus, in the act of baptism, not only does the Lord of the church appropriate to Himself the one who is baptized in His name and incorporate him into His body, but the person who is baptized also openly identifies with the Lord and His people.[37]

Once again, this is something we need to recapture in our day. Not only do people stand loose to baptism, but also to the church. Indeed the two are intimately connected. Whether it is due to our rampant individualism or our lack of theological reflection (or both!), we live in a generation of Christians who remain loosely attached to the church. Little do we see ourselves as different from the world; little do we view baptism as a defining mark of belonging to God's people. However, when we look beyond our borders to the church in other countries and discover what it means for a Christian to be baptized, for example, in a Jewish or Muslim context, the significance of baptism becomes much clearer to us. As Green reminds us: "It is extremely costly, and often involves the expulsion of a newly-baptized person from home and country. Sometimes the family holds a funeral service, to show that the baptized person no longer belongs to them in any way. He is, to all intents and purposes, dead."[38] Truly this aspect of baptism has much to say to us today, and if the truth be known, what needs to be recaptured more than anything else is the burning life and death realities of the Gospel, which baptism so beautifully signifies.

Fourth, baptism is a tremendous promise and anticipation of the fact that all things will be one day consummated through Jesus Christ our Lord. Even though there are a lot of questions surrounding the baptism of John, one thing is clear: John's baptism was an eschatological ceremony, anticipating the coming of the Messiah, the Kingdom of God, and the whole New Covenant era. Christian baptism too is eschatological, but it distinguishes itself from John's baptism in the sense that what John anticipated and longed for has now arrived in Jesus Christ; the age of fulfillment has dawned.

Thus, Christian baptism, as I have sought to argue, signifies nothing less than the fact that the believer has entered into the full realities of the New Covenant. Why? Because Christian baptism is bound up with our union with the Lord Jesus Christ, who alone has ushered in the long-awaited Kingdom and has literally inaugurated a "new creation." That is why Paul can joyfully say: "If anyone is in Christ, he is a new creation; the old has gone, the new has come!" (2 Cor. 5:17). However, it is also important to stress that Christian baptism not only looks back to the inauguration of the Kingdom and new creation in Jesus' first coming, but it also looks forward to the not yet—the consummation of all things. We still await the return of our Lord, and as such, we groan with all of creation as we await our full redemption as sons and daughters of the King (cf. Rom. 8:18ff.).

Truly, then, a Christian is one who is caught between the times. He looks back to the death and resurrection of Jesus by which the new age has come, and he looks forward in eager anticipation to the realities of the new heaven and the new earth. But in looking back, it is not as if he is a mere spectator. Rather, by baptism the believer participates in the event by which the Kingdom came. Likewise, looking forward is much more than a wishful longing for a place in the consummation. Rather, as Beasley-Murray so well puts it:

> We have been united with the Christ who brought the Kingdom in His death and resurrection and shall complete it in his *parousia*, and we have received the Spirit who mediates the powers of the Kingdom and is the binding link between the two appearings. The forward look of baptism therefore, by reason of its participation in the event that inaugurated the Kingdom, is an anticipation with joyous confidence of the event that shall consummate it. It is a "strong encouragement" for those who have fled for refuge to "seize the hope set before us" (Hebrews 6:18).[39]

Baptism, then, is an entry into the eschatological order of the new creation. This is what pervades the consciousness of the early church.

The Means of Grace: Baptism

Indeed, this is what pervades Peter's preaching at Pentecost. As he seeks to proclaim the meaning of the coming Holy Spirit, he does so by proclaiming that the new age has dawned. Jesus, who has died, is now alive. And as a result of His exaltation, He has poured out the promised Holy Spirit, the down payment of the powers of the age to come. And we participate in that age through baptism, by which we are united with Jesus Christ and sealed with the Holy Spirit for the day of redemption (Eph. 4:30).[40]

No doubt, here is an element in the meaning of baptism that desperately needs to be recovered today. In a day when so many in the church seem to flounder without direction, when there seems to be little urgency in the task of gospel proclamation, when moral and theological compromise is on every hand, we need to be reminded of these great realities. In fact, in them we need to renew our hope and confidence because in them we need to see a fresh sight of our glorious Savior-King. In this regard Beasley-Murray's comments are wise:

> Baptism means hope! . . . . Modern Christians would be strength-
> ened by a fresh grasp of this aspect of the meaning of Christian
> baptism. For men still look for ground to hope and there is no
> secure basis for it but in Christ. When we know Him to be "our
> life" (Colossians 3:4) we need no other.[41]

Certainly more could be said regarding the meaning and significance of baptism, but that, in a summary fashion, highlights much of the New Testament's teaching regarding it. While much of the biblical teaching above would meet with the agreement of many evangelicals across a wide spectrum of denominational affiliation, one basic point of division still remains. If, as the Scripture teaches, the sacrament is not effective apart from faith, on what grounds may infants who are not capable of faith be baptized? Of course, the debate and divide over this issue is vast, and I do not see a resolution in the near future, though open and candid discussion would help. Ultimately what is at dispute is not an isolated prooftext, but whole theological structures. The main point of division centers on the relationship between the Old and New Covenants and the amount of continuity and discontinuity between them.

Thus, for example, those who advocate a paedobaptist position admit that even though there is no explicit command in the New Testament to baptize infants, the practice is still legitimate due to the following:[42] (1) There is an essential unity and continuity of the covenant of grace administered to Abraham, which came to fruition in the New Covenant. (2) Since infants were included in the Old Covenant through circumcision, which was an outward sign of entrance into the covenant community, and since circumcision has been replaced by baptism in the New Covenant, then believing parents are required to administer the New Covenant sign—baptism—to their children. (3) In the Old Covenant, it is quite evident that circumcision did not necessarily mean the child was one of the elect unto salvation; they still needed to exercise faith in order to know and experience God's salvation. But it did demonstrate that God had ordered the sign before faith was present. So in the New Covenant, baptism does not guarantee that children are the elect unto salvation either; they still need to exercise repentance toward God and faith in the Lord Jesus Christ. But as in the Old Covenant, it is legitimate to give the child the sign of the New Covenant prior to faith.[43] (4) Further support for the practice of baptizing infants is found in the household baptisms reported in the New Testament.

On the other side, those who advocate that baptism should only be administered to believers argue the following:[44] (1) In Scripture, baptism is only effectual as an expression of faith, and hence the New Testament pattern—proclamation of the Gospel, believing acceptance of it, and then baptism. (2) No doubt there is a fundamental and underlying continuity between the Old and New Covenants, but there is a lot of discontinuity as well. For example, under the Old Covenant there is necessarily a distinction between the locus of the covenant community and the locus of the elect, with circumcision being the sign of the former. However, under the New Covenant this distinction has been removed. By definition, the people of the New Covenant have the law of God written on their hearts, they have experienced forgiveness of sins, and thus the locus of the New Covenant community and the locus of the elect become one. That suggests, among other things, that baptism as the sign of the New Covenant is only to be applied to those who are in the New Covenant, i.e., believers.[45] (3) The examples of household baptisms are arguments from silence. In fact, when we look at the actual examples more closely, we see

The Means of Grace: Baptism

that in a number of them there are indications of saving faith on the part
of all those baptized.[46]

Where do we go from here? Let me summarize with three concluding thoughts.

CONCLUDING REFLECTIONS

First, baptism is important, and as such, we need to be serious about it,
again. For not only is it bound up with our Lord's instruction and command to the church, but it is part and parcel of gospel proclamation—a
beautiful outward portrayal of the Gospel itself. We neglect it to our peril.

Second, in all of our disagreements over baptism, we must never forget what unites us. Most of us are quite content to acknowledge that
Christians should be baptized in obedience to God; that baptism is the
sign of the great gospel realities of union with Christ and all the glorious
benefits of New Covenant blessings; that baptism is related to our incor-
poration into the church; and that baptism, in contrast to the *ex opere
operato* view of Roman Catholicism, has no magical power, but it is by
grace alone, through faith alone, and by Christ alone that we are made
right with God. No doubt, there are profound differences among us. I
admit that paedo- and believer's baptism views cannot simultaneously be
right. I would even argue that due to the significance of our differences
we have the right to establish local congregations that emphasize one of
the views to the exclusion of the other.

However, with that said, we must never lose sight of what unites us.
And what is that? The Gospel. Baptism, though it is important, is not the
decisive issue of our day, or any day for that matter. And as such, even
though we disagree on some very important points, we need to find our
commonality in that to which baptism points—the glories of Jesus the
Christ and the full realities of the Gospel of sovereign grace. That, more
than anything, must captivate our thinking, our hearts, our churches, our
very lives, or else all is for naught.

Third, we need to recover once again the emphasis that baptism, as
the initiating rite of the church, is one of God's means of grace that He
has given to His people.[47] What this implies, of course, is that in the practice of baptism there is the blessing of God. In our obedience to Christ
and our public act of confessing Him, the Lord of the church pours His

The Present Evangelical Crisis

love and joy into our hearts. When baptism is practiced, as a sign of the believer's union with Christ, the Holy Spirit strengthens our faith and encourages us to press on. In our celebration of this sacrament in the presence of the body of Christ, the people of God are encouraged in their commitment to the Lord and to each other. Indeed, in the practice of baptism, the full eschatological realities of the Gospel are impressed upon our minds and hearts by the Spirit of God, so that we are challenged once again to view our lives from the perspective of eternity, and thus to live aright as those who have tasted the powers of the age to come. No doubt, even though baptism in and of itself does not bring us into a state of grace, it has been ordained by God as a proper means of grace that we ignore, distort, or downplay to the loss of our spiritual health, life, and mission.

NOTES

1. There are many points of disagreement between the two views of believer's baptism and paedobaptism, such as the status of households in Scripture (e.g., Acts 11:14; 16:15, 33; 18:8) and Jesus' blessing of the little children (Matt. 19:13-15; Mark 10:13-16; Luke 18:15-17). But the heart of the disagreement between the two views is theological; i.e., the main dispute centers on the relationship between the Old and New Covenants and the amount of continuity and discontinuity between them. On this important issue and the arguments given by both sides see the following: Louis Berkhof, *Systematic Theology* (Grand Rapids, MI: Eerdmans, 1941), pp. 622-643; Edmund Clowney, *The Church* (Downers Grove, IL: InterVarsity Press, 1995), pp. 276-284; Geoffrey W. Bromiley, *Children of Promise: The Case for Baptizing Infants* (Grand Rapids, MI: Eerdmans, 1979); Robert R. Booth, *Children of Promise: The Biblical Case for Infant Baptism* (Phillipsburg, NJ: Presbyterian & Reformed, 1995); John Calvin, *Institutes of the Christian Religion*, Vol. 2 (Philadelphia: Westminster, 1960), pp. 1303-1359; Donald Bridge and David Phypers, *The Water That Divides: The Baptism Debate* (Leicester, England: Inter-Varsity Press, 1977), pp. 33-70; G. R. Beasley-Murray, *Baptism in the New Testament* (Grand Rapids, MI: Eerdmans), pp. 334-344; Paul K. Jewett, *Infant Baptism and the Covenant of Grace* (Grand Rapids, MI: Eerdmans, 1978); Millard J. Erickson, *Christian Theology*, Vol. 3 (Grand Rapids, MI: Baker Books, 1985), pp. 1089-1105; Wayne Grudem, *Systematic Theology* (Grand Rapids, MI: Zondervan, 1994), pp. 966-984.

2. See Bridge and Phypers, *The Water That Divides*, pp. 73-150 for a helpful and concise summary of the historical data surrounding the baptism debate.

3. The term "low baptismal consciousness" is taken from David F. Wright's article, "Recovering Baptism for a New Age of Mission," in *Doing Theology for the People of God: Studies in Honor of J. I. Packer*, eds. Donald Lewis and Alister McGrath (Downers Grove, IL: InterVarsity Press, 1996), p. 54.

The Means of Grace: Baptism

4. Murray J. Harris, in his article "Baptism and the Lord's Supper," in *In God's Community: The Church and Its Ministry*, eds. David J. Ellis and W. Ward Gasque (London: Pickering and Inglis, 1978), p. 14 nicely contrasts baptism with the proclamation of the Word of God as the Gospel presented to the eye-gate versus the Gospel proclaimed to the ear-gate. Thus Harris states: "The submersion of the Christian in water is an acted parable of the death and burial of Christ, while his emergence from the water graphically dramatizes Christ's rising from death and entrance into new life."

5. Historically, evangelicals have differed over whether to apply the term *sacrament* to baptism and the Lord's Supper. Some evangelicals, especially Baptists, have refused to refer to baptism and the Lord's Supper as sacraments. Instead, they have preferred the word *ordinances*, primarily for two reasons: (1) Baptism and the Lord's Supper were ordained by our Lord (Matt. 28:18-20; 1 Cor. 11:24); (2) They have wanted to distinguish their view from Roman Catholicism, which has historically viewed baptism and the Lord's Supper as sacraments (along with confirmation, penance, anointing of the sick, holy orders, and marriage), which in themselves actually convey grace to people without necessarily requiring faith from the persons participating in them. This is the notion behind the Latin phrase *ex opere operato*; that is, by virtue of the work done, grace is actually given, so that it can be said that the sacraments actually confer grace in an efficacious sense, without the need for faith in the recipients. On the other hand, other evangelicals, especially those in the Anglican, Lutheran, and Reformed traditions, have been willing to speak of baptism and the Lord's Supper as sacraments, though still in contrast to the Roman Catholic view, in the sense that they are outward and visible signs of an inward grace. If one understands *sacrament* in the latter sense, it does not seem that any momentous point is at issue here. Since evangelicals clearly distinguish their view from the *ex opere operato* view of Roman Catholicism, it is legitimate to refer to baptism and the Lord's Supper as either sacraments or ordinances, and thus I will use the words interchangeably. On one specific Baptist objection to the use of the term *sacrament* see A. H. Strong, *Systematic Theology*, Vol. 3 (Philadelphia: Judson Press, 1909), p. 930. On the Roman Catholic use of the term *sacrament* see Richard P. McBrien, *Catholicism*, Vol. 2 (Minneapolis: Winston Press, 1980), pp. 731-745 and Thomas Bokenkotter, *Essential Catholicism* (Garden City, NY: Image Books, 1986), pp. 170-186. On the topic of sacraments in general see Alister E. McGrath, *Christian Theology: An Introduction*, 2nd edition (Oxford, England: Blackwell, 1997), pp. 494-520.

6. There is much discussion in the literature on the origin of Christian baptism and its relationship to Qumran, Jewish proselyte baptism, John's baptism, and the baptism of Jesus. It is certainly not the purpose of this chapter to wrestle with these issues, but they are important ones in ultimately coming to grips with the meaning and significance of Christian baptism. It seems safe to say that Christian baptism emerged out of the ministry of John the Baptist. John administered a one-time "repentance-baptism" for the forgiveness of sins (Mark 1:4) in anticipation of Messiah's baptism of Spirit and fire (Matt. 3:11). Jesus submitted to John's baptism (Matt. 3:13-17; Mark 1:9-11) to demonstrate His identification and solidarity with sinful humanity and the inauguration of His ministry as the Messiah. But once Jesus' cross-work was

The Present Evangelical Crisis

complete, the provisional nature of John's baptism reached its full and final significance in Christian baptism, bound up with the ushering in of the New Covenant age. Many have noted that due to the close connection between John's baptism and Christian baptism, one should expect to find the same stress upon personal repentance and faith in Christian baptism that we find in John. In fact, I would argue that attempts to circumvent this connection in order to find a justifiable reason to baptize those who lack personal repentance and faith put John and Jesus (and later the apostles) at odds with one another and disrupt the unique forerunner-Messiah relationship that exists between them in the New Testament. For more on these issues see D. S. Dockery, "Baptism," in *Dictionary of Jesus and the Gospels*, eds. Joel B. Green, Scot McKnight, and I. Howard Marshall (Downers Grove, IL: InterVarsity Press, 1992), pp. 55-58; Beasley-Murray, *Baptism*, pp. 1-92; Beasley-Murray, "Baptism," *NIDNTT*, ed. Colin Brown, Vol. 1 (Grand Rapids, MI: Zondervan, 1986), pp. 143-150; George E. Ladd, *A Theology of the New Testament*, rev. ed. (Grand Rapids, MI: Eerdmans, 1993), pp. 31-41; Harris, "Baptism and the Lord's Supper," pp. 16-17; Bridge and Phypers, *The Water That Divides*, pp. 15-32.

7. On the grammatical construction of this verse and issues surrounding it, see D. A. Carson, *Matthew, The Expositor's Bible Commentary*, ed. Frank E. Gaebelein, Vol. 8 (Grand Rapids, MI: Zondervan, 1984), pp. 594-599; and Beasley-Murray, *Baptism*, pp. 77-92.

8. Carson, *Matthew*, p. 597. See also Beasley-Murray, *Baptism*, pp. 90-92; G. R. Beasley-Murray, "Baptism," in *New Dictionary of Theology*, eds. Sinclair B. Ferguson, David F. Wright, and J. I. Packer (Downers Grove, IL: InterVarsity Press, 1988), p. 70.

9. This is why Paul Jewett, in his article "Baptism (Baptist View)," in *Zondervan Pictorial Encyclopedia of the Bible*, ed. Merrill C. Tenney, Vol. 1 (Grand Rapids, MI: Zondervan, 1975), p. 466 defines Christian baptism as "that initiatory washing with water in the name of the Father, the Son, and the Holy Spirit which the risen Lord commissioned His apostles to administer to all His followers as a mark of their discipleship."

10. Carson, *Matthew*, p. 597. Beasley-Murray makes the same point, though from the perspective of the apostle Paul, in his article "Baptism," in *Dictionary of Paul and His Letters*, eds. Gerald F. Hawthorne, Ralph P. Martin, and Daniel G. Reid (Downers Grove, IL: InterVarsity Press, 1993), p. 60. Beasley-Murray rightly notes that Paul's argument in Rom 6:1ff. would be groundless unless Paul assumes that he and *all* his readers have been baptized.

11. Beasley-Murray, *Baptism*, p. 92. Also see the strong emphasis on the place of divine authority in the institution and continuing practice of baptism in Berkhof, *Systematic Theology*, p. 624; John Murray, *Christian Baptism* (Philadelphia: Presbyterian & Reformed Publishing, 1962), pp. 4-8.

12. Wright, "Recovering Baptism for a New Age of Mission," p. 54.

13. Ibid., p. 55.

14. Ibid.

The Means of Grace: Baptism

15. D. A. Carson, *The Gagging of God: Christianity Confronts Pluralism* (Grand Rapids, MI: Zondervan, 1996).

16 Ibid., p. 19. Carson's observation is very similar to Francis Schaeffer's assessment that the vital and crucial issue facing the evangelical church at the end of the twentieth century is the battle over truth. See Francis A. Schaeffer, *The Great Evangelical Disaster* (Wheaton, IL: Crossway Books, 1984).

17. One remembers the often quoted statement of Allan Bloom as he began his work *The Closing of the American Mind* (New York: Simon and Schuster, 1987), p. 25: "There is one thing a professor can be absolutely certain of: almost every student entering the university believes, or says he believes, that truth is relative."

18. *Inclusivism* is the view that all who are saved are saved on account of the person and work of Jesus Christ, but that conscious faith in Jesus Christ is not absolutely necessary. Some may be saved, even though they have never heard about Jesus, by responding to the knowledge that they have around them, i.e., responding to general revelation. Others may be saved by responding to Jesus after death, i.e., post-mortem salvation. *Exclusivism*, in contrast to inclusivism, argues that only those who place their faith in Jesus Christ are saved. Exclusivism has been the historic position of the church. Inclusivism, which has been popular in Roman Catholic circles, especially since Vatican II, has increasingly become popular in evangelical circles: e.g., Clark Pinnock and John Sanders. For more on these issues see Carson, *The Gagging of God*; Ronald Nash, *Is Jesus the Only Savior?* (Grand Rapids, MI: Zondervan, 1994); John Sanders, *No Other Name: An Investigation Into the Destiny of the Unevangelized* (Grand Rapids, MI: Eerdmans, 1992); Clark H. Pinnock, *A Wideness in God's Mercy: The Finality of Jesus Christ in a World of Religions* (Grand Rapids, MI: Zondervan, 1992).

19. For a more in-depth treatment of these issues, refer to Carson, *The Gagging of God*. Also see David F. Wells, *No Place For Truth, or Whatever Happened to Evangelical Theology?* (Grand Rapids, MI: Eerdmans, 1993); Gene Edward Veith, Jr., *Postmodern Times* (Wheaton, IL: Crossway Books, 1994); David S. Dockery, ed. *The Challenge of Postmodernism: An Evangelical Engagement* (Wheaton, IL: Victor Books, 1995); and, on a more popular level, the essays in John Armstrong, ed. *The Coming Evangelical Crisis* (Chicago: Moody Press, 1996).

20. See Wright, "Recovering Baptism for a New Age of Mission," pp. 56-57. In this regard Wright states the following: "We should not imagine, however, that as the church increasingly finds itself, in Europe at least, in a primary mission field, this recovery of baptism will be straightforward. For inclusiveness is a prominent element in the religious psyche of the ex-Christian West, and baptism always marks boundaries. It is the rite whereby persons are included in the family of Christ, but only by drawing lines between church and nonchurch, between Christian and non-Christian. A baptismal ministry which seeks to be faithful to the New Testament's presentation of baptism cannot fail to run athwart the inclusivist spirit of the age. In a number of ways the pre-Constantinian experience of the church becomes more and more pertinent at the end of the second millennium. Not least is this the case for baptism."

The Present Evangelical Crisis

21. Beasley-Murray, *Baptism*, p. 101. Murray Harris, "Baptism and the Lord's Supper," pp. 19-21 makes the same point when he emphasizes that "In baptism there is a transference of the rights of possession ('into the name,' *eis to onoma*, Acts 8:16; 19:5). . . . As he submits to baptism in obedience to Christ's command, the believer gives outward evidence, by an oral and public confession, of his inward belief in Jesus Christ as the Son of God and his intent to show lifelong devotion and loyalty to his Master with whom he has died, been buried, and raised (Romans 6:1-11)." Also see F. F. Bruce, *The Book of Acts*, NICNT (Grand Rapids, MI: Eerdmans, 1986), pp. 75-78; Richard N. Longenecker, *Acts, The Expositor's Bible Commentary* (Grand Rapids, MI: Zondervan, 1995), pp. 79-81; Berkhof, *Systematic Theology*, pp. 624-626.

22. The term is taken from Beasley-Murray, *Baptism*, p. 102.

23. Ibid.

24. One of the important side-issues in the baptism debate is the proper mode of baptism. Even though the purpose of this chapter is not to deal with this issue, it is significant that those who argue for the believer's baptism position generally argue that immersion is the most adequate way to symbolize our union with Christ. On this see Jewett, "Baptism," p. 466; and Grudem, *Systematic Theology*, pp. 967-968. Of course, this is not the only factor in the discussion regarding the proper mode. Much discussion also centers around the word *baptize* and its meaning. On this see *BAGD*, pp. 131-132; Beasley-Murray, "Baptism," *NIDNTT*, pp. 144-146; cf. A. Oepke, "Baptize," *TDNT*, ed. Gerhard Kittel, Vol. 1 (Grand Rapids, MI: Eerdmans, 1964), pp. 529-546. For a contrary view see Berkhof, *Systematic Theology*, pp. 629-631 and Murray, *Christian Baptism*, pp. 9-33.

25. J. I. Packer, *Concise Theology* (Wheaton, IL: Tyndale House, 1993), p. 212.

26. Douglas Moo, *The Epistle to the Romans*, NICNT (Grand Rapids, MI: Eerdmans, 1996), p. 355. Moo picks up the suggestion of James Dunn that the early church conceived of faith, the gift of the Spirit, and water baptism as components of one unified experience, what Dunn calls "conversion-initiation." This is an important observation, and it is crucial to maintain against the *ex opere operato* view of Roman Catholicism. It is not as if baptism effects regeneration, but it is assumed that faith leads to baptism, and baptism always assumes faith for its validity. Once again, this observation underscores the importance the New Testament places on baptism, without denying the priority of salvation by grace through faith. See James Dunn, *Baptism in the Holy Spirit* (London: SCM Press Ltd., 1970), pp. 139-146; Moo, *Romans,* p. 366; Beasley-Murray, "Baptism," *NIDNTT,* pp. 146-148.

27. See Ronald Y. K. Fung, *The Epistle to the Galatians,* NICNT (Grand Rapids, MI: Eerdmans, 1988), pp. 170-175; Beasley-Murray, *Baptism*, pp. 146-151; Clowney, *The Church*, p. 280.

28. See Fung, *Galatians*, pp. 173-174. Beasley-Murray, "Baptism," *Dictionary of Paul and His Letters*, p. 62, states it this way: "The two statements in Galatians 3:26 and 27 are complementary: verse 26 declares that believers are God's children 'through faith,' and verse 27 associates entry into God's

The Means of Grace: Baptism

family upon union with Christ, and Christ sharing His sonship with the baptized. It is an example of Paul's linking faith and baptism in such a way that the theological understanding of faith that turns to the Lord for salvation, and of baptism wherein faith is declared, is one and the same." On this same point also see Richard N. Longenecker, *Galatians, Word Biblical Commentary*, Vol. 41 (Dallas: Word, 1990), pp. 154-156.

29. Moo, *Romans*, p. 354. Paul often speaks of two realms: that of sin and death, founded by Adam; and that of life and righteousness, founded by Christ. As Moo states, "All people belong in one of these realms or the other; and they are now in the one or the other because God has viewed them as participating in the founding acts of these realms: the sin of Adam and the 'obedience' of Christ. Since, in terms of salvation history, the realm of Christ has been instituted after that of Adam, we can also speak in temporal categories and call the realm of Adam the 'old age' or 'aeon' and that of Christ the 'new age' or 'aeon'" (*Romans*, pp. 351-352). In Romans 6 and elsewhere, Paul often speaks of believers as being "transferred" from the one realm to the other by virtue of being united to the redemptive work of Jesus Christ. Thus a Christian is one who has moved from the reign of sin and death to that of Christ—righteousness and life. As Moo, *Romans*, p. 352, concludes: "By using this imagery of a transfer of realms, or 'dominions,' with its associations of power and rulership, Paul makes clear that the new status enjoyed by the believer (justification) brings with it a new influence and power that both has led and must lead to a new way of life (sanctification)." For a similar view see Herman Ridderbos, *Paul: An Outline of His Theology*, trans. John R. de Witt (Grand Rapids, MI: Eerdmans, 1975), pp. 44-181.

30. Ibid., pp. 353-367. This still raises the question of the "time" of our burial with Christ. Was it at the time of His burial, or did it occur at the time of our conversion? Moo argues that the text does not allow us to focus on the cross or our own experience as the "time" of our being buried with Christ, but rather it is both. Thus, as Moo states: "We are dealing with a category that transcends time. Our dying, being buried, and being resurrected with Christ are experiences that transfer us from the old age to the new. But the transition from old age to new, while applied to individuals at their conversion, has been accomplished through the redemptive work of Christ on Good Friday and Easter. Paul's *syn* refers to a 'redemptive-historical' 'withness' whose locus is both the cross and resurrection and Christ—where the 'shift' in ages took place historically—and the conversion of every believer—when this 'shift' in ages becomes applicable to the individual" (*Romans*, pp. 364-365).

31. Ibid., p. 366.

32. Beasley-Murray, "Baptism," in *Dictionary of Paul and His Letters*, p. 62. Colossians 2:11-12 is another text that is parallel to Romans 6:1-4. On this text see P. T. O'Brien, *Colossians and Philemon, Word Biblical Commentary*, Vol. 44 (Waco, TX: Word, 1982), pp. 114-121.

33. Wayne Grudem, *1 Peter*, TNTC (Grand Rapids, MI: Eerdmans, 1988), pp. 164-165.

34. Beasley-Murray, "Baptism," *NIDNTT*, p. 148.

The Present Evangelical Crisis

35. Beasley-Murray, *Baptism*, p. 279. No doubt, in this context the question is often raised: "To which church does baptism give entry—to the local or universal church, to the visible or the invisible church?" Even though these questions are legitimate to ask, one wonders if this kind of question would have been conceivable to the New Testament. On this see the article by P. T. O'Brien, "The Church as a Heavenly and Eschatological Entity," in *The Church in the Bible and the World*, ed. D. A. Carson (Grand Rapids, MI: Baker, 1987), pp. 88-119; and D. A. Carson, "Evangelicals, Ecumenism and the Church," in *Evangelical Affirmations*, eds. Kenneth S. Kantzer and Carl F. H. Henry (Grand Rapids, MI: Zondervan, 1990), pp. 347-385.

36. Michael Green, *Baptism: Its Purpose, Practice, and Power* (Downers Grove, IL: InterVarsity Press, 1987), p. 51.

37. See Beasley-Murray, *Baptism*, pp. 279-284.

38. Green, *Baptism*, p. 52.

39. Beasley-Murray, *Baptism*, p. 292.

40. For the close connection between baptism and the Holy Spirit, see Dunn, *Baptism in the Holy Spirit*; Beasley-Murray, "Baptism," in *Dictionary of Paul and His Letters*, pp. 63-64. Once again the connection between baptism and the Holy Spirit is bound up with conversion. As Beasley-Murray states, "Conversion is not only the result of human decision, but it is enabled by the Spirit. He is not only the fruit of conversion-baptism; he is the real baptizer, the agent who makes baptism what it was meant to be: entry upon life in Christ" (pp. 63-64).

41. Beasley-Murray, *Baptism*, pp. 295-296.

42. For more on these specific arguments, consult the works found in footnote 1. In addition, other helpful resources are: J. I. Packer, *Concise Theology*, pp. 212-216; R. C. Sproul, *Essential Truths of the Christian Faith* (Wheaton, IL: Tyndale House, 1992), pp. 225-229; Geoffrey W. Bromiley, "Baptism," in *The International Standard Bible Encyclopedia*, ed. G. W. Bromiley, Vol. 1 (Grand Rapids, MI: Eerdmans, 1979), pp. 410-415.

43. There is some dispute over this within the paedobaptist community, especially over the notion of whether infant baptism leads to a kind of presumptive regeneration and the whole nature of the conditional covenant. For an interesting and important discussion of these issues, see David J. Engelsma's seven articles entitled, "A Candid Confession of the Character of a Conditional Covenant," in *The Standard Bearer* (January 1—April 1, 1997).

44. This is the position that the author takes. Consult the resources in footnote 1 for more specific data regarding the specific arguments presented here for the believer's baptism view.

45. See D. A. Carson, "Evangelicals, Ecumenism, and the Church," pp. 347-385 for the exegetical underpinnings of this argument. Much of the debate surrounds the nature of the New Covenant and its relationship to the Old. For a very helpful article that explores some of these same issues and turns the burden of proof onto the shoulders of the paedobaptist, see R. Fowler

The Means of Grace: Baptism

White, "The Last Adam and His Seed: An Exercise in Theological Preemption," *Trinity Journal* 6:1 (1985), pp. 60-73.

46. On this see Grudem, *Systematic Theology*, pp. 976-978; Beasley-Murray, *Baptism*, pp. 312-320.

47. For a helpful discussion of the means of grace, see Grudem, *Systematic Theology*, pp. 950-965.

A WORD OF THANKS

I would like to thank Kirk Wellum, Greg Strand, and Jeff Nesbitt for their healthy discussion on this issue of baptism. Their conversations and written work have been a great help to me, even though they are not responsible for any errors that have been made in this essay.

8

CHURCH DISCIPLINE: THE MISSING MARK

R. Albert Mohler, Jr.

What is pure is corrupted much more quickly than what is corrupt is purified.

—JOHN CASSIAN
(A.D. 360-435)

The decline of church discipline is perhaps the most visible failure of the contemporary church. No longer concerned with maintaining purity of confession or lifestyle, the contemporary church sees itself as a voluntary association of autonomous members, with minimal moral accountability to God, much less to each other.

The absence of church discipline is no longer remarkable—it is generally not even noticed. Regulative and restorative church discipline is, to many church members, no longer a meaningful category, or even a memory. The present generation of both ministers and church members is virtually without experience of biblical church discipline.

As a matter of fact, most Christians introduced to the biblical teaching concerning church discipline confront the issue of church discipline as an idea they have never before encountered. At first hearing, the issue seems as antiquarian and foreign as the Spanish Inquisition and the Salem witch trials. Their only acquaintance with the disciplinary ministry of the church is often a literary invention such as *The Scarlet Letter*.

And yet, without a recovery of functional church discipline—firmly established upon the principles revealed in the Bible—the church will continue its slide into moral dissolution and relativism. Evangelicals have long recognized discipline as the "third mark" of the authentic church.[1] Authentic biblical discipline is not an elective, but a necessary and integral mark of authentic Christianity.

How did this happen? How could the church so quickly and pervasively abandon one of its most essential functions and responsibilities? The answer is found in developments both internal and external to the church.

Put simply, the abandonment of church discipline is linked to American Christianity's creeping accommodation to American culture. As the twentieth century began, this accommodation became increasingly evident as the church acquiesced to a culture of moral individualism.

Though the nineteenth century was not a golden era for American evangelicals, the century did see the consolidation of evangelical theology and church patterns. Manuals of church discipline and congregational records indicate that discipline was regularly applied. Protestant congregations exercised discipline as a necessary and natural ministry to the members of the church, and as a means of protecting the doctrinal and moral integrity of the congregation.

As ardent congregationalists, the Baptists left a particularly instructive record of nineteenth-century discipline. Historian Gregory A. Wills aptly commented, "To an antebellum Baptist, a church without discipline would hardly have counted as a church."[2] Churches held regular "Days of Discipline" when the congregation would gather to heal breaches of fellowship, admonish wayward members, rebuke the obstinate, and, if necessary, excommunicate those who resisted discipline. In so doing, congregations understood themselves to be following a biblical pattern laid down by Christ and the apostles for the protection and correction of disciples.

No sphere of life was considered outside the congregation's accountability. Members were to conduct their lives and witness in harmony with the Bible and with established moral principles. Depending on the denominational polity, discipline was codified in church covenants, books of discipline, congregational manuals, and confessions of faith. Discipline covered both doctrine and conduct. Members were disciplined for behavior that violated biblical principles or congregational covenants, but also for violations of doctrine and belief. Members were considered to be under the authority of the congregation and accountable to each other.

The Present Evangelical Crisis

By the turn of the century, however, church discipline was already on the decline. In the wake of the Enlightenment, criticism of the Bible and of the doctrines of evangelical orthodoxy was widespread. Even the most conservative denominations began to show evidence of decreased attention to theological orthodoxy. At the same time, the larger culture moved toward the adoption of autonomous moral individualism. The result of these internal and external developments was the abandonment of church discipline as ever larger portions of the church member's life were considered off-limits to the congregation.

This great shift in church life followed the tremendous cultural transformations of the early twentieth century—an era of "progressive" thought and moral liberalization. By the 1960s, only a minority of churches even pretended to practice regulative church discipline. Significantly, confessional accountability and moral discipline were generally abandoned together.

The theological category of sin has been replaced, in many circles, with the psychological concept of therapy. As Philip Reiff has argued, the "Triumph of the Therapeutic" is now a fixture of modern American culture.[3] Church members may make poor choices, fail to live up to the expectations of an oppressive culture, or be inadequately self-actualized—but they no longer sin.

Individuals now claim an enormous zone of personal privacy and moral autonomy. The congregation—redefined as a mere voluntary association—has no right to intrude into this space. Many congregations have forfeited any responsibility to confront even the most public sins of their members. Consumed with pragmatic methods of church growth and congregational engineering, most churches leave moral matters to the domain of the individual conscience.

As Thomas Oden notes, the confession of sin is now passé and hopelessly outdated to many minds.

> Naturalistic reductionism has invited us to reduce alleged individual sins to social influences for which individuals are not responsible. Narcissistic hedonism has demeaned any talk of sin or confession as ungratifying and dysfunctional. Autonomous individualism has divorced sin from a caring community. Absolute relativism has regarded moral values as so ambiguous

Church Discipline: The Missing Mark

that there is no measuring rod against which to assess anything as sin. Thus modernity, which is characterized by the confluence of these four ideological streams, has presumed to do away with confession, and has in fact made confession an embarrassment to the accommodating church of modernity.[4]

The very notion of shame has been discarded by a generation for which shame is an unnecessary and repressive hindrance to personal fulfillment. Even secular observers have noted the shamelessness of modern culture. As James Twitchell comments:

We have in the last generation tried to push shame aside. The human-potential and recovered-memory movements in psychology; the moral relativism of audience-driven Christianity; the penalty-free, all-ideas-are-equally-good transformation in higher education; the rise of no-fault behavior before the law; the often outrageous distortions in the telling of history so that certain groups can feel better about themselves; and the "I'm shame-free, but you should be ashamed of yourself" tone of political discourse are just some of the instances wherein this can be seen.[5]

Twitchell sees the Christian church aiding and abetting this moral transformation and abandonment of shame—which is, after all, a natural product of sinful behavior. "Looking at the Christian Church today, you can only see a dim pentimento of what was once painted in the boldest of colors. Christianity has simply lost *it*. It no longer articulates the ideal. Sex is on the loose. Shame days are over. The Devil has absconded with sin."[6] As Twitchell laments, "Go and sin no more" has been replaced with "Judge not lest you be judged."

Demonstration of this moral abandonment is seen in mainline Protestantism's surrender to an ethic of sexual "liberation." Liberal Protestantism has lost any moral credibility in the sexual sphere. Homosexuality is not condemned, even though it is clearly condemned in the Bible. To the contrary, homosexuals get a special caucus at the denominational assembly and their own publications and special rights.

Evangelicals, though still claiming adherence to biblical standards of morality, have overwhelmingly capitulated to the divorce culture. Where are the evangelical congregations that hold married couples accountable for maintaining their marriage vows? To a great extent, evangelicals are just slightly behind liberal Protestantism in accommodating to the divorce culture and accepting what amounts to "serial monogamy"—faithfulness to one marital partner *at a time*. This, too, has been noted by secular observers. David Blankenhorn of the Institute for American Values remarked that "over the past three decades, many religious leaders . . . have largely abandoned marriage as a vital area of religious attention, essentially handing the entire matter over to opinion leaders and divorce lawyers in the secular society. Some members of the clergy seem to have lost interest in defending and strengthening marriage. Others report that they worry about offending members of their congregations who are divorced or unmarried."[7]

Tied to this worry about offending church members is the rise of the "rights culture," which understands society only in terms of individual rights rather than moral responsibility. Mary Ann Glendon of the Harvard Law School documents the substitution of "rights talk" for moral discourse.[8] Unable or unwilling to deal with moral categories, modern men and women resort to the only moral language they know and understand—the unembarrassed claim to "rights" that society has no authority to limit or deny. This "rights talk" is not limited to secular society, however. Church members are so committed to their own version of "rights talk" that some congregations accept almost any behavior, belief, or "lifestyle" as acceptable, or at least off-limits to congregational sanction.

The result of this is the loss of the biblical pattern for the church—and the impending collapse of authentic Christianity in this generation. As Carl Laney laments, "The church today is suffering from an infection which has been allowed to fester. . . . As an infection weakens the body by destroying its defense mechanisms, so the church has been weakened by this ugly sore. The church has lost its power and effectiveness in serving as a vehicle for social, moral, and spiritual change. This illness is due, at least in part, to a neglect of church discipline."[9]

HOLINESS AND THE PEOPLE OF GOD

Throughout the Bible, the people of God are characterized by a distinctive purity. This moral purity is not their own achievement, but the work of God within their midst. As the Lord said to the children of Israel, "I am the Lord your God. Consecrate yourselves and be holy, because I am holy" (Lev. 11:44a).[10] Given that they have been chosen by a holy God as a people carrying His own name, God's chosen people are to reflect His holiness by their way of living, worship, and beliefs.

The holiness code is central to the understanding of the Old Testament. As God's chosen nation, Israel must live by God's Word and law, which will set the children of Israel visibly apart from their pagan neighbors. As the Lord said through Moses: "Be sure to keep the commands of the LORD your God and the stipulations and decrees he has given you. Do what is right and good in the LORD's sight, so that it may go well with you and you may go in and take over the good land that the LORD promised on oath to your forefathers" (Deut. 6:17-18).

The nation is reminded that it is now known by God's name and is to reflect His holiness. "For you are a people holy to the LORD your God. The LORD your God has chosen you out of all the peoples on the face of the earth" (Deut. 7:6). God promised His covenant faithfulness to His people but expected them to obey His Word and follow His law. Israel's judicial system was largely designed to protect the purity of the nation.

In the New Testament, the church is likewise described as the people of God who are visible to the world by their purity of life and integrity of testimony. As Peter instructed the church: "But you are a chosen people, a royal priesthood, a holy nation, a people belonging to God, that you may declare the praises of him who called you out of darkness into his wonderful light. Once you were not a people, but now you are the people of God; once you had not received mercy, but now you have received mercy" (1 Pet. 2:9-10).

Peter continued, "Dear friends, I urge you, as aliens and strangers in the world, to abstain from sinful desires, which war against your soul. Live such good lives among the pagans that, though they accuse you of doing wrong, they may see your good deeds and glorify God on the day he visits us" (1 Pet. 2:11-12).

As the new people of God, the church is to see itself as an alien community in the midst of spiritual darkness—strangers to the world who must abstain from the lusts and enticements of the world. The church is to be conspicuous in its purity and holiness and steadfast in its confession of the faith once for all delivered to the saints. Rather than capitulating to the moral (or immoral) environment, Christians are to be conspicuous by their good behavior. As Peter summarized, "Just as he who called you is holy, so be holy in all you do" (1 Pet. 1:15).

The apostle Paul clearly linked the holiness expected of believers to the completed work of Christ in redemption: "Once you were alienated from God and were enemies in your minds because of your evil behavior. But now he has reconciled you by Christ's physical body through death to present you holy in his sight, without blemish and free from accusation" (Col. 1:21-22). Clearly, this holiness made complete in the believer is the work of God; holiness is the evidence of His redemptive work. To the Corinthian congregation Paul urged, "Let us purify ourselves from everything that contaminates body and spirit, perfecting holiness out of reverence for God" (2 Cor. 7:1).

The identity of the church as the people of God is to be evident in its pure confession of Christ, its bold testimony to the Gospel, and its moral holiness before the watching world. Nothing less will mark the church as the true vessel of the Gospel.

DISCIPLINE IN THE BODY

The first dimension of discipline in the church is that discipline exercised directly by God as He deals with believers. As the book of Hebrews warns, "You have forgotten that word of encouragement that addresses you as sons: 'My son, do not make light of the Lord's discipline, and do not lose heart when he rebukes you, because the Lord disciplines those he loves, and he punishes everyone he accepts as a son.' Endure hardship as discipline; God is treating you as sons. For what son is not disciplined by his father?" (Heb. 12:5-7). As the passage continues, the author warns that those who are without discipline "are illegitimate children and not true sons" (v. 8). The purpose of discipline, however, is righteousness. "No discipline seems pleasant at the time, but painful. Later on, however, it produces a harvest of righteousness and peace for those who have been trained by it" (v. 11).

This discipline is often evident in suffering—both individual and congregational. Persecution by the world has a purifying effect on the church. This persecution is not to be sought, but if the church is "tested by fire," it must prove itself pure and genuine and receive this suffering as the

Church Discipline: The Missing Mark

Lord's discipline, even as children receive the discipline of a father. The fact that this analogy is so foreign to many modern Christians points out the fact that discipline has disappeared in many families, as well as in the church. Children are treated as moral sovereigns in many households, and the social breakdown of the family has diminished its moral credibility. The loving discipline portrayed in this passage is as foreign to many families as it is to most congregations.

God's loving discipline of His people is His sovereign right and is completely in keeping with His moral character—His own holiness. His fatherly discipline also establishes the authority and pattern for discipline in the church. Correction is for the greater purpose of restoration and the even higher purpose of reflecting the holiness of God.

The second dimension of discipline in the church is that disciplinary responsibility addressed to the church itself. Like God's fatherly discipline of those He loves, the church is to exercise discipline as an integral part of its moral and theological responsibility. That the church can fall into moral disrepute is evident in the New Testament itself.

The apostle Paul confronted a case of gross moral failure in the Corinthian congregation that included "immorality of . . . a kind that does not occur even among pagans" (1 Cor. 5:1). In this case, apparent incest was known to the congregation, and yet it had taken no action.

"And you are proud! Shouldn't you rather have been filled with grief and have put out of your fellowship the man who did this?" Paul accused the Corinthian congregation (v. 2). He instructed them to act quickly and boldly to remove this stain from their fellowship. He also warned them, "Your boasting is not good. Don't you know that a little yeast works through the whole batch of dough? Get rid of the old yeast that you may be a new batch without yeast—as you really are" (vv. 6-7a).

Paul was outraged that the Corinthian Christians would tolerate this horrible sin. Incest, though not literally unknown in the pagan world, was universally condemned and not tolerated. In this respect the Corinthian church had fallen beneath the moral standards of the pagan world to whom they were to witness. Paul was also exasperated with a congregation he had already warned. Mentioning an earlier letter unavailable to us, Paul scolds the Corinthians:

The Present Evangelical Crisis

I have written you in my letter not to associate with sexually immoral people—not at all meaning the people of this world who are immoral, or the greedy and swindlers, or idolaters. In that case you would have to leave this world. But now I am writing you that you must not associate with anyone who calls himself a brother but is sexually immoral or greedy, an idolater or a slanderer, a drunkard or a swindler. With such a man do not even eat. What business is it of mine to judge those outside the church? Are you not to judge those inside? God will judge those outside. "Expel the wicked man from among you."

—VV. 9-13

The moral outrage of a wounded apostle is evident in these pointed verses, which call the Corinthian church to action and the exercise of discipline. They have now fallen into corporate sin by tolerating the presence of such a bold and arrogant sinner in their midst. Their moral testimony is clouded, and their fellowship is impure. Their arrogance has blinded them to the offense they have committed before the Lord. The open sin in their midst is like a cancer that, left unchecked, will spread throughout the entire body.

In the second letter to the Thessalonians, Paul offers similar instruction, combining concern for moral purity and doctrinal orthodoxy: "In the name of the Lord Jesus Christ, we command you, brothers, to keep away from every brother who is idle and does not live according to the teaching you received from us" (2 Thess. 3:6). Paul instructs the Thessalonians to follow his own example because "We were not idle when we were with you" (2 Thess. 3:7).

THE PATTERN OF PROPER DISCIPLINE

How should the Corinthians have responded to this public sin? Paul speaks in 1 Corinthians of delivering this sinner unto Satan and removing him from fellowship. How is this to be done? To the Galatians Paul wrote that "if someone is caught in a sin, you who are spiritual should restore him gently. But watch yourself, or you also may be tempted" (Gal. 6:1). This teaching is clear, indicating that spiritual leaders of the church are to confront a sinning member with a spirit of humility and gentleness, and with the goal of restoration. But what are the precise steps to be taken?

The Lord Himself provided these instructions as He taught His disciples: "If your brother sins against you, go and show him his fault, just between the two of you. If he listens to you, you have won your brother over. But if he will not listen, take one or two others along, so that 'every matter may be established by the testimony of two or three witnesses.' If he refuses to listen to them, tell it to the church; and if he refuses to listen even to the church, treat him as you would a pagan or a tax collector" (Matt. 18:15-17).

The Lord instructed His disciples that they should first confront a sinning brother in private. "Show him his fault," instructed the Lord. If the brother acknowledges the sin and repents, the brother has been won. The fact that the first step is a private confrontation is very important. This limits the injury caused by the sin and avoids a public spectacle, which would tarnish the witness of the church to the Gospel.

In the event the private confrontation does not lead to repentance, restoration, and reconciliation, the next step is to take witnesses. Jesus cited the Deuteronomic law which required multiple witnesses of a crime for conviction. Yet His purpose here seems larger than the mere establishment of the facts of the case. Jesus seems to intend for the witnesses to be an important presence in the *event* of the confrontation, thus adding corroborating testimony concerning the confrontation of a sinning brother. The brother cannot claim that he was not confronted with his sin in a brotherly context.

If the brother does not listen even in the presence of one or two witnesses, this becomes a matter for the congregation. "Tell it to the church," instructed Jesus, and the church is to judge the matter before the Lord and render a judgment that is binding upon the sinner. This step is extremely serious, and the congregation now bears a corporate responsibility. The church must render its judgment based upon the principles of God's Word and the facts of the case. Again, the goal is the restoration of a sinning brother or sister—not a public spectacle.

Sadly, this congregational confrontation may not avail. If it does not, the only recourse is separation from the sinning brother. "Treat him as you would a pagan or a tax collector," instructed the Lord, indicating that the separation is to be real and public. The congregation is not to con-

The Present Evangelical Crisis

sider the former brother as a part of the church. This drastic and extreme act is to follow when a brother or sister will not submit to the discipline of the church. We should note that the church should still bear witness to this man, but not as brother to brother, until and unless repentance and restoration are evident.

THE POWER OF THE KEYS

What is the church's authority in church discipline? Jesus addressed this issue directly, even as He declared the establishment of the church after Peter's great confession: "I will give you the keys of the kingdom of heaven; whatever you bind on earth will be bound in heaven, and whatever you loose on earth will be loosed in heaven" (Matt. 16:19). This "power of the keys" is one of the critical controversies between evangelicals and the Church of Rome. Roman Catholics believe that the pope, as Peter's successor, holds the keys, and thus the power of binding and loosing. Protestants, however, believe that the Lord granted the keys to the church. This interpretation is supported by the Lord's repetition of the matter in Matthew 18:18, "I tell you the truth, whatever you bind on earth will be bound in heaven, and whatever you loose on earth will be loosed in heaven." Here the context reveals that the power of binding and loosing is held by the church.[11]

The terms *binding* and *loosing* were familiar terms used by rabbis' in the first century to refer to the power of judging matters on the basis of the Bible. The Jewish authorities would determine how (or whether) the Scriptures applied in a specific situation and would render judgment by either binding, which meant to restrict, or loosing, which meant to liberate. The church still bears this responsibility and wields this power. John Calvin, the great Genevan Reformer, believed that the power of binding should be understood as excommunication, and loosing as reception into membership: "But the church binds him whom it excommunicates—not that it casts him into everlasting ruin and despair, but because it condemns his life and morals, and already warns him of his condemnation unless he should repent. It looses him when it receives into communion, for it makes him a sharer of the unity which is in Christ Jesus."[12]

Calvin's interpretation is fully in agreement at this point with Martin

Church Discipline: The Missing Mark

Luther, whose essay on "The Keys" (1530) is a massive refutation of papal claims and Roman Catholic tradition. Luther saw the keys as one of Christ's great gifts to the church. "Both of these keys are extremely necessary in Christendom, so that we can never thank God enough for them."[13] As a pastor and theologian, Luther saw the great need for the church to bear the keys, and he understood this ministry to be gracious in the recovery of sinning saints. As Luther reflected:

> For the dear Man, the faithful Bishop of our souls, Jesus Christ, is well aware that His beloved Christians are frail, that the devil, the flesh, and the world would tempt them unceasingly and in many ways, and that at times they would fall into sin. Therefore, He has given us this remedy, the key which binds, so that we might not remain too confident in our sins, arrogant, barbarous, and without God, and the key which looses, that we should not despair in our sins.[14]

What about a church leader who sins? Paul instructed Timothy that a church leader—an elder—is to be considered "worthy of double honor" when he rules well (1 Tim. 5:17). When an elder sins, however, that is a matter of great consequence. First, no accusation is to be received on the basis of only one uncorroborated witness. If a charge is substantiated by two or three witnesses, however, he is "to be rebuked publicly, so that the others may take warning" (1 Tim. 5:20). Clearly, leadership carries a higher burden, and the sins of an elder cause an even greater injury to the church. The public rebuke is necessary, for the elder sins against the entire congregation. As James warned, "Not many of you should presume to be teachers, my brothers, because you know that we who teach will be judged more strictly" (Jas. 3:1).

The scandals of moral failure on the part of church leaders have caused tremendous injury to the cause of Christ. The stricter judgment should be a vivid warning to those who would violate the Word of God and lead others into sin by example. The failure of the contemporary church to apply consistent biblical church discipline has left most of these scandals unresolved on biblical grounds—and thus a continuing stain on the church.

The Bible reveals three main areas of danger requiring discipline.

The Present Evangelical Crisis

These are *fidelity of doctrine, purity of life*, and *unity of fellowship*. Each is of critical and vital importance to the health and integrity of the church.

FIDELITY OF DOCTRINE

The theological confusion and compromise that mark the modern church are directly traceable to the church's failure to separate itself from doctrinal error and heretics who teach it. On this matter the Bible is clear: "Anyone who runs ahead and does not continue in the teaching of Christ does not have God; whoever continues in the teaching has both the Father and the Son. If anyone comes to you and does not bring this teaching, do not take him into your house or welcome him. Anyone who welcomes him shares in his wicked work" (2 John 9-11). The apostle Paul instructed the Galatians that "if we or an angel from heaven should preach a gospel other than the one we preached to you, let him be eternally condemned! As we have already said, so now I say again: If anybody is preaching to you a gospel other than what you accepted, let him be eternally condemned!" (Gal. 1:8-9).

The letters of 2 Peter and Jude explicitly warn of the dangers presented to the church in the form of false prophets and heretics. Jude alerts the church that "certain men whose condemnation was written about long ago have secretly slipped in among you. They are godless men, who change the grace of our God into a license for immorality and deny Jesus Christ our only Sovereign and Lord" (v. 4). Similarly, Peter warns, "There will be false teachers among you. They will secretly introduce destructive heresies, even denying the sovereign Lord who bought them— bringing swift destruction on themselves" (2 Pet. 2:1).

The church must separate itself from these heresies—and from the heretics! The permissive posture of the church in this century has allowed the most heinous heresies to grow unchecked—and heretics to be celebrated. Francis Schaeffer was among the most eloquent modern prophets who decried this doctrinal cowardice. Schaeffer emphatically denied that a church could be a true Christian fellowship and allow false doctrine. As he stated, "One cannot explain the explosive dynamite, the *dunamis*, of the early church apart from the fact that they practiced two things simultaneously: orthodoxy of doctrine and orthodoxy of community in the midst of the visible church, a community which the world can see. By the grace of God, therefore, the church must be known simultaneously for its purity of doctrine and the reality of its community."[15]

PURITY OF LIFE

The visible community of the true church is also to be evident in its moral purity. Christians are to live in obedience to the Word of God and to be exemplary in their conduct and untarnished in their testimony. A lack of attention to moral purity is a sure sign of congregational rebellion before the Lord.

Writing to the Corinthians, Paul chastised them severely: "Do you not know that the wicked will not inherit the kingdom of God? Do not be deceived: Neither the sexually immoral nor idolaters nor adulterers nor male prostitutes nor homosexual offenders nor thieves nor the greedy nor drunkards nor slanderers nor swindlers will inherit the kingdom of God. And that is what some of you were. But you were washed, you were sanctified, you were justified in the name of the Lord Jesus Christ and by the Spirit of our God" (1 Cor. 6:9-11).

When Christians sin, their sin is to be confronted by the church in accordance with the pattern revealed in Scripture. The goal is the restoration of a sister or a brother, not the creation of a public spectacle. The greatest moral danger to the church is the toleration of sin, public or private. Conversely, one of the greatest blessings to the church is the gift of biblical church discipline—the ministry of the keys.

UNITY OF FELLOWSHIP

The integrity of the church is also dependent upon the true unity of its fellowship. Indeed, one of the most repeated warnings found in the New Testament is the admonition against toleration of schismatics. The unity of the church is one of its most visible distinctives—and most precious gifts.

The warnings about this are severe: "I urge you, brothers, to watch out for those who cause divisions and put obstacles in your way that are contrary to the teaching you have learned. Keep away from them. For such people are not serving our Lord Christ, but their own appetites. By smooth talk and flattery they deceive the minds of naive people" (Rom. 16:17-18). Writing to Titus, Paul instructed that the church should "Warn a divisive person once, and then warn him a second time. After that, have nothing to do with him. You may be sure that such a man is warped and sinful; he is self-condemned" (Titus 3:10-11).

A breach in the unity of the church is a scandal in the body of Christ. The church is consistently exhorted to practice and preserve a true unity in true doctrine and biblical piety. This unity is not the false unity of a lowest-common-denominator Christianity, the "Gospel Lite" preached and taught in so many modern churches, but rather is found in the healthy and growing maturity of the congregation as it increases in grace and in its knowledge of the Word of God.

The ongoing function of church discipline is to be a part of individual self-examination and congregational reflection. The importance of maintaining integrity in personal relationships was made clear by our Lord in the Sermon on the Mount as He instructed the disciples that anger against a brother is a deadly sin. Reconciliation is a mandate, not a hypothetical goal. "Therefore, if you are offering your gift at the altar and there remember that your brother has something against you, leave your gift there in front of the altar. First go and be reconciled to your brother; then come and offer your gift" (Matt. 5:23-24).

Similarly, Paul warned against participating in the Lord's Supper amidst divisions. The Supper itself is a memorial of the broken body and shed blood of the Savior and must not be desecrated by the presence of divisions or controversies within the congregation, or by unconfessed sin on the part of individual believers. "For whenever you eat this bread and drink this cup, you proclaim the Lord's death until he comes. Therefore, whoever eats the bread or drinks the cup of the Lord in an unworthy manner will be guilty of sinning against the body and blood of the Lord. A man ought to examine himself before he eats of the bread and drinks of the cup. For anyone who eats and drinks without recognizing the body of the Lord eats and drinks judgment on himself" (1 Cor. 11:26-29).

The "discipline of the Table" is thus one of the most important disciplinary functions of the congregation. The Lord's Supper is not to be served indiscriminately, but only to those baptized believers who are under the discipline of the church and in good standing with their congregation.

Church Discipline: The Missing Mark

THE RECOVERY OF THE THIRD MARK

The mandate of the church is to maintain true gospel doctrine and order. A church lacking these essential qualities is, biblically defined, not a true church. That is a hard thing to say, for it clearly indicts thousands of American congregations who long ago abandoned this essential mark and have accommodated themselves to the spirit of the age. Fearing lawsuits and lacking courage, these churches allow sin to go unconfronted, and heresy to grow unchecked. Inevitably, the false unity they seek to preserve gives way to the factions that inevitably follow the gradual abandonment of biblical Christianity. They do not taste the true unity of a church grounded on the truth and exercising the ministry of the keys.

John Leadley Dagg, the author of a well-known and influential church manual of the nineteenth century, noted: "It has been remarked, that when discipline leaves a church, Christ goes with it."[16] If so, and I fear it is so, Christ has abandoned many churches who are blissfully unaware of His departure.

At the end of the twentieth century, the great task of the church is to prove itself to be the genuine church revealed in the New Testament— proving its authenticity by a demonstration of pure faith and authentic community. We must regain the New Testament concern for fidelity of doctrine, purity of life, and unity of fellowship. We must recover the missing mark.

NOTES

1. The identification of proper discipline as the third mark of the true church goes back at least to the Belgic Confession [1561]: "The marks by which the true Church is known are these: If the pure doctrine of the gospel is preached therein; if she maintains the pure administration of the sacraments as instituted by Christ; if church discipline is exercised in punishing of sin; in short, if all things are managed according to the pure Word of God, all things contrary thereto rejected, and Jesus Christ acknowledged as the only Head of the Church. Hereby the true Church may certainly be known, from which no man has a right to separate himself." "The Belgic Confession," in *The Creeds of Christendom*, ed. Philip Schaff, rev. David S. Schaff, Vol. 3 (New York: Harper and Row, 1931), pp. 419-420. Similarly, the *Abstract of Principles* of The Southern Baptist Theological Seminary (1858) identifies the three essential marks as true order, discipline, and worship.

2. Gregory A. Wills, *Democratic Religion: Freedom, Authority, and Church*

The Present Evangelical Crisis

Discipline in the Baptist South 1785-1900 (New York: Oxford University Press, 1997), p. 12.

3. Philip Reiff, *The Triumph of the Therapeutic: Uses of Faith After Freud* (Chicago: University of Chicago Press, 1966).

4. Thomas C. Oden, *Corrective Love: The Power of Communion Discipline* (St. Louis: Concordia, 1995), p. 56.

5. James B. Twitchell, *For Shame: The Loss of Common Decency in American Culture* (New York: St. Martin's Press, 1997), p. 35.

6. Ibid., p. 149.

7. David Blankenhorn, *Fatherless America: Confronting Our Most Urgent Social Problem* (New York: Basic Books, 1995), p. 231.

8. Mary Ann Glendon, *Rights Talk: The Impoverishment of Political Discourse* (New York: Free Press, 1991).

9. J. Carl Laney, *A Guide to Church Discipline* (Minneapolis: Bethany House, 1985), p. 12.

10. This verse is quoted in 1 Peter 1:16 and is addressed to the church.

11. *The New American Standard Bible*, revised edition, is correct in translating the Greek verb in the perfect tense. Any other translation of the verb tense confuses the meaning and can lead to a distorted understanding of Jesus' teaching. He is not stating that the church has the power to determine what shall later be decided in heaven. The verb tense indicates that as the church functions on the authority of Scripture, what it determines shall have been already determined in heaven. For a complete consideration of this issue, see Julius Robert Mantey, "Distorted Translations in John 20:23; Matthew 16:18-19 and 18:18," *Review and Expositor* 78 (1981), pp. 409-416.

12. John Calvin, *Institutes of the Christian Religion*, 2 vols., ed. John T. McNeill, trans. Ford Lewis Battles, *Library of Christian Classics*, Vol. 20 (Philadelphia: Westminster, 1960) , p. 1214.

13. Martin Luther, "The Keys," in *Luther's Works* (American Edition), ed. Conrad Bergendoff, gen. ed. Helmut T. Lehmann, Vol. 40 (Philadelphia: Fortress Press, 1958), p. 373.

14. Ibid.

15. Francis A. Schaeffer, "The Church Before the Watching World," in *The Church at the End of the Twentieth Century* (Wheaton, IL: Crossway Books, 1970), p. 144.

16. J. L. Dagg, *A Treatise on Church Order* (Charleston, SC: The Southern Baptist Publication Society, 1858), p. 274.

9

PREACHING:
THE DECISIVE FUNCTION

Arturo G. Azurdia III

In May 1991 an article appeared in *The Wall Street Journal* entitled, "Mighty Fortresses: Megachurches Strive to Be All Things to All Parishioners." The article documents some of the novel methods currently employed by local churches to boost attendance and attract the unsaved in their communities. One example cited was that of a staged wrestling match sponsored by a local church and featuring church employees. The purpose for this event was to initiate greater participation for Sunday evening services. The writer of the article notes some of the necessary preparations involved: "To train for the event, 10 game employees got lessons from Tugboat Taylor, a former professional wrestler, in pulling hair, kicking shins and tossing bodies around without doing real harm."[1]

An earlier but similar article reported that a half-million dollar special-effects system, designed to produce smoke, fire, sparks, and laser lights, had recently been installed in the auditorium of a large southwestern church. Various staff members were sent to Bally's Casino in Las Vegas to acquire the necessary skills to perform live special effects. Sometime later, the pastor of this church concluded a sermon by ascending to "heaven" via invisible wires that drew him up out of sight while the choir and orchestra added musical accompaniment to the smoke, fire, and light show.[2] About this pastor the article boasts:

> He packs his church with special effects . . . cranking up a chain saw and toppling a tree to make a point . . . the biggest Fourth of

Preaching: The Decisive Function

July fireworks display in town and a Christmas service with a rented elephant, kangaroo and zebra. The Christmas show features 100 clowns with gifts for the congregation's children.[3]

Surprisingly, these are not obscure citations from eccentric congregations. They are common occurrences in churches that are regarded as evangelically mainstream. Similar examples could be drawn from many of the most widely recognized churches across the United States. The novelty of these "ministry methodologies," however, along with their increasing receptivity and growing prominence, necessitate some discriminating consideration on the part of clear-thinking evangelicals. How are these methods of gospel ministry to be regarded? Do the Scriptures affirm that "anything goes" in the name of reaching people for Jesus Christ? Is it true, as is often stipulated, that ministry methods are of no significance to God as long as the message of the Gospel is clearly communicated? Is it accurate to conclude that style by itself is neither good nor bad, but always neutral?

From the perspective of the apostle Paul in 1 Corinthians 1—2, style is not neutral. When the Gospel is the message, the method of its presentation is not irrelevant. Paul's concern was to make evident that the cross of Jesus Christ not only establishes the *substance* of our preaching, it determines the *style* in which we communicate it. In other words, message and method must be harmonious. When they are not, the integrity of the message suffers.

Before proceeding any further, it is essential that we alert ourselves to the possibility of losing focus on the issue of concern. Our reservation concerning many of these novel ministry methodologies has nothing to do with preferring a traditional style of ministry over a more contemporary emphasis. Contemporaneity is not the issue. Effectual Christianity will always prove contemporary to the unique mission field given to it by Jesus Christ. Rather, the issue in view is *the radical inconsistency that exists between the message of the bloody cross and the slick, sophisticated, Spielberg-like methods of communicating it.* Paul's burden is to assert that true, apostolic ministry is characterized by an intimate correspondence of message and method, that thoroughgoing consistency is to exist between the word of the cross and its articulation.

The Present Evangelical Crisis

RECOVERING THE PRIORITY

Has God ordained a method for making known the message of the cross? Or is methodology something that can be shaped by the unique cultural mores of each generation? Paul appears resoundingly consistent in the context of 1 Corinthians 1—2:

> *For Christ did not send me to baptize, but to* preach *the gospel.*
>
> —1:17

> *God was pleased through the foolishness of what was* preached *to save those who believe.*
>
> —1:21

> *When I came to you . . . I* proclaimed *to you the testimony about God.*
>
> —2:1

> *My message and my* preaching *were not with wise and persuasive words . . .*
>
> —2:4

A brief examination of a Bible concordance reveals that the English words *preach, preaching, proclaim,* and *proclaiming* are used over 100 times in the New Testament Scriptures. Greidanus states that the New Testament employs as many as thirty-three different verbs to describe what we usually cover with the single word *preaching.*[4]

Despite the frequency with which the Scriptures refer to preaching, many contemporary evangelicals seem astonished by this emphasis. Some even appear to take tacit offense at this assertion of biblical truth.[5] Unfortunately, in the much-needed recovery of an every-member ministry, evangelicals have correspondingly misplaced the priority recovered by their forebears in the Reformation—namely, the centrality of preaching.[6] Some in pastoral ministry have failed to recognize the emphasis of biblical revelation that steadily establishes preaching as the primary method of communicating the message of the Gospel.

As a corrective, one should give consideration to the terms by which Jesus defined His ministry: "The Spirit of the Lord is on me, because he has anointed me to *preach* good news to the poor. He has sent me to *proclaim* freedom for the prisoners and recovery of sight for the blind, to release the oppressed, to *proclaim* the year of the Lord's favor" (Luke 4:18-19, emphasis added).

It is not surprising, then, that following His baptism, as Matthew records, "Jesus began to *preach*" (Matt. 4:17, emphasis added). The Gospel of Mark sheds further light on this priority of Jesus: "Let us go somewhere else—to the nearby villages—so I can *preach* there also. That is why I have come" (Mark 1:38, emphasis added). Two chapters later Mark records Jesus' rationale for choosing His disciples: "He appointed twelve—designating them apostles—that they might be with him and that he might send them out to *preach*" (Mark 3:14, emphasis added). Moreover, this design was to continue following His resurrection: "Go into all the world and *preach* the good news to all creation" (Mark 16:15, emphasis added). This commission was thoroughly embraced by the disciples, and especially Peter, as is made evident in the book of Acts. About this divinely appointed methodology Peter says to Cornelius, "He commanded us to *preach* to the people" (Acts 10:42, emphasis added).

Paul's conviction about preaching was equally resolute. He explained to the Jews in Antioch: "And we *preach* to you the good news of the promise made to the fathers" (Acts 13:32, NASB, emphasis added). In his letter to the Romans Paul revealed something of his desire for ministry with the Christians in Rome: "That is why I am so eager to *preach* the gospel also to you who are at Rome" (Rom. 1:15, emphasis added). This verse in particular is of noteworthy interest, given the fact that Paul desired to preach the Gospel to *Christians* (cf. Rom. 1:7). Later he wrote more specifically concerning God's saving design through preaching:

> *"Everyone who calls on the name of the Lord will be saved."*
> *How, then, can they call on the one they have not believed in? And*
> *how can they believe in the one of whom they have not heard?*
> *And how can they hear without someone preaching to them?*
>
> —ROM. 10:13-14

In 1 Corinthians 9, Paul exposes the burden of every man appointed by God to this work: "Yet when I *preach* the gospel, I cannot boast, for I am compelled to preach. Woe to me if I do not *preach* the gospel! " (v.

The Present Evangelical Crisis

16, emphasis added). To verify his rightful place among the apostles, Paul stated matter-of-factly: "Whether, then, it was I or they, this is what we *preach*, and this is what you believed" (1 Cor. 15:11, emphasis added). Finally, in anticipation of his imminent execution, the great apostle gave a concluding exhortation to young Timothy: "*preach* the Word" (2 Tim. 4:2, emphasis added). In summary, preaching was a prominent feature in the ministry methodology of Jesus, the stated reason for which He called His disciples, and the reason for which they too would be clothed with the power of the Spirit (cf. Luke 24:49). Furthermore, they continued the pattern of this methodology by exhorting subsequent disciples to this same task.[7]

How altogether different are the priorities of ministry within contemporary evangelicalism. It is a colossal understatement to suggest that preaching and preachers have fallen on hard times in recent years. Christians themselves often speak of preaching in disparaging tones. Political correctness demands that the man of God no longer be regarded as "a preacher," but instead as "a communicator." An absence of preaching is often the means now employed to attract people to the assembly on the Lord's Day. "Come to our church. Our pastor won't preach at you." Television sitcoms frequently portray preachers as irrelevant and empty-headed buffoons. "From what do these kinds of attitudes stem?" it should be asked. Some would be quick to suggest the antiauthoritarian mood of our day: "Most people will welcome a word of encouragement. Some may accept a social commentary of sorts. But few in our day, if any, will tolerate preaching that is authoritative." While for the most part this assessment is accurate, it is not my chief concern. Rather, I am convinced that preaching is held in such low esteem today because a great many preachers are so utterly inept at the task.

To what can this ineptitude be attributed? To be sure, some lack calling and giftedness. Of course, this is no reflection upon the spiritual integrity of such men, nor on the potential of their usefulness to the Kingdom of God. It is to say that some men are not suited to pulpit ministry because God in His sovereignty has not appointed them to this particular task. You may remember the scene from the movie *Chariots of Fire* when Harold Abrahams solicits the personal tutelage of a famous track and field coach, Sam Mussabini. Following Abrahams's request, Mussabini replies: "You see, Mr. Abrahams, like the bridegroom, it's the

Preaching: The Decisive Function

coach that should do the asking . . . we've an old saying in my game, son: 'you can't put in what God's left out.'"

The New Testament certainly affirms the priesthood of all believers. It does not espouse, however, a "preacherhood" of all believers. The experience of regeneration and the presence of the indwelling Spirit, matched with sincere desire, does not fit a man for the ministry of proclamation, which is rather the consequence of the sovereign calling and gifting of God.[8]

Some men are inept at preaching because they lack diligence; the pastorate is an effective hiding-place for lazy men. Other men lack understanding. That is to say, they have yet to recognize the priority of preaching in God's design. A pastor may find himself overseeing the Sunday school program, directing the Awana ministry, leading the men's Bible study, or maintaining unlimited availability for counseling. Consequently, it is not uncommon to hear: "Pastor Smith is a great guy and a genuine servant. I'm just not fed by his preaching." In defense, some would be quick to assert, "But these other ministries are important." Certainly this is true. But at this point it must be asked, what kind of priority did the original apostles give to the role of preaching when the need for other ministries became apparent? When the legitimate demands of people threatened the apostles' commitments to ministry assigned to them by Jesus, these needs were addressed by the appointment of a second group of spiritually mature men. Does this delegation reflect laziness on the part of the original apostles? Worse yet, does it betray a sense of spiritual superiority on their parts? No; it is merely a division of labor that seeks to protect the centrality of preaching in God's design. "It would not be right for us to neglect the ministry of the word of God in order to wait on tables . . . [we] will give our attention to prayer and the ministry of the word" (Acts 6:2-4).

Preachers (and their congregations!) must understand that faithfulness to God's methodology will by necessity exempt them from significant participation in most other ministry responsibilities. When referring to elders worthy of double honor, Paul describes them as men who work to the point of exhaustion[9] at "*preaching and teaching*" (1 Tim. 5:17, emphasis added). An assumption should be obvious at this point: if men such as these, given to preaching and teaching, labor unto weariness in this work, it is highly unlikely they will have significant involvement with

The Present Evangelical Crisis

other ministries, however important they may be. Faithful exposition is an all-consuming work; a faithful man must be immovable from this design. He recognizes preaching as the method ordained of God. Marcel states it as succinctly as it can be stated: *"Preaching is the central, primary, decisive function of the Church."*[10] From the historical perspective Lloyd-Jones adds:

> Is it not clear, as you take a bird's-eye view of Church history, that the decadent periods and eras in the history of the Church have always been those periods when preaching had declined? What is it that always heralds the dawn of a Reformation or a Revival? It is renewed preaching.[11]

A DECLARATION THAT DEMANDS COMPLIANCE

Why does the New Testament steadily set forth preaching as the principal method of communicating the Gospel? Simply stated, it is the method best suited to the nature of the message being made known. The Gospel is a message that declares the invasion of God into human history. God has intervened to address the human dilemma by means of His redemptive achievements. Hence, the Good News is to be announced. It is to be proclaimed. God is not negotiating with this message; He is not asking for discussion or attempting to strike a bargain. As the Lord of the universe, He is declaring a word that demands compliance from His creation. A brief consideration of the words used in 1 Corinthians 1—2 reveals this emphasis.[12] The spirit of the Gospel demands a method of communication that is authoritative: "God has acted. God has come. You must respond." Preaching then, in this sense, is not "the delivery of a learned and edifying or hortatory discourse in well-chosen words and a pleasant voice. It is the declaration of an event,"[13] "urging acceptance and compliance."[14]

It must be understood that the preacher does not *share*, he *declares*. It is for this very reason that small group Bible studies can never replace the preaching of the Gospel. Preaching is not a little talk. It is not a fireside chat. To substitute sharing and discussion for preaching is to risk the integrity of the Gospel itself. When a man stands before the people of God with the Christocentric word on his lips he must say, as it were, "Thus saith the Lord," because through the Scriptures God still speaks. This is not arrogance on the part of the preacher. Rather, it is an authoritative passion that grows out of a recognition of the nature of the message he has been sent to proclaim. Carson states: "It is not arrogant to re-present as forcefully as we can God's gospel; it is simply faithful stewardship."[15] Stott agrees:

> But we preach . . . that is, our task as Christian preachers is not subserviently to answer all the questions which men put to us; nor to attempt to meet all the demands which are made on us; nor hesitatingly to make tentative suggestions to the philosophically minded; but rather to proclaim a message which is dogmatic because it is divine. The preacher's responsibility is proclamation, not discussion. There is too much discussion of the Christian religion today, particularly with unbelievers, as if we were more concerned with men's opinions of Christ than with the honor and glory of Jesus Christ Himself. Are we to cast our Priceless Pearl before swine to let them sniff at Him and trample upon Him at their pleasure? No. We are to proclaim Christ, not to discuss Him . . . we are "heralds," charged to publish abroad a message which did not originate with us but with Him who gave it to us to publish.[16]

Preaching is the method that best suits the authoritative declaration of God's accomplishments in Jesus Christ. But greater focus is needed at this juncture. It is not wholly accurate to set forth preaching as God's method, apart from a proper understanding of the manner in which this preaching is to express itself. To be sure, Christian preaching is concerned with content. It is also concerned with the character in which the content is communicated. That is to say, Christian preaching consciously renounces all dependence upon humanly-devised techniques of persuasion. Two features were noticeably absent from Paul's preaching ministry in Corinth: "*superiority of speech*" and "*wisdom*" (1 Cor. 2:1, NASB, emphasis added). In all likelihood the first phrase refers to the *manner* of communication,[17] while the second refers to the *content*,[18] a reference to the philosophical speculations so prominent in Corinth.[19] "When I came to you I did not offer an exposition of a novel philosophical conception," Paul affirms. "For that very reason I refused to draw upon the oratorical techniques of the rhetorician."

The Present Evangelical Crisis

In verse 4 Paul further describes his preaching: " . . . *not with wise and persuasive words*" (emphasis added). The Greek word translated "persuasive" appears only here in the New Testament, though its cognate is used in Colossians 2:4 to speak of persuasion that is intentionally deceitful, "for the specious and plausible Gnostic philosophers."[20] In relationship, then, to 1 Corinthians 2:4, Robertson states: "Corinth put a premium on the veneer of false rhetoric and thin thinking."[21] Barrett describes this as "words directed by worldly wisdom."[22] This phrase is not a display of false humility on the part of Paul. Elsewhere he readily acknowledges his attempt to be persuasive (cf. Acts 14:12). Rather, Paul is reminding the Corinthians of his conscious intention to renounce the manipulative techniques of persuasion that were regularly employed in the Greek culture. Had his message been the product of his own mind, he might have drawn upon these communicative techniques.

THE HOLY CORRESPONDENCE

Suppose that a mother and father are burdened to teach the alphabet to their children. Putting on a purple dinosaur costume and singing the ABC song is an altogether legitimate method to employ. Suppose a corporation feels the need to boost profits in its fast-food chain by increasing hamburger sales. Donning a jack-in-the-box head is equally legitimate. No incongruity exists between message and method of communication. On the other hand, something would be radically inappropriate were approaches such as these employed by the parents of Jon Bonet Ramsey in making their television appeal to find their daughter's murderer. Why would these be so evidently out of place? Because there would exist an irreconcilable disparity between the message and the method of its communication.

The preacher brings to a fallen humanity the very testimony of God centered on the redemptive work of Jesus Christ, a work that by nature shatters all human self-sufficiency. To then attempt a proclamation of that message in a manner that relies upon methods reflecting the wizardry of men is to eviscerate the Gospel of its own content. The cross, implies Paul, not only determines the substance of the preacher's message—it dictates the manner in which preachers communicate it. To be sure, Paul's aspiration is to win the hearts of people. But in attempting to capture their

Preaching: The Decisive Function

affections, he leaves no room for competitors. His desire is that their hearts be captured by the Gospel, not by his sophisticated presentation of it. Consequently, Paul refrains from any technique of communication that, on its own merit, might elicit a response from his listeners. The implication is obvious: a response drawn out by anything other than the Gospel simply proclaimed will more often than not prove to be something less than a saving response.

At this very point it is essential for preachers give heed to Paul's methodology. To be sure, a true gospel preacher longs to see the experience of authentic conversion in the lives of the people to whom he preaches. However, he understands that if the response of a listener is drawn out by the dimming of the lights, the playing of soft music, the powerful stories of the preacher, or the pressure of surrounding multitudes streaming forward to the altar, it is highly unlikely that such a response will prove to be saving. Such may serve to boost the ego of the preacher, but the apostolic aim is conversion to Jesus Christ. Therefore, any technique that may confuse the latter objective with the former must be eliminated.

Where the affections of the people are at stake, there must be no competitors allowed. The Gospel must capture their hearts, not the genius of those who seek to communicate it. The Puritan John Flavel coined an important phrase: "a crucified style best suits the preachers of a crucified Christ."[23] Christian preaching demands a holy correspondence between message and method. We must always be asking of ourselves and our ministries: "Is the method I am employing to communicate the Gospel in keeping with the essence of the Gospel itself? Is this a cross-kind of communication?" John Piper writes:

> . . . the cross is the power of God to crucify the pride of both the preacher and the congregation. In the New Testament the cross is not only a past place of objective substitution; it is also a present place of subjective execution—the execution of my self-reliance and love affair with the praise of men.[24]

Well-meaning evangelicals may call this ministry methodology into question. "Well," some may say, "I appreciate your enthusiasm. I appreciate your idealism. But I am a bird of a different feather. That is to say,

The Present Evangelical Crisis

both of my feet are rooted deeply in reality, which means I recognize the need to be practical in order to survive. So, pastor, let me ask you, 'How do you expect the Gospel to succeed if you strip away all of the communicative techniques that drive every other message in our day?'" At this point the man of God can say with full apostolic precedence, "I am foolish enough to expect the Gospel to succeed by means of the power of God." About this Paul reminds his Corinthian readers: "My message and my preaching were not with wise and persuasive words, but with a demonstration of the Spirit's power" (1 Cor. 2:4).

The word "demonstration" means "proof, evidence, verification."[25] Angel asserts that through the second century this word was used in Greek culture to speak of evidence supplied by an orator to prove the validity of his argument.[26] Kistemaker refers to it as "a term used in a court of law for testimony."[27] It was employed in the Greek mystery religions to speak of the direct "intervention by a divinity."[28] Moreover, the usage of this term in extra-biblical literature reveals the efficacy of its persuasiveness. Hence, the following conclusions: "The element of showing or demonstrating implies clearly making something known . . . in a clear, convincing, and confirming manner *and therefore shown to be certain or true*."[29] Abbott-Smith defines this term as "certain proof."[30] Another suggests: "a *compelling decision demanded* by the presupposition."[31] Kistemaker summarizes: "The term signifies that no one is able to refute the proof that is presented."[32]

Paul is reminding the Corinthians that his preaching was not confirmed in them as a consequence of appropriating the most current and sophisticated techniques of communication. Rather, that which caused the message to be so forcefully persuasive and convincing was the immediate intervention and power of the Holy Spirit. The phrase "*of the Spirit and of power*" (NASB) is a hendiadys, the coordination of two ideas, one of which is dependent upon the other.[33] The two nouns in the genitive are subjective.[34] Hence, the following captures Paul's intended meaning: the Spirit, with His power, gives the demonstration. "My preaching," says Paul, "was characterized, not by manipulative techniques of communication, but by a supernatural verification that was supplied by the power of the Spirit of God."[35]

It is this power that makes the foolish message and method effectual in the lives of people—the Holy Spirit pouring out His power on the proclamation of the Christocentric word. Luther suggests that the preacher is only a mouthpiece:

> Those who are now proclaiming the gospel are not those who really do it; they are only a mask and masquerade through which God carries out His work and will. You are not the ones who are catching fish, God says, I am drawing the net myself.[36]

Calvin indicates there is no benefit from preaching "except when God shines in us by the light of His Spirit; and thus the inward calling, which alone is efficacious and peculiar to the elect, is distinguished from the outward voice of men."[37] Spurgeon has referred to the work of the Spirit in preaching as "the sacred anointing."[38] Whitefield terms it "the thunder and lightning"[39] in his sermons. Tony Sargent defines this "unction" and elaborates as follows:

> . . . (it is) the penetration and domination of the personality by the Spirit. . . . It is the preacher gliding on eagle's wings, soaring high, swooping low, carrying and being carried along by a dynamic other than his own. His consciousness of what is happening is not obliterated. He is not in a trance. He is being worked on but is aware that he is still working. He is being spoken through but he knows he is still speaking. The words are his but the facility with which they come compels him to realize that the source is beyond himself.[40]

Martyn Lloyd-Jones provides a helpful explanation:

> What is this? It is the Holy Spirit falling upon the preacher in a special manner. It is an access of power. It is God giving power, and enabling, through the Spirit, to the preacher in order than he may do this work in a manner that lifts it beyond the efforts and endeavors of man to a position in which the preacher is being used by the Spirit and becomes the channel through whom the Spirit works.[41]

This is the vitality of the Spirit—namely, His work of glorifying Jesus Christ through fallible men who faithfully proclaim the Christocentric Scriptures.

The Present Evangelical Crisis

THE SPIRIT AND THE WORD

The Scriptures repeatedly display a tight connection between the coming of the Holy Spirit and the subsequent proclamation of the Word of God. This connection is seen frequently in the Old Testament Scriptures. In Numbers 11, as a fulfillment of God's promise to Moses, the Holy Spirit was given to the seventy elders of Israel, with the attendant manifestation of their prophesying. Jealous for the unique position of Moses, Joshua emphatically pled with his mentor to restrain the seventy elders. The response of Moses is telling: "Are you jealous for my sake? I wish that all the LORD's people were prophets and that the LORD would put his Spirit on them!" (Num. 11:29). The implied connection between the gift of the Holy Spirit and the subsequent communication of the prophetic word is evident.

Numbers 24 records the coming of the Spirit upon Balaam with the result that the word of the Lord was made known through him (Num. 24:2ff.). In his final song King David declared: "The Spirit of the LORD spoke through me; his word was on my tongue" (2 Sam. 23:2). In 2 Chronicles this relationship of the Spirit to the proclaimed word is cited again: "Then the Spirit of God came upon Zechariah son of Jehoiada the priest. He stood before the people and said, "This is what God says . . ."" (24:20). Nehemiah 9 sets forth the penitent prayer of the people of Israel that recounts their repeated failures and Yahweh's subsequent mercy: "For many years you were patient with them. By your Spirit you admonished them through your prophets" (Neh. 9:30). The prophet Ezekiel writes: "Then the Spirit of the LORD came upon me, and he told me to say: 'This is what the LORD says . . .'" (11:5).

Several other references could be cited that reveal the relationship between the coming of the Holy Spirit and the consequent proclamation of the Word of God. It can be argued that a predominant ministry of the Holy Spirit as recorded in the Old Testament Scriptures was His coming upon men for the purpose of making known the Word of God.[42]

The New Testament Scriptures continue to reveal a connection between the coming of the Spirit of God and the proclamation of the Word of God. A specific phrase in Luke and Acts appears eight times, and always in relationship to a prophetic kind of speaking. The verb

Preaching: The Decisive Function

used in each of these occurrences is a Greek word meaning "that which fills or takes possession of the mind."[43] In each of these occurrences the word appears in an aoristic tense and with a passive voice. Hence, each usage of the phrase can be rendered: "filled with the Holy Spirit," or "having been filled with the Holy Spirit." In each of these eight occurrences the filling of the Spirit is presented as an event, a sovereign and spontaneous act of God related to the proclamation of truth.[44] At this point it is necessary to give brief consideration to each of these passages. The first appears in relationship to the birth announcement of John the Baptist:

> But the angel said to him, "Do not be afraid, Zacharias, for your petition has been heard, and your wife Elizabeth will bear you a son, and you will give him the name John. And you will have joy and gladness, and many will rejoice at his birth. For he will be great in the sight of the Lord, and he will drink no wine or liquor; and he will be filled with the Holy Spirit, while yet in his mother's womb."
>
> —LUKE 1:13-15, NASB, EMPHASIS ADDED

Gabriel continues by indicating that this filling is directly connected to the specific ministry given to John: "And he will turn back many of the sons of Israel to the Lord their God. And it is he who will go as a forerunner before Him in the spirit and power of Elijah" (Luke 1:16-17). John's prophetic ministry of repentance, like that of Elijah, necessitated the filling of the Spirit of God. Here is a direct parallel to what was repeatedly seen in the Old Testament: the coming of the Holy Spirit for the purpose of proclaiming God's Word.

The second and third appearances of this phrase concern Elizabeth and Zacharias, the parents of John the Baptist:

> At that time Mary got ready and hurried to a town in the hill country of Judea, where she entered Zechariah's home and greeted Elizabeth. When Elizabeth heard Mary's greeting, the baby leaped in her womb, and Elizabeth was filled with the Holy Spirit."
>
> —LUKE 1:39-41, EMPHASIS ADDED

The Present Evangelical Crisis

What follows this sudden filling of the Spirit? Elizabeth prophetically proclaims Mary to be the mother of the promised Messiah:

In a loud voice she exclaimed: "Blessed are you among women, and blessed is the child you will bear! But why am I so favored, that the mother of my Lord should come to me?"

—LUKE 1:42-43

When the Baptist is born, his father, Zechariah, has a similar experience:

His father Zechariah was filled with the Holy Spirit *and prophesied: "Praise be to the Lord, the God of Israel, because he has come and has redeemed his people."*

—LUKE 1:67-68, EMPHASIS ADDED

Here again a sudden filling of the Holy Spirit results in the proclamation of a word that has a supernatural origin.

The fourth usage of this phrase appears in the earliest portion of the book of Acts. Prior to His ascension Jesus reinforces the promise previously made to His disciples: "You will receive power *when the Holy Spirit comes on you*; and you will be my witnesses" (Acts 1:8, emphasis added). On the Day of Pentecost this promise comes to fulfillment:

Suddenly a sound like the blowing of a violent wind came from heaven and filled the whole house where they were sitting. They saw what seemed to be tongues of fire that separated and came to rest on each of them. All of them were filled with the Holy Spirit *and began to speak in other tongues as the Spirit enabled them.*

—ACTS 2:2-4, EMPHASIS ADDED

Issuing forth as a consequence of the filling of the Spirit is a supernatural kind of speaking. Luke, however, does not have unintelligible languages in view. Rather, these "tongues" were quite understandable and their content specifically focused:

> *When they heard this sound, a crowd came together in bewilderment, because each one heard them speaking in his own language. . . . "Then how is it that each of us hears them in his own native language? . . . we hear them declaring the wonders of God in our own tongues!"*
>
> —ACTS 2:6, 8, 11

The Pentecostal manifestations of "tongues" amounts to the proclamation of the redemptive accomplishments of the Triune God in languages understood by the assembled hearers. Peter then proceeds to legitimize this experience by quoting an Old Testament revelation:

> *". . . this is what was spoken by the prophet Joel: '"In the last days, God says, I will pour out my Spirit on all people. Your sons and daughters will prophesy."'"*
>
> —ACTS 2:16-17

One of the effects of the New Covenant advent of the Spirit would be the making known of the Word of God in a greater and more profusive fashion.

This phrase is employed by Luke on a fifth occasion in Acts 4 in relationship to the imprisonment of Peter and John. Following the healing of a man lame from birth (Acts 3:1-8), Peter and John begin to proclaim Jesus and His resurrection from the dead. This preaching leads to their arrest. On the following day they are placed before the Jewish leadership and are asked to supply an explanation for this healing: "By what power or what name did you do this?" (Acts 4:7). Luke then records: "Then Peter, *filled with the Holy Spirit*, said to them . . ." (Acts 4:8, emphasis added). But the attentive reader will ask the obvious question, "Was not Peter filled with the Holy Spirit in Acts 2:4? What, then, is this?"

While it must be affirmed that all Christians are indwelt by the Holy Spirit permanently (cf. John 14:16; Rom. 8:9), and all believers will experience the effects of the Spirit's presence in their lives to a greater or lesser degree (particularly as it relates to the transformation of their character into Christlikeness; cf. Gal. 5:16-24), there is another work of the Spirit directly related to the proclamation of the Word of God, a unique filling of the Holy Spirit that amounts to receiving His power. This is a spontaneous work of God attending the declaration of His Word, which is sovereignly and selectively given.

Later in chapter 4 Luke employs this phrase on a sixth occasion. When Peter and John are released by the Jewish leadership, they return to their fellow disciples. Luke then records the following experience:

> *After they prayed, the place where they were meeting was shaken. And they were all* filled with the Holy Spirit *and spoke the word of God boldly.*
>
> —ACTS 4:31, EMPHASIS ADDED

As in the aforementioned scenario with Peter, these believers were Christians in the full New Testament sense. That is to say, they had been recipients of the indwelling Spirit of God. And yet, they are suddenly *"filled with the Holy Spirit"* with the result that Word of God is spoken with great boldness.

The seventh usage of this phrase relates to the experience of Paul in Acts 9. Here Ananias informs the recently converted Saul that he has been sent by the command of the Lord Jesus so that Saul might regain his sight and *"be filled with the Holy Spirit"* (Acts 9:17, emphasis added). The reason for Paul's need of filling is implied in verse 15, where the Lord tells Ananias that Saul "is my chosen instrument to carry my name before the Gentiles and their kings and before the people of Israel" (Acts 9:15). Furthermore, this is confirmed by Paul's later recollection of Ananias' words:

> *"Then he said: 'The God of our fathers has chosen you to know his will and to see the Righteous One and to hear words from his mouth. You will be his witness to all men of what you have seen and heard.'"*
>
> —ACTS 22:14-15

It is no surprise, then, that after Paul received this filling of the Spirit Luke records the following: "At once he began to preach in the synagogues that Jesus is the Son of God" (Acts 9:20).

Finally, Luke draws upon this phrase on an eighth occasion. In Acts

Preaching: The Decisive Function

13 Paul and Barnabas are preaching the Gospel on the island of Salamis. There a Roman proconsul named Sergius Paulus summons them so that he might hear the Word of God.

> But Elymas the sorcerer (for that is what his name means) opposed them and tried to turn the proconsul from the faith. Then Saul, who was also called Paul, filled with the Holy Spirit, looked straight at Elymas and said . . .
>
> —ACTS 13:8-11, EMPHASIS ADDED

Here is Paul, a Christian and an apostle, a man possessing the indwelling Holy Spirit. Moreoever, he is a man who on at least one previous occasion had been filled with the Spirit of God. Right here, however, Luke records another occasion of this filling. Consequently, once again Paul speaks under the Spirit's direct influence.

What is this "Spirit-filling"? An examination of these passages reveals it to be the instantaneous, sudden, and sovereign operation of the Spirit of God coming upon a man so that his proclamation of Jesus Christ might be attended by holy power. This, then, appears to be the emphasis of Paul's words when he says to the Corinthians: "My message and my preaching were not with wise and persuasive words, but with a demonstration of the Spirit's power" (1 Cor. 2:4). The Spirit, by means of His power, through the words of a preacher, establishes, verifies, and confirms the Gospel in the heart of a man or woman so that he or she will respond to the truth he or she hears. Paul conveys the same idea elsewhere:

> We proclaim him, admonishing and teaching everyone with all wisdom, so that we may present everyone perfect in Christ. To this end I labor, struggling with all his energy, which so powerfully works in me.
>
> —COL. 1:28-29

> . . . because our gospel came to you not simply with words, but also with power, with the Holy Spirit and with deep conviction.
>
> —1 THESS. 1:5

The Present Evangelical Crisis

Peter similarly adds:

It was revealed to them that they were not serving themselves but you, when they spoke of the things that have now been told you by those who have preached the gospel to you by the Holy Spirit sent from heaven.

— 1 PET. 1:12

Martyn Lloyd-Jones refers to this work of the Spirit as "the smile of God"[45] upon the preacher. To be sure, there are occasions when the preacher himself is conscious of the attending power in the act of preaching. More often than not, however, it is the congregation that recognizes the voice of the Spirit of God.

Ministers may give voice and utterance to the Bible which is the word of God. Like James and John they may be sons of thunder to impenitent sinners. They may pour forth a tempest of impassioned, eloquent declamation. They may proclaim all the terrors of the Lord; represent the earth as quaking and trembling under the footsteps of Jehovah; flash around them the lightnings of Sinai; borrow, as it were, the trump of the archangel, and summon the living and the dead to the bar of God . . . and still God may not be there; His voice may not be heard either in the tempest, the earthquake, or the fire; and if so, the preacher labored in vain; his hearers, though they may for the moment be affected, will receive no permanent salutary impressions. Nothing effectual can be done unless God be there, unless he speaks with his still, small voice. By this still, small voice we mean the voice of God's Spirit; the voice which speaks not only to man, but in man; the voice, which, in stillness and silence, whispers to the ear of the soul, and presses upon the conscience those great eternal truths, a knowledge and belief which is connected with salvation. . . . Large congregations often sit and hear a message from God, while perhaps not a single individual among them feels that the message is addressed to himself, or that he has any personal concern in it. But it is not so when God speaks with his still, small voice. Every one, to whom God thus speaks, whether he be alone, or in the midst of a large assembly, feels that he is spoken to, that he is called, as it were, by name. The message comes home to him,

Preaching: The Decisive Function

and as Nathan said to David, Thou art the man. Hence, while
multitudes are around him, he sits as if he were alone. At him
alone the preacher seems to aim. On him alone his eye seems to
be fixed. To him alone every word seems to come. . . . No scene,
on this side of the bar of God, can be more awfully, overpower-
ingly solemn, than the scene which such an assembly exhibits.
The Father of spirits is present to the spirits he has made; present
to each of them, and speaking to each. Each one feels that the eye
of God is upon him, that the voice of God is speaking to him.
Each one therefore, though surrounded by numbers, mourns solitary and apart. The powers of the world to come are felt. Eternity,
with all its crushing realities, opens to view, and descends upon
the mind. The final sentence, though uttered by human lips,
comes with scarcely less weight, than if pronounced by the Judge
himself. All countenances gather blackness, and a stillness,
solemn and profound, and awful, and pervades the place, interrupted by only a stifled sob, or a half repressed sigh. My hearers,
such scenes have been witnessed. Within a few years they have
been witnessed in hundreds of places.[46]

It may be surprising for some to discover that when the Spirit of God
powerfully attends the preaching of the Word, one of the common indi-
cators is a heightened sense of quiet; not shouts and ecstasies, but rather
an unnatural silence. The ever-present coughing ceases. The incessant
movement of people is overcome by dramatic stillness. And suddenly,
though the features of the preacher's face and the timbre of his voice are
still identifiably his, the words coming forth from his mouth seem to have
been sent from heaven itself.

Near the conclusion of his excellent book on preaching, John R. W.
Stott provides an illustration worthy of great consideration.

I have before me, as I write, a photograph of the massive central
pulpit from which Spurgeon preached in the Metropolitan
Tabernacle. The photograph is reproduced in the second volume
of his *Autobiography*. Fifteen steps led up to it on each side, in a
great sweeping curve, and I have heard it said (but have been
unable to confirm) that as Spurgeon mounted those stairs, with
the measured tread of a heavily built man, he muttered to him-

The Present Evangelical Crisis

self on each one, "I believe in the Holy Ghost." We may be quite sure that, after fifteen repetitions of this creedal affirmation, by the time he entered the pulpit, he *did* believe in the Holy Spirit. He also urges us to do the same.[47]

Are you a preacher? If so, allow me to ask you directly: Is this what you affirm when you wake up on the Lord's Day morning? "I believe in the Holy Ghost." Is this what you affirm when you drive into the church parking lot? "I believe in the Holy Ghost." Is this what you affirm when you kneel in your study just before entering the sanctuary? "I believe in the Holy Ghost." Is this what you affirm when, with all your overwhelming limitations, you step behind the sacred desk to proclaim the majestic infinities of Jesus Christ? "I believe in the Holy Ghost." Do you long for the voice of God to be heard when you preach? Then this must be your credo: "I believe in the Holy Ghost."

It is not enough to possess the proper message. Nor is it enough to embrace the proper method. Gospel preachers desperately need the divinely appointed means, the clothing with power from on high.

O God, on the basis of the merits of Your Son, give us this, we pray.

NOTES

1. R. Gustav Niebuhr, "Mighty Fortresses: Megachurches Strive to Be All Things to All Parishioners," *The Wall Street Journal*, May 13, 1991, Sec. A, p. 6.

2. Robert Johnson, "Heavenly Gifts: Preaching a Gospel of Acquisitiveness, a Showy Sect Prospers," *The Wall Street Journal*, December 11, 1990, Sec. A, pp. 1-8.

3. Ibid., Sec. A, p. 8.

4. Sidney Greidanus, *The Modern Preacher and the Ancient Text* (Grand Rapids, MI: Eerdmans, 1988), p. 6.

5. Contrarily, evangelicals need to heed the perspective of Bonhoeffer: "The congregation which is being awakened by proclamation of the Word of God will demonstrate the genuineness of its faith by honoring the office of preaching in its unique glory and by serving it with all its powers; it will not rely on its own faith or on the universal priesthood of all believers in order to depreciate the office of preaching, to place obstacles in its way, or even to try to make it subordinate to itself." Dietrich Bonhoeffer, *Ethics* (New York: Macmillan, 1955), p. 260.

6. "We are living in an age which is querying about everything, and among

Preaching: The Decisive Function

these things it is querying the place and the value and the purpose of
preaching. In increasing numbers people seem to be depreciating the value
of preaching, and they are turning more and more to singing of various types
and kinds, accompanied with various kinds of instruments. They are also
going back to dramatic representations or recitals of Scripture, and some are
going back even to dancing and various other forms of external
manifestations of the act of worship. All this is having the effect of
depreciating the place and value of preaching. . . . Now we know that the
Reformation—even before you come to the particular Puritan emphasis—
swept away all such things. It swept away the medieval 'mystery plays' as
they are called, and dramatic performances in the church. The Reformation
got rid of all that and it is very sad to observe that people who claim an
unusual degree of spirituality should be trying to lead us back to that which
the Reformers saw so clearly had been concealing the gospel and the Truth
from people. If you mime the Scriptures, or give dramatic representation of
them, you are distracting the attention of people from the truth that is
conveyed in the Scriptures; whereas preaching . . . is essentially concerned
with bringing out the truth in Scriptures." D. Martyn Lloyd-Jones, *The
Puritans: Their Origins and Successors* (Carlisle, England: Banner of Truth,
1987), p. 373.

7. "Our Lord was a preacher. John the Baptist, the forerunner, was also a
preacher primarily. In Acts we find the same: Peter on the day of Pentecost
got up and preached, and he continued to do so. Paul was pre-eminently a
great preacher. We see him preaching in Athens, as he *declares* the Truth to
the Athenians. That was the essential view of preaching held by the Puritans
. . . and all who believe in the supremacy of preaching have always claimed,
that this was our Lord's own method of teaching the Truth." Ibid., pp. 374-
375.

8. "I believe that there should be a place in the church for the exercise of any
gift that any individual church member may chance to have; but I am certain
that all Christians are not given the gift of expounding the Scriptures. All are
not called or meant to preach. This is something peculiar and special, and
we must get rid of the idea which opposes the preaching of one man who is
called to work." Ibid., pp. 373-374.

9. The verb referred to here means "to be tired or weary, as the result of hard
or difficult endeavor." Johannes P. Louw and Eugene A. Nida, *Greek-
English Lexicon of the New Testament Based on Semantic Domains*, Vol. 1
(New York: United Bible Societies, 1989), p. 260.

10. Pierre Ch. Marcel, *The Relevance of Preaching* (Grand Rapids, MI: Baker,
1963), p. 18.

11. D. Martyn Lloyd-Jones, *Preaching and Preachers* (Grand Rapids, MI:
Zondervan, 1971), p. 24.

12. The word translated "preach" in 1 Corinthians 1:17 means "to announce
good news . . . proclaim, to preach." William F. Arndt and F. Wilbur
Gingrich, *A Greek-English Lexicon of the New Testament and Other Early
Christian Literature* (Chicago: University of Chicago Press, 1979), p. 317.
In 1:23 Paul writes, "we preach Christ." Here he employs a Greek word
meaning "to proclaim aloud, to publicly announce . . . an authoritative and

The Present Evangelical Crisis

public announcement that demands compliance." C. Brown, *The New International Dictionary of New Testament Theology*, ed. Colin Brown, Vol. 3 (Grand Rapids, MI: Zondervan, 1979), pp. 44, 48. Paul then speaks of "proclaiming" God's testimony (1 Cor. 2:1). The word used here means "to announce, with focus upon the extent to which the announcement or proclamation extends." Louw and Nida, *Semantic Domains,* Vol. 1, p. 411. Finally, in 1 Corinthians 2:4 Paul refers to "phenomena of a call which goes out and makes a claim upon the hearers." C. Brown, *DNNT*, Vol. 3, pp. 48, 53.

13. Gerhard Friedrich, *Theological Dictionary of the New Testament*, ed. Gerhard Kittel, Vol. 3 (Grand Rapids, MI: Eerdmans, 1965), p. 703.

14. Louw and Nida, *Semantic Domains*, Vol. 1, p. 417.

15. D. A. Carson, *The Cross and Christian Ministry: An Exposition of Passages from 1 Corinthians* (Grand Rapids, MI: Baker, 1993), p. 37.

16. John R. W. Stott, *The Preacher's Portrait* (Grand Rapids, MI: Eerdmans, 1961), p. 110.

17. The phrase here refers to words that are pompous and high-sounding. Louw and Nida, *Semantic Domains*, Vol. 1, p. 736. Conzelmann renders this: "Not in such a way as to distinguish myself"; Hans Conzelmann, *1 Corinthians* (Philadelphia: Fortress Press, 1975), p. 53.

18. Gordon D. Fee, *The First Epistle to the Corinthians* (Grand Rapids, MI: Eerdmans, 1987), pp. 90-91.

19. "It has been persuasively argued that Paul is alluding to the sophists of his day. Many intellectual movements greatly prized rhetoric. Philosophers were as widely praised for their oratory as for their content. But the sophists brought these ideals to new heights. Following fairly rigid and somewhat artificial conventions, these public speakers were praised and followed (and gained paying students!) in proportion to their ability to declaim in public assembly, to choose a theme and expatiate on it with telling power, and to speak convincingly and movingly in legal, religious, business, and political contexts. They enjoyed such widespread influence in the Mediterranean world, not least in Corinth, that public speakers who either could not meet their standards, or who for any reason chose not to, were viewed as seriously inferior." Carson, *The Cross*, pp. 33-34.

20. A. T. Robertson, *Word Pictures in the New Testament*, Vol. 4 (Grand Rapids, MI: Baker, 1931), p. 83.

21. Ibid.

22. C. K. Barrett, *The First Epistle to the Corinthians* (Peabody, MA: Hendrickson, 1968), p. 65.

23. John Flavel, *The Works of John Flavel*, Vol. 6 (Carlisle, England: The Banner of Truth Trust, repr. 1968), p. 572.

24. John Piper, *The Supremacy of God in Preaching* (Grand Rapids, MI: Baker, 1990), p. 33.

25. Louw and Nida, *Semantic Domains*, Vol. 1, p. 341.

26. G. T. D. Angel, "ἀπόδειξις," *The New International Dictionary of New Testament Theology*, ed. Colin Brown, Vol. 3 (Grand Rapids, MI: Zondervan, 1979), p. 570.

27. Simon J. Kistemaker, *Exposition of the First Epistle to the Corinthians* (Grand Rapids, MI: 1993), p. 76.

28. Arndt and Gingrich, *A Greek-English Lexicon of the New Testament and Other Early Christian Literature*, p. 89.

29. Louw and Nida, *Semantic Domains*, Vol. 1, p. 341.

30. G. Abbott-Smith, *A Manual Greek Lexicon of the New Testament* (Edinburgh: T & T Clark, 1981), p. 49.

31. Fritz Rienecker, *A Linguistic Key to the Greek New Testament* (Grand Rapids, MI: Zondervan, 1980), p. 390.

32. Kistemaker, *Corinthians*, p. 76.

33. See F. Blass and A. Debrunner, *A Greek Grammar of the New Testament and Other Early Christian Literature* (Chicago: University of Chicago Press, 1961), p. 228.

34. The nouns in the genitive act as the subject of, or do the action implied in, the noun to which they stand related.

35. Here we discover the trinitarian basis for a New Testament preaching ministry: gospel preachers proclaim God's testimony concerning His *Son*, verified by the power of the *Holy Spirit*.

36. Martin Luther, *Luther's Works*, Vol. 17 (St. Louis: Concordia, 1956), pp. 262-263.

37. John Calvin, *Commentaries on the Epistle of Paul the Apostle to the Romans* (Edinburgh: Calvin Translation Society, 1849), pp. 400-401.

38. Charles Haddon Spurgeon, *Lectures to My Students* (Pasadena, TX: Pilgrim Publications, repr. 1990), p. 96.

39. Cited without reference by D. M. Lloyd-Jones, *The Puritans: Their Origins and Successors* (Carlisle, England: The Banner of Truth Trust, 1987), p. 122.

40. Tony Sargent, *The Sacred Anointing* (Wheaton, IL: Crossway Books, 1994), p. 29.

41. Lloyd-Jones, *Preaching and Preachers*, p. 305.

42. "Here [in the Old Testament] . . . He [the Spirit of God] is presented as the source of all the supernatural powers and activities which are directed to the foundation and preservation and development of the kingdom of God in the midst of the wicked world. . . . We are moving here in a distinctly supernatural atmosphere and the activities which come under review belong to an entirely supernatural order. . . . Prominent above all other theocratic gifts of the Spirit, however, are the gifts of supernatural knowledge and insight, culminating in the great gift of Prophecy. This greatest of gifts . . . is the free gift of the Spirit of God to special organs chosen for the purpose of the revelation of His will." Benjamin Breckinridge Warfield, *Biblical Doctrines* (Grand Rapids, MI: Baker, repr. 1991), pp. 112, 114. See also Wilf

The Present Evangelical Crisis

Hildebrandt, *An Old Testament Theology of the Spirit of God* (Peabody, MA: Hendrickson, 1995), pp. 151-192.

43. Abbott-Smith, *A Manual Greek Lexicon*, p. 360.

44. This must not be confused with a similar phrase that appears six times in Luke and Acts (Luke 4:1; Acts 6:3, 5; 7:55; 11:24; 13:52). In each of these occurrences either the adjective πλήρης ("full") or the verb πλήρόω ("to make full" or "to fill") is used. See Arndt and Gingrich, *A Greek-English Lexicon*, pp. 669-670. These phrases, in contradistinction with the aforementioned eight phrases, refer to an abiding state or condition of fullness over against an event of being filled. Using Acts 4:8 as an example Bruce states: "We should distinguish between this use of the aorist passive, denoting a special moment of inspiration, and the use of the adjective *pleres* ('full') to denote the abiding character of the Spirit-filled man (cf. Stephen in 6:5)." F. F. Bruce, *Commentary on the Book of Acts* (Grand Rapids, MI: Eerdmans, 1970), p. 99.

A distinction should also be made between these eight phrases and the singular Pauline phrase in Ephesians 5:18, "be filled with the Spirit," which employs the present passive imperative of πλήρόω. Moreover, in all the Luke-Acts passages the genitive is used πνεύματος ἁγίου, the case typically employed with verbs of filling to stress the *content* of whatever is being filled. See Blass and A. Debrunner, *A Greek Grammar*, p. 95. In contrast, the Pauline text employs the dative (πλεύματι) with the preposition ἐν, supplying a locative emphasis. Hence, the verse could be translated "be filled in (the) Spirit"—i.e., "be filled in the realm of the Spirit/spirit," which, as the context makes clear, will consequently issue forth in certain behaviors (5:19-21). A second possibility for this phrase exists if ἐν with the dative is taken in an instrumental sense: "be filled with (by means of) the Spirit." In other words, the Holy Spirit is not the content of the filling but is the instrument God uses to fill the believer with some other content. In summary the New Testament never employs ἐν πλεύματι to express the content with which something is filled.

45. D. Martyn Lloyd-Jones, *Revival* (Wheaton, IL: Crossway Books, 1987), p. 295.

46. Edward Payson, "God Heard in the Still Small Voice," as cited in Iain Murray, *Revival and Revivalism: The Making and Marring of American Evangelicalism* (Carlisle, England: Banner of Truth, 1994), pp. 212-213.

47. John R. W. Stott, *Between Two Worlds: The Art of Preaching in the Twentieth Century* (Grand Rapids, MI: Eerdmans, 1982) p. 334.

10

RICHARD SIBBES AND THE UNION OF THE HEART WITH CHRIST: LESSONS ON GODLINESS[1]

Paul R. Schaefer, Jr.

In a very insightful article, J. I. Packer has written the following on why we modern evangelicals need "Puritans":[2]

> The answer, in one word, is maturity. Maturity is a compound of wisdom, good will, resilience, and creativity. The Puritan exemplified maturity; we don't. We are spiritual dwarfs. A much travelled leader, a Native American (be it said), has declared that he finds North American Protestantism, man-centered, manipulative, success-oriented, self-indulgent and sentimental, as it blatantly is, to be 3000 miles wide and a half an inch deep. The Puritans, by contrast, as a body were giants. They were great souls serving a great God. In them clear-headed passion and warm-hearted compassion combined.[3]

The author of this article highly concurs with Packer's assessment of the situation, and in this chapter the hope is to focus on some of the very important themes from one Puritan in particular—namely, Richard Sibbes (1577-1635), who in his life and work exemplified all these qualities that Packer extols as marking Puritan reflections on Christian godliness.[4] All too often when we modern evangelicals think about the Puritans (if we think of them at all!), we think about negative traits that sometimes were actually there and that sometimes are myths of our own imaginations.[5] When actually reading the Puritans, we find, however, that these negatives almost vanish in the air, and what we discover instead are lessons that if regarded will bring needed reformation to our personal walks and the lives of our congregations and will give us a vision for a robust and living Christianity of head and heart that we can proclaim to a dying world in need of a message of grace.

Sibbes had a long and industrious career that at different times included such callings as Fellow at St. John's College, Cambridge, preacher at Gray's Inn, London, Master of St. Catharine's Hall, Cambridge, and vicar of Holy Trinity Church, Cambridge. In his preface to Sibbes's detailed exposition of 2 Corinthians 1, Thomas Manton, a Puritan of the next generation, wrote: "[Sibbes had an] excellent and peculiar gift . . . in unfolding and applying the great mysteries of the gospel in a sweet and mellifluous way; and therefore was by his hearers usually termed *The Sweet Dropper*, sweet and heavenly distillations usually dropping from him with such a native elegance as is not easily imitated."[6] Sibbes himself spoke this way on the importance of opening the Word of God:

> For God by the preaching of the gospel sets us at liberty. . . . Those, therefore, that are enemies of the dispensation of the gospel in the ministry, they are enemies to spiritual liberty; and it is an argument that a man is in bondage to Satan when he is an enemy any way of the unfolding of the word of God. . . . [W]ith the dispensation of divine truth Christ comes to rule in the heart; by the outward kingdom comes the spiritual kingdom. . . . Therefore those that would have the spiritual kingdom of God, by grace and peace to rule in their hearts till they reign for ever in heaven, they must come by this door, by the ministry, by the outward ordinance.[7]

In turning now to the actual content of Sibbes's preaching, we will notice a depth of maturity, true devotion, and spiritual insight all too lacking in much of contemporary evangelicalism.

GRACE ALONE: PREACHING HOW CHRIST'S "RULE IN THE HEART" IS ESTABLISHED

Some modern scholars have remarked on Sibbes's relative silence in handling the sovereignty of God in the salvation of sinners.[8] It should be noted, however, that Sibbes spent much of his career in a situation in which preaching on the deep points of the sovereignty of grace was actually forbidden by law.[9] Given these strictures, what appears remarkable is not so much Sibbes's relative silence as his bold advocacy of the absolute necessity and efficacy of God's grace in bringing souls into union with Christ. This is especially seen when he made points connected to human need. Sibbes spoke of redemption not in anthropocentric (alas, an all too commonplace focus today) but rather theocentric and trinitarian terms:

> See here, for our comfort, a sweet agreement of all three persons: the Father giveth a commission to Christ; the Spirit furnisheth and sanctifieth to it; Christ himself executeth the office of a Mediator. Our redemption is founded upon the joint agreement of all three persons of the Trinity.[10]

Passivity, not activity, marked Sibbes's teachings on a person's transformation from a state of misery to a state of glory: ". . . in the chain of salvation [Romans 8:30] you have passive words in them all. . . . So here [2 Cor. 3:18] we are transformed from glory to glory, all is by the Spirit of God, the third person. . . . We do all by the Spirit, as all things are wrought in us by the Spirit."[11]

Sibbes warned his listeners that beliefs that taught that one could "with his own industry water his own ground with somewhat in himself" actually "rob[bed] God of his due glory." Only "the dew of heaven" given freely by the Spirit could water the heart, for "a Christian life [is] nothing else but a gracious dependence."[12] Mere morality never sufficed. He attacked those who preached such "mere morality," saying that such teaching resembled "the dark times" when the church was under "popery." Moral reform might bring about a reformation of "many abuses" and give "reward and respect among men," but it never produced Christians. Ultimately, such preaching "veiled" and "obscured" Christ and the proclamation that salvation was found in Him alone. The times called for something different: "Those ages wherein the Spirit of God is most, is where Christ is most preached, and people are always best where there is most Spirit; and they are most joyful and comfortable and holy, where Christ is laid open to the hearts of people."[13]

Richard Sibbes and the Union of the Heart with Christ

The reason for Sibbes's denunciations of a purely moral approach for salvation arose not only from his concern that "mere morality" robbed God of due glory, but also from his reflections on human nature apart from grace. In his sermon "The Dead Man," an exposition of Ephesians 2:1, Sibbes described our fallen condition as a pervasive and radical corruption: ". . . a death of all the powers: we cannot act and move according to that life that we had at the first; we cannot think; we cannot will; we cannot affect; we cannot do anything [that] savours of spiritual life."[14] By stating the depravity of human agents so baldly, Sibbes declared his aversion to any anthropology that placed any native ability toward spiritual good in any faculty—whether understanding, will, or affections— of the soul. One notices in his language not only an inability *to do good works* but actually an inability *even to desire* anything pleasing to God apart from supernatural grace.

Calling the "proneness to sin" in all men "a natural inclination" that will always "break out with greater violence" until "our natures be altered" meant that in the bent and habits of their lives all humans in their natural estate voluntarily chose to rebel. Such corruption, Sibbes cautioned, while "necessary to us" was nevertheless "no violent necessity from an outward cause, but a necessity that we willingly pull upon ourselves. . . ." In other words, one can never blame God for one's sin or even proclaim that God forced one to sin. Sibbes warned that one could not blame Adam either, for rather than stopping the downward spiral into which the sin of Adam had plunged us, "we feed and strengthen it . . . and by that means we justify Adam's sin . . . and shew that if we had been in Adam's [prelapsarian] condition ourselves, we would have made that ill choice which he made." The blame for sin fell on all and every, and thus for one to be saved, Sibbes declared, one desperately needed to "come under the government of grace."[15]

Sibbes demanded that "[g]race is not glorious if we add the least thing of our own to it."[16] He rebuked those who thought that grace could "be commanded by the creature," contending instead:

> . . . this perfect gift, the grace of God [for salvation], comes from above, from the Father of lights. *There is no principle of grace naturally within a man.* It is as childish to think that grace comes from any principle within us, as to think that the dew, which falls

The Present Evangelical Crisis

upon a stone is the sweat of the stone, as children think that the stone sweats, when it is dew that has fallen upon it. Certainly our hearts, in regard of themselves, are barren and dry.[17]

In an exposition of 2 Corinthians 3:17, Sibbes acknowledged that all humans as created beings possessed a freedom of a sort, but added that such freedom was limited to its own "sphere." The Fall marred all humanity, but it did not obliterate the "natural power and endowment that God hath put upon the soul, and so the will is alway free in earth and in hell." The understanding also possessed a certain amount of "liberty" in the same way. Sibbes denied, however, that such "liberty" extended toward the "spiritual good." In his natural sinful estate, man "can do nothing but naturally." To grasp the spiritual was out of anyone's natural reach, and thus no person attained naturally that "liberty as it is taken for power and ability to do good." Regarding this spiritual liberty, Sibbes exhorted, "The will of man is slavish altogether." Indeed "the soul of man" as a whole "hath no liberty at all to that which is spiritually good."

Into this bleak situation, the Spirit of God "puts a new life into the soul[s]" of the elect. In doing so, the Spirit brought sinners into a new sphere by granting a "supernatural principle" absent in the natural estate: "we cannot do particular actions without the exciting power of the Spirit of God. The Spirit stirs up to every particular thing, when the soul would be quiet of itself. The moving comes from the Spirit of God." Through such an "efficacious and effectual" working, Sibbes argued, the Spirit "robs not the soul of liberty, but perfects that liberty."[18] A new "principle" given by the Spirit of God, and thus outside nature, had to be implanted by grace alone in order for a person to have any power for union with Christ and to live spiritually.[19]

In "The Christian Work," an exposition of Philippians 2:12-13, Sibbes reminded his hearers that not only the "power" to do God's will but the "very act of willing and doing" came from God: ". . . we [can]not think a good thought without the Spirit of God working in us. For we have no life at all, but are 'dead in sins and trespasses', much less can we have any motion to that which is good for ourselves." Nevertheless, Sibbes knew that the sensitive saint would inquire "how" the work "we do" could be all God's, yet also ours. He answered this by recognizing

Richard Sibbes and the Union of the Heart with Christ

that "in every work . . . done, there is God's power and man's joined together." Such doing, however, arose not from a "co-ordinate" synergism but from a grace-empowered and "subordinate" response by the human. When "we think or will," he admonished, such actions are ours; nonetheless, whenever we "think or will that which is good, that is from God." In so doing, God deals with the "creature" as one with an understanding and willing heart. In bringing a person to true freedom that "consists not in doing this or that *ad libitum*" but a true liberty to do things "out of a sound judgment, . . . God enters into the heart, changes the stony heart into a heart of flesh, takes away all rebellious dispositions of our heart, and makes them pliable to his will" (cf. Ezek. 36). Only the powerful efficacy of grace could do this, not some spark of initiative (however small) on the part of the creature.[20]

Sibbes also used covenant terminology to explain both the absolute efficacy of grace and the responsibility to respond piously to God's call. In doing so, he followed that line of Reformed thinking that recognized two covenants given by God to mankind:[21] a prelapsarian "covenant of works" that continued to be felt by all since God, who "would not have it forgotten," renewed it in the giving of the law at Sinai; and, a "new covenant [of grace]" given by God "after [the] fall" in order to "recover again man's communion and fellowship with God."

The first covenant continued to be felt by all of Adam's posterity, but only as a "curse" because "we cannot fulfill the law which requireth personal obedience, perfect obedience, and exact obedience. . . . The law then findeth us dead and killeth us. It findeth us dead before, and not only leaves us dead still, but makes us more dead." Discussing the continued operative work of the law in this way enabled Sibbes to emphasize once again his recognition of both human inability as well as human responsibility to respond to God. Men were different from other "creatures." "God . . . framed man," Sibbes explained, "[as] an understanding creature," one "fit to have communion and intercourse with" God. Such human constitution remained after the Fall. What had now changed was the human ability to use God's original means ("the covenant of works") as a way toward such union and communion. That way—personal, perfect, and exact obedience to the commands of the law—had been closed.

An entirely new approach for communion with God was needed, and this God had provided in the "new covenant" through which he entered "into new conditions with us." Sibbes believed that God put this covenant into effect right after the Fall, and thus only one covenant of grace existed whereby persons could have fellowship with God. Although God had renewed the prelapsarian covenant through giving the law at Sinai, the "covenant of grace" worked right alongside that closed path to salvation and stood as the only true means of fellowship now available. The first covenant merely left everyone, including the children of Israel, without excuse.

Sibbes explained this notion of only one covenant of grace through reflections on sacred history. Prior to the giving of Christ, "who is the ground of the covenant, and so of our communion and fellowship with God," God declared this covenant in the historical stages of promise, ceremony, and testament. From Adam to Abraham, God called this covenant of grace "a promise of the blessed seed"; from Abraham to Moses, he portrayed the "covenant" through the "ceremony" of circumcision; finally, from Moses to Christ, it figured as a "testament . . . established by [the] blood" of types. Through the shadows of covenant-promise, covenant-ceremony, and testament-type, God pointed His ancient people to Christ, who alone, through His death as the mediator of the covenant of grace, fulfilled their need for a newly established fellowship. With the advent of Christ, this "covenant of grace is most clear . . . and is now usually called the New Testament. . . ."

Before speaking in any way about stipulations to be fulfilled on the part of the elect as members of this covenant, Sibbes centered his thinking about "new conditions" for communion with God around the fulfilment of the covenant by the "testator": ". . . without the death of Christ there could be no satisfaction, and without satisfaction there could be no peace with God." Indeed, Sibbes apparently desired to move his listeners away from thinking about "covenant" in overtly contractual terms *by pointing out that this covenant, as a "testament [which is] indeed a covenant, and something more,"* must have the death of the testator "before it can be of force." This covenant of grace as "testament" meant that God *"bequeatheth good things merely of love."* Sibbes further contended: "A covenant requireth something to be done. In a testament, there is nothing but receiving the legacies given."

Such language had shock value for his lawyer listeners at Gray's Inn. It forced them to sit up and take notice. Covenant and testament language formed a part of the regular discourse of government and commerce, certainly, but the language as Sibbes used it took a decidedly different twist since he combined covenant and testament together:

> In covenants, ofttimes it is for the mutual good one of another, but a testament is merely for their good for whom the testament is made, to whom the legacies are bequeathed. . . . God's covenant now is such a testament, sealed with the death of Christ, made out of love for our good; for what can God receive of us? All is legacies from him; and though he requireth conditions, requireth faith and obedience, yet he himself fulfilleth what he asketh, giveth what he requireth, giveth it as a legacy. . . .

Through using the ordinary language of the marketplace, Sibbes turned everyday meanings upside-down and pointed to the absolute uniqueness of God's "agreement" with the elect in Christ. His remarks served to reorient one's spiritual thinking if one was tempted to think he could relate to God in the same way he related to others in business.[22]

Sibbes knew his audience. He contended that "God deals with men as men by way of commerce—he propounds [promises] by way of covenant and condition." Nevertheless, even in giving promises based upon conditions, such as "the promise of forgiveness of sins" given "if they believe, if they repent," God never supposed some natural ability to respond on the part of sinners: "They [God's promises] are propounded conditionally, but in the performance they are absolute, because God performs the covenant himself; he performs our part and his own part too. . . . Faith and repentance is his gift."[23]

A covenant that had a repentant faith as a sole condition *as well as* an absolute gift had ramifications for the heart's union with Christ. God used faith as "an uniting virtue to knit us to the mediator . . . because it empties the soul of all conceit of worth or strength. . . ." In this way, man gave "all the glory to God," which Sibbes deemed proper since "[i]n the covenant of grace, God intends the glory of his grace above all."[24] Such covenant union required "supernatural sight" or "else we shall have a natural knowledge of supernatural things." Therefore, Sibbes contended, "the Spirit only works faith to see that Christ is mine."[25] With such a sight of such a gracious covenant, the heart once bound in darkness could answer. Sibbes would only have wanted to add the caveat: ". . . he makes the heart to answer."[26]

The triumph of God's grace in the heart and life of the regenerate through faith-union with Christ brought the believer, on his own dead and blinded by sin, new life and new sight that now could and would by grace through the power of the Spirit lead him to live truly to the glory of God. God applied Christ's redemption for this union by the Spirit: "So the Spirit is a quickening and a cherishing Spirit, and maketh the heart, which is a barren wilderness, to be fruitful."[27]

LIVING UNDER CHRIST'S RULE: UNION AND COMMUNION WITH CHRIST

The question arises, however: if a person played a role in the Christian life, however minor, subordinate, and dependent, what characterized the answering quality and subsequent fruitfulness of that person's heart? To answer this, four areas upon which Sibbes reflected need to be examined briefly. The first has to do with the heart itself and its relationship to the faculties of the soul as understood in seventeenth-century terms. Second, what did progress in godliness entail, and how did it relate to union with Christ given by grace through faith? The third area explores how Sibbes used the "means of grace" as helps in such progress in godliness. Fourth, if Sibbes demanded such progress, which it appears he did, how did this affect the question of assurance?

The Heart and the Faculties of the Soul

Like other Puritans, Sibbes demanded that authentic Christianity had to be wholehearted, the believer being intimately involved in growing in grace.[28] At the same time, he never forgot to admonish active saints that in the "spiritual marriage between Christ and us," Christ Himself through the Spirit "gives . . . not only the power to will and to do, but the very act of willing and doing; and this he doth out of his free grace and pleasure."[29] This work of sheer grace deeply affected the heart.

Sibbes regularly spoke of the heart as a metaphor for the whole soul. For example:

Richard Sibbes and the Union of the Heart with Christ

The word heart, you know, includes the whole soul, for the understanding is in the heart, 'an understanding heart,' Job xxxviii.36.
To 'lay up things in our hearts', Luke ii.51, there it is memory; and
to cleave in heart is to cleave in will, Acts xi.23. To 'rejoice in heart',
Isa. xxx.29, that is in the affection. So that all the powers of the
soul, the inward man, as Paul calleth it, 2 Cor. iv.16, is the heart.[30]

Yet Sibbes also used *heart* as a synonym for "will and affections":

To have him in the brain to talk, and in the tongue to discourse,
and to keep the heart for worldly lusts and such things, I account
not this an inbeing of Christ to any purpose, to any comfort.
Where Christ is comfortably, he takes his throne and lodging in
the heart, he dwells in it by faith. By heart, I mean, especially the
will and affections. He draws the will to cleave to him, to choose
him for the best good. . . . For he dwells in the heart and affections, especially the will. The will chooseth him to be an head and
husband.[31]

Was this a contradiction? The answer from the evidence that Sibbes
himself provided must be no. Sibbes, here and in other places where he
talked about heart as will and affections, had a concern in mind deeply
embedded in his historical context as a preacher of "visible reformation"
(a phrase used by William Perkins [1558-1604], the great Puritan patri-
arch, as a major goal of his preaching[32]—and it might be added, all Puritan
preaching). Sibbes's thoughts on these matters meant not so much a separation of the understanding as distinct from the heart, but a concern to
warn his listeners that one should never content oneself with a mere
"notional faith." True Christian knowledge, saving Christian knowledge,
meant more. It meant a knowledge that deeply affected both head and
heart: "The heart must be moved, but the brain must be instructed first.
There is a sympathy between these two parts; as in nature, so in grace."[33]
    While Sibbes most definitely deemed a volitional taking of Christ cru-
cial to a true Christianity, two points need to be kept in mind. First,
remembrance must be given to Sibbes's reflections on natural inability
apart from grace, discussed in the preceding section. Second, Sibbes
viewed the work that God did on the heart as always starting with the
illumination of the understanding. A hint of this was seen in the quota-

tion about the brain being instructed first. Sibbes spoke of this often. For example, he contended that "there is no sanctifying grace in the affections but it comes by enlightening the understanding";[34] "when the Spirit sets a man at liberty . . . this is out of largeness of understanding";[35] "the understanding, where it hath full light, it carries the will to choose";[36] "[g]race, glory, and comfort come from above; and draw our minds up to have our conversation and our desires above";[37] and, "[t]he way to expel wind out of our bodies is to take some wholesome nourishment, and the way to expel windy fancies from the soul is to feed upon serious truths."[38] One finds no conception of anti-intellectual or anti-doctrinal Christianity in the writings of Richard Sibbes (or all the great Puritans for that matter). True godliness was always nurtured through knowledge of God found in the Scriptures.

Union with Christ and Its Benefits of Justification and Sanctification

Wakefield has written: "The 'mystical union' [i.e., union with Christ] of which the Puritans write is not the goal of the Christian life only, but its beginning."[39] This faith-union itself, which arose by the effectual call of God the Father who by the Spirit and the Word regenerated the heart through applying Christ's redemption, brought to the person the great benefits of the work of Christ—namely, justification and sanctification.

Sibbes, like Puritan thinkers before and after him (and we might note John Calvin here as well),[40] used the "double grace or double benefit" idea to describe the Christian's entrance into spiritual life and his subsequent fruitfulness: "*. . . the Christian needs not only converting but establishing grace.*"[41] This contention arose in the context of admonitions that one "set upon nothing in [one's] own strength": "Man naturally affects a kind of divinity, and will set upon things in confidence of his own abilities, without prayer and seeking God's help. He thinks to compass great matters, and bring things to a good issue by his own wit and discretion. Oh! delude not yourselves. This cannot be."[42]

True to his concern that spiritual revival take place in the heart, Sibbes excoriated those "who profess themselves Christians . . . [who] partake the name, but not the anointing of Christ. . . . [W]e cannot behold the Sun of righteousness, but we shall be changed and enlightened." Nevertheless, right in the same passage that demanded spiritual and

Richard Sibbes and the Union of the Heart with Christ

moral change of the highest order came the ground: "For what we do we do, but we are patients first to receive power from the Spirit." Moreover, Sibbes contended that the Holy Spirit who brought illumination to us in the first place also "is efficacious" as the "Spirit . . . of sanctification."[43]

Sibbes preached in years that witnessed the rise of a number of anti-nomian teachers in England.[44] Such antinomianism was indeed attractive to those nurtured in the free grace teachings of Puritan and Reformed thinkers like Sibbes. Sibbes, nevertheless, wanted to distance his under-standing of free grace from theirs: "When the soul desires the forgiveness of sin, and not grace to lead a new life, that desire is hypocritical; for a true Christian desires power against sin as well as pardon for it. If we have not sanctifying grace, we have not pardoning grace. Christ came as well by water to regenerate as by blood to justify."[45] He also contended: "[The words of Song of Solomon 6:3] serve to instruct us therefore in the nec-essary connection of these two, justification and sanctification, [so that we will not sever them]. . . . We hold here that whensoever Christ is ours, there is a spirit of sanctification in us, to yield all to Christ, though this resignation be not presently perfect."[46] To use the language of our day, Sibbes contended that true faith always brought forth a confession of Christ as *both* Savior *and* Lord.

Yet, while unwilling to separate justification and sanctification, Sibbes held that they also must be distinguished: "There is an order of working in the soul. God giveth justification before sanctification; and before he freeth from the guilt of sin, he giveth grace to confess sin. . . . Where these go before, [sanctifying] grace will follow; and where they do not, there will be no sanctification."[47] Later in the same treatise Sibbes argued, ". . . *first men must have spiritual life, and be just, before they can walk*. . . . It is a conceit of the papists, that good works do justify a man. Luther says well, that a 'good man doth good works'. Good works make not the man. Fruit makes not the tree, but the tree the fruit. So we are just first, and then we walk as just men."[48] Sibbes pointed to such jus-tification in Christ alone as the ground of comfort:

> So justification is not only a sentence of pardon, but it is also . . . a title to life everlasting. . . . What serves my faith but for my com-fort, to shew me that my title is in Christ? My strength and ground of comfort is in him, not in myself. . . . Enlarge it your-

The Present Evangelical Crisis

self. If man be not sound in this point, all he does is nothing. This is all in all. Our sanctification without this is nothing. This is the ground of all. Be careful of this, to look to Christ's obedience, life, death, and sufferings, and those comforts flowing from our interests therein.[49]

Moreover, Sibbes consistently linked both the benefits of justification and sanctification directly to Christ and faith in Christ:

Faith hath two branches, it doth give as well as take. Faith receives Christ, and says, Christ is mine; and the same faith saith, I am Christ's again. Indeed, our souls are empty; so that the main work of faith is to be an empty hand . . . a beggar's hand to receive. But when it hath received it gives back again, both ourselves and all that we can do. . . . This discovers a great deal of false faith in the world; for undoubtedly if it were true faith there would be a yielding back again. . . . [There is] a mutual coherence of justification and sanctification, and the dependence one upon another. . . . Christ is mine; his righteousness is mine for my justification. . . . But is that all? No. . . . There is a return of faith in sanctification. The same Spirit that witnesseth Christ is ours, [he] sanctifies and alters our disposition. . . . This . . . helps us . . . understand the covenant of grace . . . not only what God will do to us, but the duty we are to do to him again, though we do it in his strength. A covenant holds not on one side, but on both. Christ is mine, and I am Christ's again. . . . The covenant of grace is so called because God is so gracious as to enable us to perform our part.[50]

Sibbes grounded the effectual means and accomplishment for such response in the Atonement, for only in "the blood of Christ" was there "the fountain of all cleanness." One immersed oneself in this fountain "not like a moral man, to labour by multitude of acts to get a new habit," but by the outstretched and empty hand of faith. Only "the blood of Christ" could "wash me from sin." Not only so, but as one applied the blood through faith in Christ "for justification to free thee from the guilt of sin," so also one "let [such] faith work, as it may be applied to sanctification, to wash away the spots and pollutions of sin." Sibbes con-

Richard Sibbes and the Union of the Heart with Christ

cluded: "This is certainly the most effectual means that can be imagined. Go to the well head; look to that main principal beginning, like a Christian, and not like a moral man: that though thou art polluted and defiled, yet the blood of the Lord Jesus will purge thee from all sin, spot as well as guilt. . . ."[51]

So what did it mean to live by faith in Christ and thus grow in grace daily? Sibbes declared that a "Christian is a strange person. . . . He consists of contraries. . . . He grows downwards and upwards at the same time; for as he dies in sin and misery, and natural death approaching, so he lives the life of grace, and grows more and more till he end in glory."[52] To live this life, Sibbes commended mortification and vivification: ". . . we should much endeavour *the mortification of our lusts*. . . . [When Satan] solicits us, he finds a correspondency betwixt our corrupt hearts and himself, whereby having intelligence what we haunt, and what we love, he will be sure to molest us. The less we have of the works of Satan in us, the less will be our trouble; and the more we do the will of God, and strive against our corruptions, the more will be our comfort."[53]

Progress in Godliness Through Godly Means

To grow in grace, God gave godly means both public and private. One found the "sweetness of Christ" conveyed to the soul through "the ordinances": "His sacraments are sweet, his word sweet, the communion of saints sweet. . . . [W]hen Christ comes and shows his presence and face to the soul, he refresheth and delights it. . . . Those that hate and undermine the ordinances of God, they hinder the comfort of their own souls."[54] Nevertheless, Sibbes hardly reserved his fire for those who despised the ordinances of God. He reproached in a similar manner those who used them formally, even complaining that "it is the sin of this age, this formality." Those who "conformed" to religious practices merely for the sake of conformity lived in a "dead formality." So as one approached the ordinances, ". . . we ought to join with all the ordinances of God, a desire that Christ would join his Spirit, and make them effectual. We ought to come to the ordinances in dependence on Christ for a blessing upon them, and for his presence in them, who is the life and scope of all; and then we should not find such dullness and deadness in them."[55]

Indeed, the means of grace (the preaching of the Gospel, the sacra-

ments, Christian fellowship, etc.) served as God's way actually to help one
from "plodding in duties" because they turned the mind back to the fountain of grace, Jesus Christ: ". . . when we have distemper in our souls, let
us come to this light of God's love in Christ, and by oft meditation of
God's word, see there how he presents himself to us a father in covenant;
not only a friend, but a gracious father. . . ."[56] Sibbes even called the ordinances of God His "kisses."[57]

While he held that sacraments had no power in themselves to purify,
as this was the work of the Spirit working with the Word preached,[58] and
that in sacramental feeding the mind should be directed to the Word and
not the titillation of the senses,[59] Sibbes continued nevertheless that as
seals of the covenant of grace, they confirmed the Word and helped the
saints renew themselves in the covenant.[60] He even waxed lyrical: "That
which makes the house of God beautiful more especially, *is the means of
salvation*: not only God's presence, but the means, solemn and public
prayer, the word and sacraments, and likewise the government, that
should be in purging the church—all make the church of God beautiful
and lovely. All the ordinances of God in the church of God have a delight
in them to spiritual senses."[61]

Sibbes also deemed the communion of saints essential to Christian
godliness. The people of God needed one another: "Every Christian hath
a beauty severed in himself; but when all meet together, this is more excellent."[62] More than that, the communion of saints provided strength as
well. Sibbes warned of the dangers of neglecting the communion of saints
in the visible church: "There must be a union with Christ the head and
with the rest of the members before we can have the Spirit to strengthen
us and anoint us. Those that rend themselves from the body, cannot hope
for stablishing from the head."[63] Sibbes decried the concept of "a solitary
Christian, [who] will stand alone by himself." He concluded: "As we are
knit to Christ by faith, so we must be knit to the communion of saints by
love. That which we have of the Spirit is had in the communion of
saints."[64]

Sibbes, therefore, while certainly advocating a robust personal
Christianity, was hardly an individualist when it came to discussions of
Christian growth. He did, however, advise individual Christians to use
private means such as personal prayer and morning devotions as helps
to growth in grace.[65] Part of one's "every day's exercises" should be

Richard Sibbes and the Union of the Heart with Christ

". . . to see ourselves in Christ, and so see him and ourselves one."[66] Notice once again here Sibbes's Christ-centeredness. Whether talking about the edification of Christian fellowship, the importance of preaching, the work of God in conversion, the blessedness arising from the sacraments, the nature of faith, the call to private devotions—the list could go on, Sibbes never tired of calling his listeners outside of themselves to the greatness and tenderness of God in Christ.

One final means of growth should be mentioned—namely, Sibbes's attitude toward the role of the law of God for the Christian, the so-called *tertius usus legis*. While he did not make many detailed arguments about the use of the law in this way, he did hold that the law had a continuing function in our lives as Christians. He proclaimed:

> We are now by the Spirit set at liberty to delight in the law, to make the law our counsellor, to make the word of God our counsellor. That that terrified and affrighted us before, now it is our direction. . . . [T]he law that terrified and whipped us when we were in bondage, till we be in Christ—it scares us to Christ—that law after comes to be a tutor, to tell us this we shall do, to counsel us, and say this is the best way; and we come to delight in those truths, when they are discovered to us in the inward man.[67]

In calling men to himself, Christ called them to purity. Sibbes pointed to Christ as "the glass we should imitate" and as the "pattern to which we should conform ourselves" in this pursuit of godliness. He continued: ". . . so . . . the life of our Saviour Jesus Christ, and the word of God, must be our pattern. But you will say, how am I to attain to this? I answer, the law of God prescribes to us a perfect form of obedience, though it be not possible for me to fulfill it, and so the life of our Saviour Christ, we are not able to express the virtues in him, and his purity; yet there cannot be a better pattern than the law, and the life of our Saviour Christ."[68]

Sibbes certainly desired no one to think he had any claim on God because of outward morality; he constantly decried the "mere morality" and living "civilly" of many in his day. Nevertheless, Sibbes demanded that godly desires, which themselves had been wrought through the illuminating work of the Spirit and the Word, must lead to holy actions. The law helped here in showing what God required. The law was not the way

The Present Evangelical Crisis

to salvation. In coming to Christ for redemption, the law could only show us our failings and our desperate need of a Savior. Nonetheless, once regenerated, the law served as the pattern of godliness that the regenerate were called to follow.

Am I Saved? The Question of Assurance

Sibbes generally followed the pattern of assurance laid down in treatises by his forebears in the Puritan way such as William Perkins and Paul Baynes (the man whose preaching the Holy Spirit used to bring Sibbes to Christ). Like them, he used the *actus reflexus* as a counseling technique to advise the weak in faith:[69] "And so, many of the dear children of God, sometimes they can hardly say that they have any assurance, but yet, notwithstanding, they can say [by a reflex act], if they do not belie themselves and bear false witness against themselves, that they have cast themselves on God's mercy, that they have performed the first act of faith [the direct act whereby the soul relies upon God as reconciled in Christ, and relies upon Christ as given by God, and relies upon the promise], and this faith is not fruitless altogether."[70] The bracketed material in the preceding quotation came from Sibbes's thoughts just prior to the quote itself and set the context. Sure, the saint could use the experience of grace as a way to see the hand of God in one's life, but what really mattered was reliance on "*God as reconciled in Christ*" and reliance "upon the promise."[71]

In fact, Sibbes more times than not pointed believers away from contemplation on themselves for assurance and toward contemplation of Christ and his work on the cross:

> Aye, but what shall we do if the waters [of the sanctification of the Spirit] be troubled in the soul, as sometimes there is such confusion in the soul that we cannot see the image of God upon it in sanctification, we cannot see the stamp of God's Spirit there, there is such a chaos in the soul? . . . Then go to the blood of Christ! There is always comfort. The fountain that is opened . . . to wash in is never dry. Go therefore to the blood of Christ, that is, if we find sin upon our consciences, if we find no peace in our consciences, nor sanctification in our hearts, go to the blood of Christ

which is shed for all those that confess their sins, and rely on him for pardon, though we find no grace. For howsoever as an evidence that we are in Christ, we must find the work of the Spirit; yet before we go to Christ it is sufficient that we see nothing in ourselves, no qualification; for the graces of the Spirit they are not the condition of coming to Christ, but the promise of those that receive Christ after. Therefore go to Christ when thou feelest neither joy of the Spirit, nor sanctification of the Spirit; go to the blood of Christ, and that will purge thee, and wash thee from all sins.[72]

Rather than an isolated occurrence, such counsel was part of the steady diet he delivered to his hearers.[73]

Even when demanding that the children of God "not only live the life of faith in justification, but also sanctification," Sibbes reproached those who "set upon grace, and killing corruptions by their own strength." The same "fulness" of Christ that one needed for justification also served as the ground of any sanctification: "He is made unto us sanctification . . . when we lack fulness, let us not despair, but fetch the large vessel of faith." Here Sibbes recognized that varying degrees of assurance were possible because of the difference in the "largeness of faith."[74] Still, Sibbes admonished those, whatever their "gifts and graces," however strong or weak their faith: ". . . we honour God most, whatsoever our graces are, in casting ourselves upon Christ, and ending our days in mercy, making an appeal to mercy; whereas the graces of sanctification and excellent parts are excellent for the good of others, but if we place too much affiance in them, it is just with God we should oftentimes go mourning to our graves. Therefore we must set them in a right place, take them as signs and evidences of our comfort, but not to forget to rely rightly on our free justification. . . ."[75]

Richard Sibbes was a preacher of grace and grace alone. Through his reflections on themes such as preaching law and gospel, the covenant, the sacraments, the Christian's personal walk and life in the communion of saints, the nature of assurance, as well as others, Sibbes points us again and again to the sovereign Triune God who alone brings salvation and keeps His people. Indeed, it does not appear hyperbolic in the least to pray in our day that God would grace us with preachers like Richard

The Present Evangelical Crisis

Sibbes who would turn our attention once again to the glory, the majesty, and the holiness of our God as well as to the greatness of His love. Such a recaptured vision is urgently needed for the compromised church and will certainly point the way to restored vitality.

NOTES

1. I have used *godliness* instead of the more common *spirituality* of our day as the most fitting term for the Puritans' reflections on the Christian life. I do this not only because the term *godliness* was their term, but also because it is a stronger term than the more obscure term *spirituality*. The term itself points out the goal.

2. The books and articles on Puritanism are legion. Indeed, the whole concept of the exact nature of "puritanism" is one hotly debated by scholars. Just who exactly were the "Puritans"? What theological, social, political, etc. ideas held them together? To help the reader who is interested in digging deeper, the following list is submitted. The books themselves will give you information on where to go for further study. *On Puritanism in general:* John Adair, *Founding Fathers: The Puritans in England and New England* (Grand Rapids, MI: Baker, 1982); Patrick Collinson, *The Elizabethan Puritan Movement* (Oxford: Oxford University Press, 1967); Susan Doran and Christopher Durston, *Princes, Pastors, and Prelates: The Church and Religion in England, 1529-1689* (London: Routledge, 1991); William Haller, *The Rise of Puritanism* (New York, 1938); J. I. Packer, *A Quest for Godliness: The Puritan Vision of the Christian Life* (Wheaton, IL: Crossway Books, 1990); Leland Ryken, *Worldly Saints* (Grand Rapids, MI: Zondervan, 1986). *On specific points of Puritan theology:* John L. Carson and David W. Hall, eds., *To Glorify and Enjoy God: A Commemoration of the Westminster Assembly* (Edinburgh: Banner of Truth, 1994); Horton Davies, *The Worship of the English Puritans* (Ligonier, PA: Soli Deo Gloria, 1997); Paul Helm, *Calvin and the Calvinists* (Edinburgh: Banner of Truth, 1982)—this book is a critical analysis of R. T. Kendall, *Calvin and English Calvinism to 1649* (Oxford: Oxford University Press, 1979); Brooks Holifield, *The Covenant Sealed: The Development of Puritan Sacramental Theology in Old and New England* (New Haven, CT: Yale, 1974); Ernest Kevan, *The Grace of Law: A Study in Puritan Theology* (Grand Rapids, MI: Baker, 1976); John von Rohr, *The Covenant of Grace in Puritan Thought* (Atlanta: Scholars Press, 1986); Gordon Wakefield, *Puritan Devotion* (London: Epworth Press, 1957); Dewey Wallace, *Puritans and Predestination* (Chapel Hill, NC: University of North Carolina, 1982).

3. Packer, *Quest for Godliness*, p. 22.

4. For by far the most complete biographical and theological portrait of Sibbes, see Mark Dever, "Richard Sibbes and the 'Truly Evangelicall Church of England': A Study in Reformed Divinity and Early Stuart Conformity." Ph.D. Dissertation, Cambridge University, 1992.

5. For a fine outline of this problem, see Ryken, *Worldly Saints*, pp. 1-21.

Richard Sibbes and the Union of the Heart with Christ

6. Thomas Manton, "To the Reader," in Richard Sibbes, "Exposition of II Cor. 1," *Works*, Vol. III (Edinburgh: 1862-1864 [original London, 1655]), p. 4.

7. Richard Sibbes, "The Excellency of the Gospel Above the Law," *Works*, Vol. IV (Edinburgh: 1862-1864), p. 228, hereafter "Excellency." For Sibbes's *Works*, the nineteenth-century Grosart edition has been used (now republished by Banner of Truth). This edition is quite reliable and is generally used in scholarly treatments. From this point forward, all Sibbes references will point to the particular treatise and the volume and page numbers only.

8. See, e.g., Kendall, *Calvin and English Calvinism*, pp. 103-105, and Larzar Ziff, *The Career of John Cotton.* (Princeton, NJ: 1962), pp. 31-32.

9. See Dever, "Richard Sibbes and the 'Truly Evangelicall Church of England,'" pp. 69-70; Julian Davies, *The Caroline Captivity of the Church* (Oxford: Oxford University Press, 1993); H. Gee and W. J. Handy, *Documents Illustrative of English Church History* (London: 1896), pp. 516-518; and J. R. Tanner, *Constitutional Documents of the Reign of James I* (Cambridge: Cambridge University Press, 1961), pp. 80-82.

10. "The Bruised Reed and the Smoking Flax," I:43, hereafter "Bruised Reed."

11. "Excellency," IV:293.

12. See "The Returning Backslider," II:335.

13. "A Description of Christ," I:24. See also: (1) "Commentary on II Cor. 4," IV:340-341, hereafter "II Cor. 4": "Therefore, if we will make men leave sin on good grounds, teach the gospel; else we shall bring them into a civil compass which is good . . . but we should not rest there. Holy duties, and abstaining from gross sins, is a great deal more groundedly enforced from the gospel than the law"; and (2) "The Saint's Privilege," VII:360: "We have not a righteousness of our own; for there are diverse things to be satisfied, God himself, and the law, and our own consciences, and the world. Perhaps we may have a righteousness to satisfy the world, because we live civilly. Oh but that will not satisfy conscience. . . . Conscience will not be contented but with that which will content God, when conscience sees there is such a righteousness found out by the wisdom of God, that contents him. . . . The Spirit convinces that [the righteousness of Christ] belongs to all believers . . . and it is such a righteousness, that when we are clothed with it, we may go through the justice of God."

14. "The Dead Man," VII:400.

15. "The Soul's Conflict," I:174.

16. "Excellency," IV:244.

17. "The Returning Backslider," II:331, emphasis mine.

18. See "The Dead Man," VII:401: "No man by nature hath fellowship with the second Adam till he be grafted into him by faith, which is a mere supernatural thing. In these regards [i.e., union and communion with Christ] every man naturally is dead."

19. All references except note 18 in the two preceding paragraphs are from "Excellency," IV:224. Sibbes's language is reminiscent of Augustine, the

The Present Evangelical Crisis

great Church Father of the fourth and fifth centuries. For a discussion of Augustine on this topic, see Alister E. McGrath, *Iustitia Dei* (Cambridge: 1986), I:25-36. McGrath quotes Augustine on p. 26: "The free will taken captive (*liberum arbitrium captivatum*) does not avail, except for sin; for righteousness, it does not avail, unless it is set free and aided by divine action."

20. All references in this paragraph are from "The Christian Work," V:16-17.

21. Scholars debate the origin of the "covenant of works" terminology in Reformed divinity. Some, like D. A. Weir, argue that Calvin neither used nor taught the idea of "covenant of works" and thus it must have developed later. Others, such as A. A. Woolsey, argue that while the particular phrase might not have been used by Calvin, the idea was nevertheless present in incipient form. My purpose here is not to enter that debate since by the time Sibbes wrote, Reformed thinkers in England concerned with covenantal language generally assumed the existence of these two covenants. For a survey of the debate, see D. A. Weir, *The Origins of the Federal Theology in Sixteenth Century Reformation Thought* (Oxford: Oxford University Press, 1990), and Andrew Woolsey, "Unity and Continuity in Covenantal Thought: A Study in the Reformed Tradition to the Westminster Assembly." Ph.D. Dissertation, University of Glasgow, 1988.

22. All quotations from the preceding six paragraphs are from "The Faithful Covenanter," VI:3-6, emphases his.

23. "II Cor. 1," III:394. Also see "Bowels Opened," II:174: "In the new covenant God works both parts, his own and our parts too. Our love to him, our fear of him, our faith in him, he works all, even as he shews his own love to us."

24. "Divine Meditations," VII:189.

25. Ibid., VII:211.

26. "The Faithful Covenanter," VI:9.

27. "Bowels Opened," II:8.

28. See "II Cor. 1," III:478: ". . . if the Spirit doth all, how shall we know then that we have the Spirit? . . . If we have the Spirit of God to seal us, and to be an earnest . . . even as in our souls, how may a man know that he hath a soul? *by living and moving, by actions vital, &c.*, so we may know he hath the Spirit of God by those actions that come only from the Spirit, which is to the soul as the soul is to the body. . . . [T]he Spirit is in us in the nature of fire . . . *in transforming*. Wheresoever the Spirit dwells, he transforms the soul, he transforms the party like himself holy and gracious" (emphases his).

29. "The Christian Work," V:14.

30. "Bowels Opened," II:46. For other instances where Sibbes equated "heart" with "soul," see, for example, "The Soul's Conflict," I:246, and "Lydia's Conversion," VI:525.

31. "The Matchless Love and Inbeing," VI:403, hereafter "Inbeing." For other places where Sibbes spoke in a similar manner, see "Bruised Reed," I:83; "The Soul's Conflict," I:179; "The Church's Visitation," I:374; and "The Tender Heart," VI:31.

Richard Sibbes and the Union of the Heart with Christ

32. See William Perkins, "A Faithfull and Plaine Exposition Upon the Two First Verses of the Second Chapter of Zephaniah," *Works*, Vol. III (Cambridge: Legate, 1611), 2.425.

33. "The Dead Man," VII:398. What McGrath has written of Calvin could be applied to Sibbes as well: "We are not, therefore, being asked to believe harder that God is loving; we are being asked to allow our lives and wills to be shaped by our faith in a loving God. We are not asked to have more faith in eternal life; we are being asked to allow our faith in eternal life to affect us more deeply here and now. If faith remains something which affects only our minds, it will be prone to doubt and indecision. It must transform our wills and our lives—and by doing so, the quiet confidence of true Christian faith results. As Calvin put it, 'Faith is not a naked and frigid awareness of Christ, but a living and real experience of his power, which produces confidence.'" Alister McGrath, *Roots That Refresh* (London: Hodder, 1992), p. 111.

34. "Lydia's Conversion," VI:525.

35. "Excellency," IV:226.

36. Ibid.

37. "Bowels Opened," II:123.

38. "The Soul's Conflict," I:181.

39. Wakefield, *Puritan Devotion*, p. 102.

40. The scholarly phrase for this double benefit is *duplex gratia Dei* (the double grace of God). For an excellent study of Calvin's understanding of the relationship between justification and sanctification, see Cornelis Paul Venema, "The Twofold Nature of the Gospel in Calvin's Theology: The *Duplex Gratia Dei* and the Interpretation of Calvin's Theology." Ph.D. Dissertation, Princeton Theological Seminary, 1985.

41. "Precious Promises," IV:126, emphasis his.

42. Ibid.

43. All references in this paragraph are from "Excellency," IV:238. For some other places where Sibbes discussed passivity first and activity after in grace, see ibid., IV:205, 221, 230, and "The Pattern of Purity," VII:510-511.

44. See W. K. B. Stoever, *"A Faire and Easie Way to Heaven"* (Middletown, CT: Wesleyan Press, 1978), pp. 138-183.

45. "Divine Meditations," VII:221. For another place where Sibbes argued in a similar manner that one could not have Christ and continue in one's lusts, see "Salvation Applied," V:391.

46. "Bowels Opened," II:183, emphasis mine.

47. "The Returning Backslider," II:334.

48. Ibid., II:425, emphasis his. For Luther on this point, see Martin Luther, "The Freedom of the Christian," in *Three Treatises* (Philadelphia: Fortress Press, 1941).

The Present Evangelical Crisis

49. "The Life of Faith," V:364.

50. "Bowels Opened," II:183.

51. All references in this paragraph are from "The Pattern of Purity," VII:512. For other places where Sibbes linked Christ's life, death, and resurrection to the efficacious and meritorious accomplishment of justification and sanctification, see "The Bruised Reed," I:79; "The Spouse," II:201; "Excellency," IV:254; and "Inbeing," VI:387.

   Note especially, "The Hidden Life," V:209: "*How is Christ our life?* He is every way the cause of the life of grace and glory. And not only so, the cause, but the root and spring in whom it is. We have it from Christ and in Christ. We have it in Christ as a root, and from Christ as a working cause, and by Christ as mediator. For Christ procured life at God's hands, by his sacrifice and death. We have it in Christ as a head, from him as a cause, together with both other persons; and through him as mediator, who by his death made the way to life, appeasing the wrath of God. So we are reconciled and pardoned by the death of Christ" (emphasis his).

52. "The Hidden Life," V:206.

53. "The Difficulty of Salvation," I:400, emphasis his. Also consult "The Returning Backslider," II:390: ". . . when God's children are once converted, *they have a new nature put into them*, like unto Christ, whose Spirit they have. What he hates, they hate. He hates all sin, and nothing but sin. . . . So in the soul of a Christian, so far as grace is renewed, there is an antipathy, aversation, and abhorring of that which is contrary. . . . When grace hath altered the disposition of a man's heart, then sin and he are two; two indeed, in the most opposite terms that may be. . . . We are two now, for we were before nothing but sin" (emphasis his).

54. "Bowels Opened," II:152.

55. All quotations since footnote 54 are from "Excellency," IV:211.

56. "Inbeing," VI:398.

57. "The Spouse," II:207.

58. See "The Pattern of Purity," VII:513.

59. See "Excellency," IV:249.

60. See "The Faithful Covenanter," VI:22-24.

61. "A Breathing After God," II:232, emphasis his. Sibbes continued: "And so the beginning of glory here; for all is not kept for the life to come. For God distils some drops of glory beforehand. We see the beauty of God here, marvellously, even in this world, in regard of the beginning of glory. For upon justification, and the beginning of holiness wrought in our nature by the Spirit, we have inward peace of conscience, and joy and comfort in all discomforts whatsoever. We have not only the oil of grace, but the oil of comfort. Oh! the comfort of the children of God, that are members of the church, that are so in the church, that they are of the church too, that are of the church visible, so as they are of the church invisible. Oh! the comfort that belongs to them, all the comfort in God's book. So you see the wondrous

Richard Sibbes and the Union of the Heart with Christ

sweet prerogatives and privileges we have in all the passages of salvation in the house of God, and in God reconciled in Jesus Christ."

62. Ibid., II:233.

63. "II Cor. 1," III:433.

64. Ibid. See "Bowels Opened," II:133 for another discussion of the communion of saints, this time in "holy conferences."

65. See "The Soul's Conflict," I:186.

66. "The Saint's Privilege," VII:365.

67. "Excellency," IV:223.

68. "The Pattern of Purity," VII:515-516.

69. Some scholars seem to focus too much on this aspect of the Puritans' counsel to those with a weak faith. It is true that they did use the counsel that one could by a "reflex act" see God's work in one's life through the window of one's experience. Nevertheless, the Puritans more often than not pointed the same inquirer to Christ alone as the only mediator and the one whose atonement was fully sufficient to bring those to God who come in faith. For more on the variety that marked Puritan counsel on the question of assurance, see my doctoral dissertation (especially Chapter 3): Paul R. Schaefer, "The Spiritual Brotherhood on the Habits of the Heart: Cambridge Protestants and the Doctrine of Sanctification from William Perkins to Thomas Shepard." D.Phil. Dissertation, Oxford University, 1994.

70. "II Cor. 1," III:467.

71. Ibid., emphasis mine.

72. Ibid., III:464.

73. See, for example, "The Soul's Conflict," I:138 ("Another cause of disquiet is, that men by a natural kind of popery *seek for their comfort too much in sanctification*, neglecting justification, relying too much on their own performances" [emphasis his]). Also, "The Returning Backslider," II:385 (". . . all grace is promised upon our entry and coming into the covenant of grace, upon our believing, when we come with empty hearts and empty hands. . . . Those that are in a state of grace oftentimes want [lack] that comfort in the main point of justification and acceptation to life everlasting, which they should have, because they look to their imperfections, seeing this and that want, and so are swallowed up of discomfort; whereas if we had all the graces in the world, yet we must live by faith, relying upon the merits of Christ. For good works bring us not to heaven, as a cause, but only are helps and comforts to us in our walking to heaven. . . . Therefore, in trouble of conscience we must not look either to our good or ill, but to God's infinite mercy, and to the infinite satisfaction of our blessed Lord Jesus Christ: there, as it were, losing ourselves, seeing our sins as mountains drowned in the infinite sea of his mercy. The blood of Christ! That will pacify and stay the conscience. Nothing else can give rest to our souls. . . . And look to the all-sufficiency of God in Christ, and the promises, whereby we honour God in giving him the glory of his truth, and depart with comfort"). Also, "The Hidden Life," V:207 ("Faith will see God's glorious countenance. Faith

The Present Evangelical Crisis

makes it a glorious life though it be secret. Therefore let us not judge ourselves nor others by appearance. And it is also a *sure* life . . . mark on what grounds it is sure. First, it is hid in *heaven*. No enemy can come there. . . . And it is safe, because it is hid in *Christ*, who purchased it with his blood; who hath trampled upon all opposite powers, over death, and hell itself" [emphases his]). Also, ibid., V:210 ("Therefore in all want of grace, in all temptations and assaults, let us go to the fountain, to the fulness of God's love in Christ. . . . And to this end let us be stirred up to see those means wherein Christ will be effectual, whereby, as by veins, the blood of this spiritual life is conveyed, as the word and sacraments, the communion of saints and all sanctified means, whereby the life of grace and comfort may be conveyed to us"). Also, "The Spiritual Jubilee," V:240 ("When we look upon our sins, let us not so much look upon them in our consciences, as in our surety, Christ. . . . So, whatever is terrible, look on it in Christ first, and see a full discharge of all that may affright thy conscience, and trouble thy peace any way."). Also, "Salvation Applied," V:407 ("Caution 1. *Be not discouraged at thy small measure whatsoever, if in truth, so as to fly off from applying the riches of thy Saviour and sweet husband unto thee*; in whom, whatsoever thy poverty be, if married to him, thou art complete . . . . Caution 2. *Whatsoever pitch of sanctification or mortification thou obtainest, rest not in that, but on the all sufficiency of thy blessed Lord Jesus*, who is thine, and so with him all his obedience, righteousness, and merits of his life, death, and resurrection. . ." [emphases his]).

74. "The Life of Faith," V:369.

75. "Salvation Applied," V:395.

UNITY OF
DOCTRINE AND DEVOTION

Donald S. Whitney

I was the guest preacher for a few days at a church on the West Coast recently, and the pastor took me sightseeing. Our longest stop on this warm autumn day was the bookstore of one of the largest and best-known evangelical seminaries in the country. Since we didn't have the luxury of half a day or more to browse, I headed straight for the section on spirituality and Christian living (I teach the courses in this field at the seminary where I'm a professor). I was delighted to find eight entire bookcases devoted to the subject. Shelf by shelf, however, my delight evaporated into disbelief, then discouragement. Seven of the eight bookcases were crammed with volumes dubiously connected with biblical and evangelical Christianity. Most were written by scholars or churchmen with impressive academic credentials, but who would not sincerely subscribe to one of the established confessions of faith found in historic Christian orthodoxy. These books championed things such as the pursuit of mystical experiences, adopting New Age meditation methods, blending Buddhist thought and devotion with Christianity, incorporating Native American spirituality into the church, harmonizing karma with the Bible, and to one degree or another showing sympathy with Hinduism, shamanism, paganism, and eco-spirituality. The lesson: errors in theology tend to breed errors in spirituality.

Granted, a well-stocked seminary bookstore or library may offer numerous texts outside its own tradition for purposes of research, comparison, or refutation. What troubled me was the presence of so *many* books *so far* from historic evangelical moorings, especially in compari-

Union of Doctrine and Devotion

son with the small percentage of titles from recognized and proven evan-
gelical writers. Why so many Catholics, mystics, New Agers, Quakers,
Hindus, and Buddhists, and why so little from the likes of Bunyan,
Edwards, Müller, and other Reformation-heritage evangelicals?

I started reading in the area of Christian spirituality in the mid-1970s.
I have observed through the years a steady increase in the number of
books by writers *from the evangelical mainstream* whose work betrays
the influence of men and women whose spirituality is not rooted in an
evangelical understanding of God's revelation. They quote extensively
those who speak more of *direct* experiences with God than Scripture-
inaugurated ones. When they discuss prayer, it doesn't sound at all like
the prayers of the New Testament, but rather mystical encounters. Their
meditation techniques sometimes remind you more of relaxation methods or Eastern religions than the Bible. This kind of spiritual counsel is
found not only in obscure books from a seminary far away, but in best
sellers at your local Christian bookstore. Many are probably in your own
library or that of your church. They are penned by people whose names
are common to ministers and laypeople alike.

Nowadays I almost never pick up a book by an evangelical on
Christian spirituality that doesn't rely heavily on Catholic and other non-
evangelical sources. I have on my desk at the moment a new book on the
Christian spiritual disciplines. It is written by one of the pastors of one
of the ten largest churches on the continent. The list of endorsers on the
back jacket reads like a Who's Who of contemporary evangelical leaders. By my count there are, except for Scripture citations, 152 footnotes
in the book where others are quoted. Of these, approximately 108 references are from presumably Christian sources. Only half this number are
from writers who would be considered evangelical, even in the most gen-
erous definition of the term. Twenty percent of the religious quotations
are from Catholic sources. Almost one in eight are from Quakers.

This book is not an exception. Rather, it is typical of books on spirituality from evangelical writers and publishers today. True, this pas-
tor/author doesn't quote from the more outrageous books I saw at the
seminary. In fact, I'm very confident he would speak adamantly against
almost everything I oppose in them. So would nearly all evangelicals. But
he does, like many other evangelicals, lean frequently upon sources that
differ primarily in *degree*, and not necessarily in kind, from the most haz-

ardous writers on spirituality. If errors in theology tend to breed errors in spirituality, and if evangelicals are learning their spirituality from teachers with an aberrant theology, we have a serious problem.

As the rest of this book makes plain, despite all her real and apparent successes, these are not the best days of the church. Part of the contemporary crisis in evangelicalism is the frequent separation of a couple married in Scripture. Who is this couple? They are devotion and doctrine, the Christian life and the Christian mind, spirituality and theology. But it's as though the church has come to believe that the Bible declares, "Choose you this day which you will serve—devotion *or* doctrine." In reality it says, "Watch your life *and* doctrine closely" (1 Tim. 4:16, emphasis added). One of the great needs of the church in every age, but especially today, is a spirituality that is theological and evangelical, as well as an evangelical theology that is spiritual.

A SPIRITUALITY THAT IS THEOLOGICAL AND EVANGELICAL

Each person's spiritual practices are, of course, informed and shaped by his theology. In one sense then, there is no such thing as a spirituality that is not theological. A man or woman prays (or doesn't), for example, on the basis of what he or she believes about God and prayer. Furthermore, the *way* that man or woman prays—reciting Hail Marys, following the A-C-T-S or some other formula, devoting extensive time to praise or the confession of sin, praying through a passage of Scripture, viewing prayer as either primarily supplication or contemplation—reflects that person's theology, though he or she may have never perceived the relationship between belief and prayer.

I contend that we should be more *consciously* theological in our spirituality, striving for clear, overt connections between our doctrine and our devotion. Certain forms of prayer should be rejected and others practiced, not merely because of church tradition or novelty or how they make us feel, but as a direct result of what we believe the Bible teaches. Otherwise our spirituality will be shaped primarily by the theology of others— namely, those whose practices we adopt. And while their spiritual ways and methods may appeal to us, what if they are the fruit of heterodox or erroneous theology? The truth is, many of today's evangelical writers unwittingly usher us to these errors when they say that some of the best

Union of Doctrine and Devotion

models and teachers of Christian spirituality are also the very ones who deny evangelical beliefs.

I am also pleading for evangelicals to practice a distinctly evangelical spirituality. In his book *The Crisis of Piety*, Donald G. Bloesch observed, "In the history of the Christian church two basic types of spirituality can be discerned, the mystical and the evangelical."[1] When, as here, most of Christendom is divided into two enormous groups, it's obvious that precise definitions will be impossible. Broadly speaking, mystical spirituality has been more associated with Catholic, Orthodox, and Quaker streams of spiritual thought, while evangelical spirituality has belonged to the Protestant tradition and/or those groups who have espoused evangelical beliefs (as described elsewhere in this volume).

This is not to say that mystical spirituality and evangelical spirituality don't have many points in common, for they do. The boundary line between them is not always a high, demarcating wall, but sometimes a wide plain of mutually held territory where you are in one as much as in the other. In recent decades, however, evangelicals have increasingly welcomed representatives from the mystical and unorthodox side, inviting them to teach in and even govern certain "spiritual" areas. Despite the confidence of evangelicals that this mystical influence can be confined to supposedly well-marked spiritual enclaves within a person's life, in reality it is hard to allow such infiltration without compromising the borders of doctrinal protection. Mystics are what they are and do what they do because of what they believe. It is virtually impossible to assimilate much of their spirituality without giving ground to the theology that permeates it. The result is that the distinctives of evangelicalism become blurred, and, as Arthur Johnson forewarns in his book on the dangers of mysticism, "If this challenge [of mysticism] is not successfully met evangelicalism will cease to be evangelical."[2]

So what is mysticism? Who are these mystics whose quotations and ideas and methods fill evangelical books on spirituality? As I've indicated, to comprehensively define mysticism is impossible. It has existed for millennia and has manifold connotations. Some hear the term and think of the occult, while others apply it only to mysterious or ecstatic spiritual experiences. Some associate mysticism with eastern religions or secret societies. Unlike these uses of the term, the mystics quoted so deferentially by evangelicals historically are considered *Christian* mystics. An evangelical writer with more sympathies than I to mysticism has character-ized it this way: "Christian mysticism seeks to describe an experienced, direct, nonabstract, unmediated, loving knowledge of God, a knowing or seeing so direct as to be called union with God."[3] With this under-standing, I want to comment on four of the dangers of mysticism.

THE DANGERS OF MYSTICISM

1. Mysticism tends to overemphasize direct, subjective experiences with God rather than experiences rooted in and interpreted by Scripture and reason.

In addition to the reference to "direct" experiences with God in the definition above, notice the same terminology used by Michael Cox in his *Handbook of Christian Spirituality*. A proponent of mysticism, he writes of "the strict and generally accepted definition of mysticism—that is—the direct personal experience of Ultimate Reality, of God."[4] Evelyn Underhill, whose book *The Mystics of the Church* is a standard text on the subject by a devotee, also characterizes mysticism as finding God "through the soul's secret and direct experience."[5] While mysticism can't be reduced to a single and identical experience, "direct experiences with God" typify it as much as anything. For this reason I will devote more space to this danger than to the others.

The direct experiences with God encouraged by mystics are dis-tinguished from those that the Holy Spirit mediates through Scripture. Rather than beginning with a specific passage of God's revelation of Himself and a reasoned understanding of and reflection upon that, mystics often find greater depth and spiritual riches in meditative expe-riences that spring from a sanctified imagination. In spiritual matters, the intuitive experience begins to take priority over the cognitive one. The inevitable result of this kind of spirituality is that the importance of the Bible is to some degree depreciated, despite assurances to the contrary.

This is not to say that believers do not have "direct" experiences with God the Holy Spirit. Nor am I saying there is no use for God's gift of the imagination in prayer and meditation. Further, I am not suggesting that every valid experience with God must start with a time of Bible reading.

Union of Doctrine and Devotion

I believe every Christian has moments every day when the Holy Spirit spontaneously prompts him or her with thoughts about God or the things of God. It is every believer's privilege to improve such moments by dwelling on these Spirit-initiated thoughts, and this may lead to profound encounters with the Lord. Beyond this, even things such as a glorious sunset, the sparkling radiance of the stars, and the free laughter of children are often the means of transporting us directly to experiences of fellowship with Him. And sometimes the Lord sovereignly manifests a sense of His presence in ways that are almost atmospheric. Countless accounts from church history bear witness to the nearly tangible presence of the Spirit of God during times of true revival. Haven't you had occasions in both public and private worship when you have had an unusual spiritual awareness that "the Lord is here"?

Yes, direct experiences with God are valid, but what is *normative*? Evangelicals with a consciously theological spirituality would assert that encounters with God that begin with *Scripture* should have the central place in our spiritual experiences. Scripture-induced experiences with God should be the norm in our spirituality, not the exception; and the Scriptures are the standard by which all other spiritual experiences are evaluated.

Try as we might, our spiritual life does not begin by attempting to experience God in some direct way, but by God working toward us through Scripture. The apostle Paul put it this way: "For since in the wisdom of God the world through its wisdom did not know him, God was pleased through the foolishness of what was preached to save those who believe" (1 Cor. 1:21). The evangelistic method of Jesus and the apostles was not to urge people to seek direct experiences with God; instead they went about preaching and teaching the Scriptures (see, for instance, Mark 1:14-15). And Jesus did not say that once we have spiritual life we live by direct mystical experience with God; rather, we "live . . . on every word that comes from the mouth of God" (Matt. 4:4). "All Scripture is God-breathed and is useful for teaching, rebuking, correcting and training in righteousness, *so that* the man of God may be thoroughly equipped for every good work" (2 Tim. 3:16-17, emphasis added). That includes the "good work" of growing in the knowledge of God and likeness to Christ.

So in Scripture the normative method of meeting God is *through Scripture*. This is true not just because of the great wisdom in the Bible or the intellectual stimulation we gain from deep thought on it, but because by the Holy Spirit we *experience* Christ through the Scriptures (see John 5:39). The inspired words do not merely inform us; rather, "the word of God is living and active" (Heb. 4:12). The truths inflame our minds and burn in our hearts, but not in the same way that the reading of Shakespeare or Churchill's Battle of Britain speeches might. The Spirit of God works through the words of God to help us grow in the new life He's given us. We hear God speaking through them to us in ways that nourish us, encourage us, and give us hope that no mortal can.

We read, say, of "Christ, who is your life" in Colossians 3:4, and meditating on that, our hearts turn to Christ like flowers to the sun. Our souls are refreshed by Him. Our hearts are flooded with joy; our lips overflow with thanksgiving and adoration. Our desire to live for Him and speak of Him is freshly kindled. This is the sort of spiritual experience we need, and it comes when we seek Him through the way He has revealed Himself to us—that is, through Scripture. This is spirituality rooted in theology—first the revelation of God, then the response of the spirit of the believer. The heart is ignited by the flame of truth burning through the mind.

Suppose I decided to pursue a more mystical method. I want to spend some time in meditation, and, being a good evangelical, I do some Bible reading first, maybe even reading Colossians 3 before I begin to meditate. But instead of meditating on what the Bible says about Christ in Colossians 3:4, I decide simply that I want to meditate on Christ and experience Him directly. Is this possible? Certainly. Is this ever valid? Yes. One more question, though. What will guide my meditation? I can't meditate on Christ unless I know who He is and what He is like. That information must come from my mind, and my mind must have acquired it from the Bible. Otherwise my meditation is feeling in the dark of my imagination, looking for a "Christ" about whom I know nothing. In fact, I may have a mystical experience that is out of this world and believe that I've encountered Christ. But how will I know what or whom I've encountered? By what standard will I interpret and understand the experience? We are ultimately cast back upon Scripture and Spirit-illuminated reason, not just a sanctified imagination.

Perhaps the most influential book on spirituality in the twentieth century is Richard Foster's *Celebration of Discipline*. The first (1978) edi-

Union of Doctrine and Devotion

tion of his work was criticized because of his overly mystical approach in certain areas, particularly meditation. To his credit, Foster responded in the revised edition by removing his more controversial meditation techniques involving the imagination. In their place he included new material on "Sanctifying the Imagination." He did not suggest detailed methods this time; rather, he contrasted an active use of the imagination in meditation with "a merely cerebral approach."[6] I, too, am opposed to a "merely cerebral approach," and I think the giants of historic evangelical spirituality would rise up in chorus with me.

I would also insist that to give primacy to reason over the imagination in a spiritual experience is not to have "a merely cerebral approach." Whatever role the imagination plays, it must be informed by Scripture and guided by reason. A theological and evangelical spirituality is rational before it is emotional. God has made us in such a way that we are to be Spirit-filled, Scripture-saturated people steering by reason, with imagination and emotion, crucial as they are, filling supportive, but not directive, roles. We want to be rational, yet not excessively so as to be rational*istic* on the one hand, nor led by imaginative speculation on the other. This is true in our experiences with God just as it is in all our other daily activities and responsibilities.

Foster's Quaker pen has done much good, but I know of no other writer who has so successfully introduced evangelicals to mystical writers. I am concerned when I read quotations like the one he cites from the seventeenth-century French mystic, Madame Jeanne Guyon: "May I hasten to say that the kind of prayer I am speaking of is not a prayer that comes from your mind. It is a prayer that begins in the heart. . . . Prayer offered to the Lord from your mind simply would not be adequate. Why? Because your mind is very limited. The mind can pay attention to only one thing at a time. Prayer that comes out of the heart is not interrupted by thinking!"[7]

Is this the way Jesus taught us to pray? Does the New Testament teach that there is "prayer that comes from your mind" and that it is inadequate when compared to a completely different kind of prayer, heart prayer? Doubtless one may speak words in prayer that are not heartfelt or sincere, but that's not the same as claiming that the heart can communicate directly with God and the mind know nothing about it. How do you know when your heart is praying? How do you know that what your heart is doing is praying and not something else? Again, we cannot accept these mystical distinctions, as devout as they sound, and we must hold fast to the priority of the Christian mind.

Has some of this sounded a bit esoteric to you? Are you unconvinced of the influence of mysticism in mainstream evangelical life? True, you may never find yourself in the same pew with a monkish-looking person in a hooded robe, dressed as you might imagine some medieval mystic would. But you probably can see mysticism at your church, albeit wearing modern clothing. A common way you'll see mysticism expressed today is in the desire of some to minimize preaching in order to pursue "more dramatic" experiences with God. Apparently they think that the experiences they seek are *more* the work of the Holy Spirit than His life-giving work through the proclamation of Scripture.

Another evidence of mysticism may occur when a woman uses the Bible primarily for daily inspirational thoughts, or when a man views it mainly as a collection of principles for successful living, loving, working, or parenting. Even the familiar evangelical distinction between "head knowledge" and "heart knowledge" is a reflection of distinctives emphasized in mysticism. As we have seen, use of this terminology implies that you can "know" something in your heart without any conscious or subconscious involvement of your mind. It's true that you can have the knowledge of something, such as the work of Christ, without believing it. You can even believe that all the Bible says about Jesus is factually true without committing yourself to Him. But this is quite different from saying you have a mystical faculty to perceive truth about Jesus that bypasses the mind.

And as I've said, if you really want proof of mysticism's penetration into evangelicalism, pick up a book on spirituality or the spiritual disciplines. Look for the quotations by Gregory of Nyssa, Dionysius the Areopagite, Meister Eckhart, John Ruysbroeck, Julian of Norwich, *The Cloud of Unknowing*, Teresa of Avila, John of the Cross, Francis de Sales, George Fox, Madame Guyon, Francois Fenelon, John Woolman, Thomas Merton, etc.

In contrast to the *modus operandi* of many mystics, one of the driving principles of the Protestant Reformation was *sola Scriptura*—that is, Scripture alone is the final authority. This was set against the claim of the Roman clergy that the collective wisdom and experience of the church

Union of Doctrine and Devotion

was equal in authority with Scripture. While most evangelicals would reject Rome's claim, they affirm it in practice when they seek experiences with God that are self-generated and self-interpreted and therefore imply that the Bible is at best supplemental to the experience. A spirituality descended from the Reformation maintains that the only infallible guide to any spiritual experience is in the inspired written Word.

One of the godliest and most powerful preachers of the twentieth century was Martyn Lloyd-Jones of London. No stranger to deep experiences with God, he proposed:

> Let us imagine I follow the mystic way. I begin to have experiences; I think God is speaking to me; how do I know it is God who is speaking to me? How can I know I am not speaking to man; how can I be sure that I am not the victim of hallucinations, since this has happened to many of the mystics? If I believe in mysticism as such without the Bible, how do I test my experiences? How do I prove the Scriptures; how do I know I am not perhaps being deluded by Satan as an angel of light in order to keep me from the true and living God? I have no standard. . . .
> "Very well," says someone, "if that is your criticism of mysticism, what is the evangelical way in order that I may come to this knowledge and fellowship with God?" It is quite simple, and it is this: It always starts with the Scriptures; it says that the Scriptures are my only authority and final standard with regard to these matters, with regard to a knowledge of God. The evangelical doctrine tells me not to look into myself but to look into the Word of God; not to examine myself, but to look at the revelation that has been given to me. It tells me that God can only be known in His own way, the way which has been revealed in the Scriptures themselves.[8]

I was discussing my concerns about mysticism with Minneapolis pastor/scholar/author John Piper. After telling him about my disturbing experience in the West Coast seminary bookstore, I asked, "Where do we draw the line? At what point can we objectively say that a person goes too far in seeking an experience with God?"

Piper answered, "When he closes his Bible."

Sola Scriptura.

The Present Evangelical Crisis

2. *Mysticism tends to assume too much about man's natural condition.*

Every definition of mysticism that I've found, including those listed above, seems to assume that all people have a natural capacity to experience God. Similarly, Catholic mystics are part of a religious environment that assures people they have the power to combine their efforts with God's grace in matters of salvation. Both positions are categorically rejected by evangelicals. Mystics seldom write from the position that justification by the grace of God alone through faith alone in Christ alone is a prerequisite for communion with God. For that matter, Catholic mystics develop their spirituality in a tradition that officially rejects this doctrine.

Bloesch protests that evangelicals would "be surprised at the strong defense of free grace that we find among many of these people."[9] Of the five he cites as evidence, two lived prior to the Reformation debate on this matter. The small minority of Catholic mystics who might be shown to trust in Christ alone without any mixture of their works for salvation are anomalies, holding their positions in contradiction to the established dogma of their own church.

Notice the assumption of man's innate spiritual abilities in the following examples. The widely quoted Meister Eckhart (ca.1260-1327), for example, spoke of the divine "spark" in every soul, a spark "that is indistinguishable from God Himself."[10] Matthew Cox, a Catholic who has written on Eckhart, says of this soul spark: "Here the presumption is that God is already within the soul, which equates with the Hindu conception of Brahman the universal deity and Atman, the eternal deity within each individual soul."[11]

George Fox, the father of Quakerism and patron saint of Quaker spirituality, believed he was given a divine revelation from God—namely, that a divine Light shone in every person that they could follow to salvation. "This," says a note in *The Journal of George Fox*, "is the central teaching of George Fox. Everything else comes out of this elemental truth."[12] Fox believed he "was commanded to turn people to that inward Light, Spirit, and Grace, by which all might know their salvation and their way to God; even that Divine Spirit which would lead them into all truth, and which I infallibly knew would never deceive any."[13] In *Christian Mysticism*, which Cox calls "one of the great books of Christian mysticism,"[14] W. R. Inge says, "The Divine spark already shines within us. . . ."[15]

Mysticism reflects this optimism about the human condition by its frequent use of words such as "ladder," "ascent," "climbing," etc., which speak of self-effort. This is also assumed in the traditional three stages of mystical progress. As Cox explains: "Classically, the Mystic Way—the ladder of perfection or *scala perfectionis*—has been divided into three stages: The Purgative Life, the Illuminative Life and the unitive or Contemplative Life."[16] Some contemporary writers see no difficulty in modifying this approach to fit evangelical spirituality.[17] While passages supporting the biblical experiences of confession and repentance, illumination, and meditation abound, nowhere do we find these given as stages of the Christian life. In contrast, when evangelical theology has spoken of stages in the Christian experience it has been in terms of the biblical categories of justification, sanctification, and glorification.

The Bible does not speak of any "divine spark" of life, but rather says that man's natural condition is, "you were dead in your transgressions and sins . . . we were by nature objects of wrath" (Eph. 2:1, 3). Furthermore, "The man without the Spirit does not accept the things that come from the Spirit of God, for they are foolishness to him, and he cannot understand them, because they are spiritually discerned" (1 Cor. 2:14). That's why, contrary to what many mystics purport, "There is no one who understands, no one who seeks God" (Rom. 3:11) until, by grace, the Holy Spirit begins to work through the Gospel to bring a person to Christ.

Scripture is clear that communion with God does not come through some mystical effort at ascending to God, or descending deep within oneself to find God, but through hearing and believing the Word of God. "But the righteousness that is by faith says: 'Do not say in your heart, "Who will ascend into heaven?"' (that is, to bring Christ down) 'or "Who will descend into the deep?"' (that is, to bring Christ up from the dead). But what does it say? 'The word is near you; it is in your mouth and in your heart,' that is, the word of faith we are proclaiming" (Rom. 10:6-8).

3. Mysticism tends to misunderstand the purpose of the work of Jesus Christ.

The definition of Christian mysticism at the beginning of this section spoke of it as an experience that is "unmediated," in other words, without any mediator between the mystic and God. While the mystic would confess that Jesus is God, terms such as "unmediated" imply no dependence upon Christ to make the experience possible. Not that Christ is ignored; for some He is all their focus. Underhill classifies mystics as either "theocentric" or "Christocentric." But even the "Christocentric" ones, according to Underhill, tend to view "the Risen and Exalted Christ" as "Master, Companion, and Helper of the soul." She refers to Jesus as the "Founder" of Christianity and reports that He "is to His closest followers not merely a prophet, pattern of conduct, or Divine figure revealed in the historic past, but the object here and now of an experienced communion of the most vivid kind."[18] While Christ is all these things, there is no emphasis on Him as Redeemer, which is His most important work. He is mentioned as "Risen and Exalted," not primarily because of our justification as the Scripture emphasizes (Rom. 4:25), but for other reasons.

After broad exposure to the mystics, Donald Bloesch concludes, "Christian mystics are inclined to speak of Jesus more as the exemplar of piety than as the Saviour from sin."[19] Martyn Lloyd-Jones agrees: "The danger of mysticism is to concentrate so much on the Lord's work *in* us that it forgets the Lord's work *for* us. In other words, it is so concerned about this immediate work upon the soul that it quite forgets the preliminary work that had to be done before anything could be done upon the soul."[20] If, through repentance and faith in the life and death of Christ, a person has not experienced the benefits of this "preliminary work," no mystical experience will be of any benefit beyond the pleasure of the moment.

What is "of first importance," wrote Paul, is "that Christ died for our sins according to the Scriptures" (1 Cor. 15:3). Spiritual communion with God is impossible until a person comes in faith to Christ for access to the Father. No amount of "spirituality" can bring anyone to God, but only the work of Him who said, "No one comes to the Father except through Me" (John 14:6).

Union of Doctrine and Devotion

Lloyd-Jones's warning about the mystics' view of Christ is even more bold:

> Indeed, I do not hesitate to go further and say that mysticism, as a whole, even tends to make our Lord Himself unnecessary. That is a very serious statement, but I am prepared to substantiate it. There have been people who have been mystical and who claim that their souls have immediate access to God. They say that just as they are, they have but to relax and let go and let God speak to them and He will do so; they do not mention the Lord Jesus Christ.[21]

As there are so many mystics and such diversity among them, Lloyd-Jones's comments wouldn't apply universally. Yet evangelicals who read the mystics, or read those who celebrate them, should not seek "unmediated" experiences with God, "For there is one God and one mediator between God and men, the man Christ Jesus" (1 Tim. 2:5).

4. Mysticism tends to overemphasize the introspective, individual, and detached elements of spirituality to the detriment of the outward, corporate, and everyday aspects of the Christian life.

It is possible to overgeneralize with mystics, just as it is with evangelicals or any other large group. Numerous mystics were not isolationists. Eckhart, Francis, Catherine of Genoa, and Catherine of Sienna are outstanding examples. Still, even an admirer of the mystics like Margaret Furse admitted, "Asceticism seems to be the ever-present companion of mysticism."[22] Sometimes it is objected that mystics were not disconnected individuals but usually were members of monastic communities. But even this is an admission that, unlike the spirituality of the Reformers and the Puritans, mystical spirituality was configured in the cloister and not the everyday world of most Christians.

"The emphasis upon detachment and separation," opines Bloesch,

> . . . . accounts for the glorification of celibacy in mystical religion and the disparagement of marriage. Some mystics, such as Nicolaus of Flue, left their wives and children in order to culti-

The Present Evangelical Crisis

vate the interior life of devotion. Angela of Folino even prayed for the death of her family so that she might be free to give her life wholly to God. John Cassian said that is impossible for married people to reach the heights of contemplation.[23]

The same apostle who affirmed "Christ in you, the hope of glory" (Col. 1:27) also declared, "God was reconciling the world to himself in Christ" (2 Cor. 5:19). The biblical Christian will have a multidirectional orientation: both selfward and Godward, inward and outward, to himself and to others, including his family, his church, his neighbor, and his world. This is the way of Christ.

This means that believers won't wrap themselves in a spiritual cocoon and separate from all organized bodies of believers. Some want to become virtual evangelical monks, poring over mystical writings in their home monastery, disdaining the "unspiritual" people down at the church. This is neither biblical, nor evangelical.

More broadly, this means evangelicals won't isolate themselves in their Christian village to practice their spirituality. As Alister McGrath wrote in *Spirituality in an Age of Change*: "Just as the Reformers rejected a retreat to the monasteries, so their modern heirs must reject a retreat into the narrow withdrawn confines of Christian subculture. The world at its worst needs Christians at their best."[24]

PAY ATTENTION TO YOUR DOCTRINE

The same day I visited the seminary bookstore, I perused the shelves of a sizable Christian bookstore on the campus of one of America's most famous churches. While there were plenty of books on practical Christian living by popular evangelical authors, serious theological works were almost as scarce as books advocating atheism. Why were the shelves so fat with pragmatic books on dieting, prayer, finances, and sports figures, and so lean of theological works from Luther and Calvin or pastor/scholars like the seventeenth-century Puritans or the twentieth-century's Martyn Lloyd-Jones?

Remember the command of 1 Timothy 4:16, "Watch your life *and* doctrine closely." Our spirituality goes arm in arm with our theology. One of the reasons many evangelicals who write on spiritual-

Union of Doctrine and Devotion

ity esteem the mystics so highly is because they have read the Reformers, the Puritans, and doctrinal preachers like Lloyd-Jones so comparatively little.

C. S. Lewis once wrote of the benefit he had received from mystical books such as *On the Imitation of Christ, Scale of Perfection,* and *Revelations.* He refers to them as books of devotion. (Let me reiterate that there is a mixture of much devotional good in many of these volumes.) Then he added, "For my part, I tend to find the doctrinal books often more helpful in devotion than the devotional books, and I rather suspect that the same experience may await many others. I believe that many . . . would find that their heart sings unbidden while they are working their way through a tough bit of theology."[25]

We must pay attention to our doctrine because it is the fuel for the fire that burns in the heart. Heart-fires that burn only on emotion or experience will flame out soon after the experience or once the emotion is replaced by another. R. C. Sproul is right: "There can be nothing in the heart that is not first in the mind. Though it is possible to have theology in the head without its piercing the soul, it cannot pierce the soul without first being grasped by the mind."[26]

The truth of God is the surest foundation for passion for God. "Not to care about truth," John Piper warns, "is not to care about God. To love God passionately is to love truth passionately."[27] Do you long for the Spirit of God to give you deeper experiences of fellowship with the Father? Expect Him to minister these to you only through the truth of Scripture, for God the Spirit is "the Spirit of truth" (John 15:26; 16:13). Remember, too, that Jesus said that those who worship God "must worship in spirit *and* in truth" (John 4:24, emphasis added).

This balance of devotion and doctrine is illustrated repeatedly in the life of the apostle to the Gentiles. Paul was never more doxological than when he was his most theological. It was after eleven chapters of the most theologically deep material he ever wrote that he rapturously exclaimed, "Oh, the depth of the riches of the wisdom and knowledge of God! How unsearchable his judgments, and his paths beyond tracing out! For from him and through him and to him are all things. To him be the glory forever! Amen" (Rom. 11:33, 36). Do you want similar experiences of enjoying God? Delight yourself in the truth of God as Paul did.

The Present Evangelical Crisis

AN EVANGELICAL THEOLOGY THAT'S SPIRITUAL

After Paul finished the theology and doxology of the first eleven chapters of Romans, he then launched into a discourse on practical spirituality. Even when the theology is right, there's still a need for intentionality in spirituality. Paul combined both elements in 1 Timothy 4:16, "Watch your life *and* doctrine closely." For the Christian, to "watch your life" in this context means, "Watch your *spiritual* life," for that relates to everything in life. I've been asserting that we evangelicals need to be consciously evangelical and theological in our spirituality, and I think that is the larger problem in today's compromised church. But it is always wise to follow the biblical pattern and balance this concern with the reminder that we should *demonstrate* our theology with a godly *life*.

Obviously those who are drawn to mystical spirituality, both the writers of evangelical spirituality books as well as those who read them, turn to the mystics because they find something in these older authors they aren't getting elsewhere. They attend (or lead) churches, whether sedate or lively, with theologically vacuous worship, so they rarely sense the presence of God there. The preaching they hear is either orthodoxy without passion or style without substance. Very little in their weekly evangelical orbit feeds the fire of their affection for God. Then somewhere they read a snippet from a mystic whose expression of ardor for God puts into words their own spiritual longings, and they feel as though they've at last found a kindred spirit. The more they read, the more they realize how evangelicalism has spiritually undernourished them.

It doesn't take long before these people believe that while evangelicals are tops in evangelism and Bible study, no one compares with the spirituality of the mystics (or those who quote them). McGrath echoes, "People need help with prayer, devotion, and personal discipline—and if evangelicalism is not providing it, is it really surprising that they may turn elsewhere?"[28] They won't have to go elsewhere when their church fills the worship and preaching with much of God and teaches them how to "discipline [themselves] for the purpose of godliness" (1 Tim. 4:7b, NASB).

Lloyd-Jones believed that mysticism "almost invariably comes in as a protest against a sort of formalism and deadness in the Church. . . . Mysticism is also a protest against rationalism and a tendency to over-intellectualise the Christian faith. . . . Mysticism then is concerned to put

Union of Doctrine and Devotion

emphasis upon the reality of the knowledge of God and communion with Him."[29] If he is right, then the return of interest in mysticism is itself a testimony to the reality of the current crisis in evangelicalism and of the need for reformation and revival.

WHAT SHOULD WE DO?

1. Choose role models and teachers of spirituality who are solid theologically.

Think what we imply when we accept as great masters of spirituality those who have serious errors in their theology. It's as though we're saying, "If you want to know Jesus, come to us, for we evangelicals have the true Gospel. But to know Him *intimately*, let us direct you to people we know do *not* proclaim the true Gospel." In other words, our ministry becomes, "Come hear *us* proclaim the message of *justification*; then go read *them* for the message of *sanctification*. Hear *our* message to *know* Christ; then read *theirs* to be *like* Christ." Do you see how inconsistent this is?

Many of the mystics invoked by evangelicals today are post-Reformation Catholics, including Teresa of Avila, John of the Cross, Francis de Sales, Madame Guyon, Francois Fenelon, Therese of Lisieux, Thomas Merton, Henri Nouwen, etc. Why do we want to send our hungriest disciples to those who do not preach justification by faith alone, who pray to Mary and the saints, and who believe that the Bible is not the only source of God's infallible truth? I am not saying there is nothing we can learn from these writers. I am simply wondering why, if our time for reading is so limited, we should go to the mystics *first*.

Evangelicals have an unsurpassed heritage of teachers and models of spirituality waiting to be discovered. Read Reformers like Luther and Calvin, both their doctrinal and devotional works. We wrongly picture them only as professors who toiled over ponderous theological tomes. They were among history's most brilliant theologians, but they were also pastors and men of deep piety. They forged both their theology and spirituality, not in the ivory towers of academia, but often under persecution and in the turbulence of great cities in a rapidly changing time. McGrath comments, "The spirituality of the Reformation was organically related to its theology.[30] . . . Reformation spirituality represents a challenge to return to the roots of our faith. . . . [It] is young at heart, with a long and distinguished future ahead of it—if we are prepared to use it and act upon it. It is like a seed, dormant but not dead, which has lain inactive for many years but is capable of being reactivated and of growing."[31]

Other giants of devotion and doctrine were the Puritans. Those who know the least about the Puritans, I have learned by asking, deride them the most. Leland Ryken's *Worldly Saints: The Puritans As They Really Were*[32] reveals that what most people dislike about the Puritans is myth. In his *Quest for Godliness: The Puritan Vision of the Christian Life*, J. I. Packer writes that the Puritans stand like the California redwoods in the forest of church history. He has said elsewhere that corporately they lived more like the church in the New Testament than any other large group of Christians since the days of the New Testament. Why not find out why Packer makes such an audacious claim? Read John Bunyan's allegories, *The Pilgrim's Progress* or *The Holy War*. Dig into John Owen's masterpiece on *The Mortification of Sin*, or *Spiritual Mindedness*, *The Glory of Christ*, or *Communion with God*. You will find your heart soaring as you pray your way through *The Valley of Vision: A Collection of Puritan Prayers and Devotion*.[33] Banner of Truth has published a series of "Puritan Paperbacks" that serves as a delicious introduction to the Puritan theology/spirituality.

There's no greater American figure displaying the fusion of reason and fire than Jonathan Edwards. Most associate his name only with his great sermon, "Sinners in the Hands of an Angry God," unaware that he preached more often on the sweetness of Christ and of heaven than anything else. Read his sermon "Concerning the End for which God Created the World" or his accounts of the glorious revivals that occurred under his ministry.[34] He also edited the enormously influential *Life and Diary of David Brainerd*. I've read nothing in years that so overwhelmed me with a sense of the glory of God as his sermon "Nothing Upon Earth Can Represent the Glories of Heaven."[35]

No one is more godly than these men and women. No one is more prayerful than an evangelical hero like George Müller who recorded 50,000 specific answers to prayer.[36] No one whom we could read or quote is unassailable in life or doctrine, which is all the more reason why our lives and doctrines should focus primarily on Christ and the Bible. While I have criticized Catholic, Quaker, and other mystic sources quoted by

Union of Doctrine and Devotion

many evangelical writers on spirituality, it would also be easy to find fault with the lives and doctrines of the Reformers, Puritans, and those of their doctrinal and spiritual heritage. This is because all but Christ are sinners and imperfect, both inwardly and outwardly. However, the Bible itself commands us in Hebrews 13:7, "Remember your leaders, who spoke the word of God to you. Consider the outcome of their way of life and imitate their faith." Thus while Christ is our Lord and Savior and ultimate example, we should also remember, consider, and imitate those who have been spiritual leaders and have given us the Word of God. Clearly the better examples are those whose lives and doctrines, while not perfect, as a whole are the most faithful to God's Word. To be true to Scripture and our heritage, evangelicals cannot say the most faithful examples come from the ranks of the mystics.

It is one thing for evangelicals to be aware of mystical spirituality and, where it is consistent with Scripture, to appreciate its strengths. It is another to embrace it without realizing that it can never be fully separated from the family of beliefs that produced it. As Arthur L. Johnson, author of *Faith Misguided: Exposing the Dangers of Mysticism*, explained, "To adopt mysticism as a legitimate way of approaching God is to reject the basis of the Protestant Reformation and the basis of evangelicalism."[37]

2. Devote ourselves to both doctrine and the disciplines.

My observation is that most of those in both the pulpit and the pew are not studying doctrine. Consequently, we are impoverishing our intimacy with God, our discernment of error, and our growth in grace. Church leaders express concern that if they emphasize doctrine, people will lose interest. But who wants to fill a church with spiritually weak people? If the leadership does not manifest a contagious love of theology, who will? Without it we have a congregation of spiritual "infants, tossed back and forth by the waves, and blown here and there by every wind of teaching" (Eph. 4:14).

As to discipline, it is more easily admired in our spiritual heroes than imitated. And yet, the only way forward to spiritual maturity is down the path of the classic congregational and personal spiritual disciplines.[38] "Discipline yourself," is the word, "for the purpose of godliness" (1 Tim. 4:7b, NASB). The spiritual disciplines are not an end in themselves,

The Present Evangelical Crisis

as evangelicals have sometimes made them. They are a means, and the end is godliness—i.e., growth in the knowledge and likeness of Christ. But there is no godliness without them.

Devotion and doctrine. Let the reunion begin!

NOTES

1. Donald G. Bloesch, *The Crisis of Piety* (Grand Rapids, MI: Eerdmans, 1968), p. 95.

2. Arthur L. Johnson, *Faith Misguided: Exposing the Dangers of Mysticism* (Chicago: Moody Press, 1988), p. 43.

3. D. D. Martin, "Mysticism," in ed. Walter A. Elwell, *Evangelical Dictionary of Theology* (Grand Rapids, MI: Baker, 1984), p. 744.

4. Michael Cox, *Handbook of Christian Spirituality*, rev. ed. (San Francisco: Harper & Row, 1985), p. 14.

5. Evelyn Underhill, *The Mystics of the Church* (London: James Clarke & Co., n.d.), p. 15.

6. Richard J. Foster, *Celebration of Discipline*, rev. ed. (San Francisco: Harper & Row, 1988), p. 25.

7. As quoted in Richard J. Foster and Kathryn A. Yanni, *Celebrating the Disciplines* (New York: Harper Collins, 1992), p. 87.

8. D. Martyn Lloyd-Jones, *Fellowship with God* (Wheaton, IL: Crossway Books, 1993), p. 95.

9. Donald G. Bloesch, "Is Spirituality Enough?" in John H. Armstrong, ed. *Roman Catholicism* (Chicago: Moody Press, 1994), p. 158.

10. Margaret Lewis Furse, *Mysticism* (Nashville: Abingdon, 1977), p. 104.

11. Cox, *Handbook of Christian Spirituality*, p. 22.

12. George Fox, *The Journal of George Fox*, with an introduction by Henry J. Cadbury (Richmond, IN: Friends United Press, 1976), p. 101.

13. Ibid., p. 103.

14. Cox, *Handbook of Christian Spirituality*, p. 27.

15. W. R. Inge, *Christian Mysticism* (New York: Charles Scribner's Sons, 1933), p. 7.

16. Cox, *Handbook of Christian Spirituality*, p. 28.

17. M. Robert Mulholland, Jr. devotes an entire chapter to these stages in what he calls "The Classical Christian Pilgrimage," in *Invitation to a Journey* (Downers Grove, IL: InterVarsity, 1993), pp. 79-101.

18. Underhill, *The Mystics of the Church*, pp. 23-24.

19. Bloesch, *The Crisis of Piety*, p. 117.

Union of Doctrine and Devotion

20. Lloyd-Jones, *Fellowship with God*, p. 94.

21. Ibid.

22. Furse, *Mysticism*, p. 104.

23. Bloesch, *The Crisis of Piety*, p. 103.

24. Alister E. McGrath, *Spirituality in an Age of Change* (Grand Rapids, MI: Zondervan, 1994), p. 56.

25. C. S. Lewis, *God in the Dock*, ed. Walter Hooper (Grand Rapids, MI: Eerdmans, 1970), pp. 204-205.

26. R. C. Sproul, *Essential Truths of the Christian Faith* (Wheaton, IL: Tyndale, 1992), p. xx.

27. John Piper, *A Godward Life* (Sisters, OR: Multnomah, 1997), p. 106.

28. McGrath, *Spirituality in an Age of Change*, p. 14.

29. Lloyd-Jones, *Fellowship with God*, pp. 91-92.

30. McGrath, *Spirituality in an Age of* Change, p. 32.

31. Ibid., pp. 190-191.

32. Leland Ryken, *Worldly Saints: The Puritans As They Really Were* (Grand Rapids, MI: Zondervan, 1986).

33. Arthur Bennett, ed., *The Valley of Vision* (Edinburgh: The Banner of Truth, 1975).

34. All of these are found in the two-volume *The Works of Jonathan Edwards* published by The Banner of Truth. Some of these titles can be obtained separately.

35. Jonathan Edwards, "Nothing Upon Earth Can Represent the Glories of Heaven," in *The Works of Jonathan Edwards*, Vol. 14, *Sermons and Discourses 1723-1729*, ed. Kenneth Minkema (New Haven, CT: Yale, 1997), pp. 134-160.

36. See Roger Steer, *George Muller* (Wheaton, IL: Harold Shaw, 1981).

37. Johnson, *Faith Misguided: Exposing the Dangers of Mysticism*, p. 149.

38. On the corporate spiritual disciplines, see Donald S. Whitney, *Spiritual Disciplines Within the Church* (Chicago: Moody Press, 1996). Regarding the personal spiritual disciplines see Whitney, *Spiritual Disciplines for the Christian Life* (Colorado Springs, CO: NavPress, 1991).

EVANGELICAL MINISTRY:
THE PURITAN CONTRIBUTION

Sinclair B. Ferguson

Few epochs in the history of the Christian church can boast so many out-standing examples of Christian pastoral ministry as the Puritan period of the late sixteenth and the seventeenth centuries when such men as William Perkins, Richard Sibbes, Thomas Goodwin, John Owen, Thomas Watson, and many others ministered in England. To turn to their writings today is to enter a different order of reality from the one to which we are accustomed. Reading their teaching on the pastoral ministry for the first time can be as demanding as altitude climbing without the benefit of either oxygen or previous training. In such an atmosphere we struggle for breath.

Yet the climb, however demanding, is more than worth it. For if applied to the work of the ministry today the Puritan vision and commitment would have a profound, albeit disturbing, impact on the life of the contemporary evangelical church.

THE MINISTER

What was this Puritan view of the ministry? No more famous cameo portrait exists than the one given to us in *Pilgrim's Progress*. We come upon Bunyan's hero, Christian, at the point at which he has entered Interpreter's House where he sees a picture:

> Christian saw a picture of a very grave person hung up against the wall, and this was the fashion of it: it had eyes lift up to

Evangelical Ministry: The Puritan Contribution

Heaven, the best of books in its hand, the law of truth was written upon its lips, the world was behind its back; it stood as if it
pleaded with men, and a crown of gold did hang over its head.

Interpreter himself explains its significance:

The man whose picture this is is one of a thousand; he can beget
children, travail in birth with children, and nurse them himself
when they are born. And whereas thou seest him with his eyes lift
up to heaven, the best of books in his hand, and the law of truth
writ on his lips, it is to show thee that his work is to know, and
unfold dark things to sinners even as also thou seest him stand as
if he pleaded with men; and whereas thou seest the world as cast
behind him, and that a crown hangs over his head, that is to show
thee that slighting and despising the things that are present, for
the love that he hath to his Master's service, he is sure in the world
that comes next to have glory for his reward . . . this is the only
man whom the Lord of the Place whither thou art going hath
authorized to be thy guide in all difficult places thou mayest meet
with in the way.[1]

All the essential ingredients of the Puritan view of the ministry are
present in this single portrait: a heart to serve; devotion to the Scriptures
and an ability to preach them; a life of prayerfulness coupled with unreserved devotion to and care for the people of God. Gifts and holy unction always took priority over mere office.[2]

TIMES OF STRESS

The sixteenth and seventeenth centuries were no times to be committed
to biblical ministry if earthly comforts featured high on one's list of priorities. True, some Puritans were comfortably endowed, on occasion
through marriage; but secular historians suggest that less than 10 percent
of churches provided a salary remotely commensurate with the educational qualifications of a university graduate.[3] Furthermore, at the end of
the sixteenth century few ministers listed a study as part of their house,
for they possessed little in the way of contents for such a room. The commonplace notebooks in which they stored materials from their reading,

particularly in student days, constituted a major part of their libraries. Add to this the struggles that would, by 1662, lead to the ejection of some 2,000 Puritan ministers from their livings for non-conformity and one realizes that however competent these men were in this world, they did not live for it. Comfort was by no means their aspiration in life.

HOLY MINISTERS

What, then, marked out these individuals? Herbert Palmer (1601-1647), the gifted upper-class bachelor who became one of the Assessors of the Westminster Assembly and was widely believed to be its best catechist, knew the answer from childhood. Asked when he was only a five-year-old what he wanted to be, he replied that he hoped to be a minister. When some tried to dissuade him, telling him that ministers were "hated, despised, and accounted as the offscouring of the world," little Palmer nobly replied, "It was no matter for that; for if the world hated him, yet God would love him."[4]

Such commitment to godliness lay at the heart of the Puritan vision. Recurring notes in their thinking are the apostolic injunctions to "Keep watch over yourselves" (Acts 20:28) and to "Watch your life" (1 Tim. 4:16). A minister's lifestyle was therefore of supreme importance. Thus wrote Richard Bernard, author of one of the best known Puritan treatises on the gospel ministry:

A minister's carriage [deportment, behavior] should be such as the well disposed should love him, the indifferent should stand in awe, and the worst should be kept more in than perhaps they would, and not commit daily such outrages, as they in their hearts desire.[5]

Similarly, Robert Traill was speaking for all Puritans when he preached at the Cripplegate Morning Exercise on 1 Timothy 4:16 and noted: "Thou art set in a high office, in a dangerous place; take good and narrow heed, look well to thyself, thy heart and way."[6] It was an axiom among them that those who best obeyed the Word would be those who would best expound it. As John Owen noted: "No man preacheth that sermon well to others that doth not first preach it to his own heart."[7]

Evangelical Ministry: The Puritan Contribution

GODLY LEARNING

Training in godliness was therefore the fundamental necessity. Seminary was not as yet part of ministerial preparation. Rather, the Puritan pastors were university-trained men who further equipped themselves by personal study and often by the process of apprenticing themselves to well-proved gospel ministers, with whom they might live,[8] and by attendance at the famous "prophesyings" that for all practical purposes became seminars in faith and preaching skills for younger men.[9]

The results were striking. Even at a relatively young age men possessed the *sine qua non* of being a gospel minister—that is, a deep knowledge of God and His Word. Thus one of their number, John Carter, when asked at his ordination exam whether he had read through the entire Bible, replied: "Yes, I have read the Old Testament twice through in the Hebrew, and the New Testament often through in the Greek." (Nor was Carter a mere bookish individual; he would in later years give away most of his clerical income to the needy. Indeed, his kindness even to animals became such a byword that it was said in half-jest, half-truth that if one were a cow, horse, pig, or dog, one would give a great deal to have Carter as master!)[10]

To love any other book or books more than the Bible was, in Puritan eyes, simply to demonstrate one's unfittedness for pastoral office.[11] Yet they were by no means anti-intellectual and were very far from being anti-doctrinal. Indeed, some of them had a remarkable acquaintance with the best theological authors, from the Church Fathers through to the Reformers. They saw theology as an essentially practical discipline: "the science of living blessedly for ever" (Perkins); "the science of living to God" (Ames). To them, systematic theology was to the pastor what a knowledge of anatomy is to the physician. Only in the light of the whole body of divinity (as they liked to call it) could a minister provide a diagnosis of, prescribe for, and ultimately cure spiritual disease in those who were plagued by the body of sin and death.

The inordinate expense of books also made them careful readers. Furthermore, it safeguarded them from the modern obsession with the most recent publication and kept them focused on the best, most tried, and most thought-shaping authors. They themselves therefore learned chiefly by *thinking* rather than by an eclectic rearranging of others' ideas.

Significantly, they developed spiritually through sitting under the preaching of others and through the investment that other ministers made in their lives. The immense fruitfulness of this model should serve as a word to wise ministers in our own day.

Long and personal familiarity with the application of Scripture was a key element in the Puritan ministerial makeup. They pondered the riches of revealed truth the way a gemologist patiently examines the many faces of a diamond. Nor was this done for purely professional reasons (the "output" of sermons); rather, these men studied to know God, and out of the rich fullness of the biblical knowledge they developed they were able to speak powerfully.

PREACHING

Many seventeenth-century writers were, especially in their younger days, impressive controversialists (witness the powerful works of George Gillespie on Popish ceremonies, Samuel Rutherford on [or better, *against*] the divine right of kings, John Owen on all things Arminian). They were also experts at what the patriarchal William Perkins called "ripping up the conscience."

But edification, not destruction, was the central feature of the Puritans' ministry. Fertility in "nice questions," noted Sibbes, tends to mean barrenness in true religion.[12] Unmask gospel hypocrites they certainly did (as is always necessary in days when church attendance is mandated by law or social convention); but their central burden was to preach Jesus Christ and Him crucified, and this they did with great winsomeness and grace. Offering Christ was thus the essence of their task, and to it they devoted the very best of their energies and imaginative powers.[13]

Modern evangelical preaching is often at its weakest where theirs was at its strongest. It has a tendency to give energy and imaginative power to exploring man, his needs, and his improvement. In stark contrast to the oft-belittled Puritans, shamefully little evangelical preaching and writing today has God as Trinity, the ministry of Christ and His cross as its center. Our age of Christians is instead obsessed with getting our personal act together and confuses the organized self with the sanctified self. Sadly, even in discussing the latter, self may remain at the center. The cross can all too easily be sidelined; trinkets and trivia can frighteningly soon

Evangelical Ministry: The Puritan Contribution

be substituted for truth and holiness. As David Clarkson commented (alluding to an idea of Boniface), when we have golden chalices, we have wooden preachers; when we have wooden chalices, we have golden preachers.[14]

The Puritans believed that our basic need is to be divinely deconstructed by the law of God preached in searching and penetrating depth, pardoned through the word of the cross, and then reconstructed by the riches of grace that are made over to us in Jesus Christ, the divine storehouse. This they both knew and practiced—first for themselves, then for others.

THE CENTRALITY OF PREACHING

The chief instrument in the Puritan pastor's work was, therefore, the preaching of the Word of God. He was its appointed interpreter. But he was not first and foremost an orator. Rather, his call was to feed and defend his sheep; the predominant means by which he did this was by preaching. For that reason, Puritan manuals on the ministry focused most of their energy on how to handle the Word of God both privately and publicly.

Puritan preaching is often described as exemplifying the so-called "plain style." But this should not be misunderstood. Puritan preaching styles varied from the rugged, bare, and intellectually demanding to the eloquent and aesthetically pleasing. What was common to all forms, however, was the adoption of the motto of Paul: preach nothing but Christ; use not the wisdom of this world; eschew the enticing aesthetics of the schools of rhetoric (cf. 1 Cor. 2:1-5). No oratorical interest must ever be allowed to obscure the truth of the Gospel. The exposition of Scripture, the opening of the preacher's heart, and the unveiling of the conscience of the hearer were all simultaneously in view.

THE CHARACTERISTICS OF PURITAN PREACHING

In the light of this, three features came to mark the Puritan sermon. First, the text was "opened"—explained in its context in Scripture. Second, it was "divided"; like diamond miners blasting in the depths of the earth,

The Present Evangelical Crisis

they brought to the surface great chunks of Christian truth and held them up before the eyes of their congregations. Third, the appropriate "uses" were expounded. The key practical question was then asked and answered: How does this apply to me?

In all three of these areas the Puritans were masters. They were exegetes; but their preaching was not merely an explanation of words. They were theologians, but their aim was not the display of philosophical erudition, for they believed that all Scripture and therefore all theology belonged to all the people of God. They were counselors, but they realized that the best counselor is the Holy Spirit who applies the Word of God to the minds, consciences, emotions, dispositions, affections, and lives of God's people.

In fact, many Puritan ministers spent long hours in personal counseling and even held congregational counseling meetings in which they dealt with "cases of conscience," expounding biblical teaching on Christian patterns of behavior and especially encouraging and strengthening the weak. They did their counseling most frequently from the pulpit, believing that through applicatory preaching the Holy Spirit works without further limited human mediation to apply the Word of God to individual situations. The proof that this often took place is illustrated by the accusations made against some of them by members of their congregations that they must have paid someone to spy on their hearers!

In connection with their preaching, they often employed the "modern" pastoral tool of a "preaching grid"—taking their lead from their Lord Jesus Christ's categorization of the different heart conditions (soil) into which the Word of God (seed) came (was sown) (see Mark 4:1-20). The Puritan pastor was very conscious that those who listened to him came in a variety of categories, conditions, and needs. Some form of applicatory preaching grid was therefore valuable.

Here, as in other respects, the whole Puritan tradition was stimulated by the great William Perkins's work *The Art of Prophesying*.[15] Perkins divided hearers into seven categories:

1. Ignorant and unteachable unbelievers.
2. Ignorant but teachable.
3. Knowledgeable but unhumbled.
4. The humbled—either partly or thoroughly.

   5. Those who are already believers.
   6. Backsliders—of various kinds.
   7. Congregations containing a mixture of believers and unbelievers.

What is significant here is not so much the details of Perkins's division (although it retains its value) but his sensitivity to the differing spiritual conditions of those to whom he ministered the Word of God. While he was far from being needs-oriented in his preaching (he was more interested in *creating* a sense of need than in pandering to the needs already existing), he clearly shaped his application of Scripture to the specific conditions of his hearers. Sibbes would later write in a similar vein: "Ministers . . . are *to learn their duty hence, to observe the dispositions of people, and what bars they lay to their own salvation.*"[16]

It was this aspect of exposition that the Westminster Divines described sweetly as most "painful"[17] for preachers, for it demanded the greatest knowledge of and sensitivity to the human heart and its foibles. It also laid the greatest demand on their ability to "woo" the hearts of their listeners to Christ (an idea frequently found in Puritan writings, which they traced back at least as far as Gregory's *Life of Athanasius*). It was evident to the hearers of such preachers that—at least in imagination—these ministers had placed themselves in the pew and listened to their own exposition for themselves and also for others.

Never driven by the "how to" questions, the Puritans did not fail to answer them. That was the hallmark of their mastery of pastoral skills. Nor did they simply berate or beat their sheep into greater self-effort. Instead they set on display the mercy and sufficiency of God in Christ and the power of the Holy Spirit and thus led them on, showed them the way, and held them up as they took their first steps, pointing them, always, to grace. They recognized that though powerful sermons can be preached by those who grasp what the law demands, life-transforming expositions come only from those who have a firm grasp on how the wonder of grace operates.

GUIDELINES FROM THE WESTMINSTER ASSEMBLY

Specific guidelines were suggested by the Westminster Divines as a help in such ministry. In two and a half tightly packed pages they provided an

The Present Evangelical Crisis

outline that could fruitfully be engraved on the desk of every preacher of the Gospel.[18] With considerable wisdom they framed their instruction in a way that is applicable to a whole range of preaching methods and styles (a range, incidentally, to which the Puritans themselves gave rich expression; multi-formed and many-faceted biblical preachers, not homiletical cloning, was their goal). These fundamental principles were, in their view, equally applicable to preaching from one text, an entire passage, a key doctrinal statement, or systematically through a section or entire book of Scripture, although with characteristic sagacity they note:

> This method is not prescribed as necessary for every man, or upon every text [he is likely to be homiletically disadvantaged who has not heard powerful sermons that seem to break most homiletical rules!]; but only recommended, as being found by experience to be very much blessed of God, and very helpful for the people's understandings and memories.

With this in view, a brief introduction led the preacher to a summary or paraphrase of the preaching segment and to the principal burden of the exposition. In particular the following rules were considered fundamental:

1. What is taught must be biblical truth; in addition it must be clearly drawn from the text or passage so that people can see for themselves that it is biblical and learn how they themselves can draw that truth from the same Scripture.

As a general rule, Christians read the Bible privately in terms of the model of exposition they hear publicly. Principles of hermeneutics tend to be learned by osmosis. That is why this principle is not only essential to the integrity of pastoral preaching but central to the whole ethos of a congregation's life.

2. The teaching on which the passage focuses should then be highlighted, expounded, and illustrated, and honest, relevant difficulties (intellectual or practical) dealt with. The minister is not a purveyor of novelties, nor is his task to titillate his congregation with the latest deviation in the evangelical world. He is behind the "sacred desk" to teach and to nourish the flock. As a general principle, therefore, whatever is not edifying and spiritually nourishing he should not be expounding.

3. Stage three brings the preacher-in-the-study to his knees. He must now seek to take his exposition of the passage and

> . . . bring it home to special use, by application to his hearers . . . a work of great difficulty to himself, requiring much prudence, zeal and meditation, and to the natural and corrupt man . . . very unpleasant; yet he is to endeavour to perform it in such a manner, that his auditors may feel the word of God to be quick and powerful, and a discerner of the thoughts and intents of the heart; and that, if any unbeliever or ignorant person be present, he may have the secrets of his heart made manifest, and give glory to God.

It is not surprising, therefore, albeit it is enormously impressive, to hear of such preachers as Thomas Hooker who, it was said, seemed to grow so large when he was preaching that "one would have thought he might pick up a king and put him in his pocket!"

APPLICATORY PREACHING

How is a preacher to learn to apply God's Word in such "practical divinity"? The Westminster masters provide further guidelines.

1. The gospel minister spells out the "duties" found in Scripture. *Duty* is an endangered word in our modern evangelical subculture where all is "spirit." Intriguingly, that was an element of the ethos in which both the Reformers and the Puritans found themselves. In Calvin's day, "The Spiritual Ones" were a major thorn in the flesh to biblical reformation. Calvin despaired of helping people who felt the need to mention the Spirit in every second sentence they spoke! For the Puritans, the "Inner Light" movement constituted a similar danger. In both cases "what the Spirit said" and "what the [human] spirit heard" were divorced from and then exalted over the Word. Put more brutally, subjective feeling and emotion reigned supreme over the objective revelation of Scripture. Similarly, today the subjective, experiential, self-oriented, "touchy-feely" secular mind of the 1960s has come home to roost in the evangelical world of the 1990s.

In stark contrast to such confusion, the Puritan minister realized that divine indicatives always lead to and imply divine imperatives. Paul's letters on *gospel grace* are full of exhortation to *gospel duty*. Failure to

The Present Evangelical Crisis

understand this makes guidance an endemic problem among Christians. By contrast for the Puritans, most guidance questions were resolved by an intimate knowledge of the duties Scripture lays before us and the others by learning a patient, biblical willingness to go on applying the principles of divine revelation to every divine providence. By contrast with the mystical path to fulfillment, they believed in the covenantal path to obedience. Hence some 50 percent of the Shorter Catechism was devoted to expounding Christian duties. Whereas today the foul play flag marked *Legalism* is thrown down in the face of such a statistic, the Puritan recognized that this was the good old biblical way to God-given freedom and joy. That was why they had so much internal moral fiber!

But here the minister of the Gospel must go further into Scripture: he must indicate how these duties may be fulfilled. We are, for example, to love fellow believers, and we are to pray. But what do the Scriptures teach us about *how to* love and *how to* pray? In our day only those with rich personal and experiential acquaintance with the Scriptures can answer such questions without resort to mere anecdote or an appeal to the latest paperback offering a new key to spiritual advance. The Puritans realized that a deep conviction of the timeless relevance of the Scriptures and a real working knowledge of them saved them and their people from endless pseudo-spiritual diversions and fads.

2. The gospel minister must further uncover the true nature of sin with its misery, danger, and remedy. Virtually every Puritan sermon strikes this note in one form or another. Anselm's words to Boso, the theological stooge in *Cur Deus Homo*, echoed from every Puritan pulpit in the seventeenth century: "You have not yet considered the greatness of the weight of sin."[19]

The Puritans operated with the same pastoral formula as Anselm (although their interpretation of the Atonement was richer and more fully biblical than that of the great scholastic): grace makes sense to us only in light of the sin to which it provides the remedy. Consequently, only those made sensitive to sin, its greatness, misery and danger, will grasp clearly the wonder of God's salvation. Grace is only "amazing" when we see that it is a "wretch like me" that it saves.

3. Puritan preachers were marked by a further characteristic: in their preaching they gave "notes of trial." Here the Westminster Divines'

description of this aspect of preaching illumines the practical value of reflecting on the Perkinsian "categories" mentioned earlier:

> It is sometimes requisite to give some notes of trial (which is very profitable, especially when performed by able and experienced ministers, with circumspection and prudence, and the signs clearly grounded on the holy scripture,) whereby the hearers may be able to examine themselves whether they have attained those graces, and performed those duties, to which he exhorteth, or be guilty of the sin reprehended, and in danger of the judgments threatened, or are such to whom the consolations propounded do belong; that accordingly they may be quickened and excited to duty, humbled for their wants and sins, affected with their danger, and strengthened with comfort, as their condition, upon examination, shall require.

THE PREACHER

This, then, was the Puritan preaching "method." As we have noted, this was not regarded as an unbreachable preaching rule or a formula for cloning preachers. No one familiar with their sermons would confuse John Owen with Thomas Watson, for example! In whatever style the Scriptures were truly expounded and applied, the key lay in the extent to which the preacher himself was given over to the Spirit to employ as He saw fit. What did this imply? Seven things:

1. A commitment to the hard work of studying, meditating on, and applying to oneself the truth of Scripture.

2. A concern to speak God's truth to all of God's people, however simple they might be. The great Puritans were well-educated and highly intelligent ministers; but they knew that the concealment of art is also an art (*artis etiam est celare artem*, as Perkins delighted to say).

3. Preaching the whole counsel of God, for the conversion, sanctification, and glorification of men and women, for the glory of God alone in whose presence both the great and obscure must be exposed as sinners.

4. Manifesting wisdom in teaching and applying the Word of God, as well as the grace of God in the very spirit of the preaching, without "passion or bitterness."

5. A sense of the *gravitas* that ought to characterize a servant of God, which will in turn influence both physical demeanor and even voice and speech. The preacher is neither joker nor trifler.

6. Yet neither is the preacher to be lugubrious and censorious, but rather filled with a loving affection for those to whom he speaks. Nothing is better calculated to win hearers than their knowledge that their minister has "a hearty desire to do them good." The Puritans knew that people will take a great deal from such a man.

7. All this must be backed up by a life that is consistent both in private and in public with the message that is preached.

PRAYER

The ministry of the Word, in apostolic fashion, was always coupled with prayer, without which the wheels of the chariot in which Christ was conveyed to the congregation (i.e., the preaching)[20] would not run on smooth ground.

It cannot be emphasized too much how central this was in Puritan thinking. They saw it as the chief duty of a pastor to give himself to "prayer and the ministry of the word" (Acts 6:4). Not only the combination, but the *order* was significant to them. If a pastor was not a man of prayer, he should not be a pastor. Thus Robert Traill was able to say in his famous sermon "By What Means May Ministers Best Win Souls?":

> Ministers must pray much if they would be successful . . . some ministers of meaner gifts and parts are more successful than some that are far above them in abilities; not because they preach better, so much as because they pray more. Many good sermons are lost for lack of much prayer in study.[21]

The evidence of this in Puritan ministries was seen in the importance they placed on corporate prayer in the life of the fellowships in which they served. Richard Baxter was by no means unique in seeing it as so vital that he devoted one night every week to gathering together the younger people in his congregation in order that they might learn how to pray. John Carter, whose name has already been honorably noted, was renowned for the effectiveness of his intercession. On one occasion the husband of a woman whose life was endangered during childbirth instinctively ran to Carter to ask him to pray for her!

Personalized Ministry

Puritan ministry always moved from general principles to specific applications: How does this part of Scripture apply to these people at this time? But this was taken one stage further: the minister was responsible to apply the Scriptures particularly—i.e., to his congregation individually in personalized instruction and evangelism. How was this accomplished? The consensus was: by catechizing. This, in many ways, was a profound form of what we might call "pastoral explosion."

It was in large measure due to his vision for this work that, in 1656, Richard Baxter wrote his justly famous *The Reformed Pastor*. The experiences that brought him to this conviction are telling:

> It hath oft grieved my heart to observe some eminent able preachers, how little they do for the saving of souls, save only in the pulpit; and to how little purpose much of their labor is, by this neglect.[22]

Baxter had come to the sobering realization that considerable numbers of his hearers took in very little of what he preached; he needed to deal with them one by one to help them understand the message of the Gospel and to see its significance for their lives. In a moment of tremendous ministerial candor he wrote:

> For my part, I study to speak as plainly and movingly as I can . . . and yet I frequently meet with those that have been my hearers eight or ten years, who know not whether Christ be God or man, and wonder when I tell them the history of his birth and life and death, as if they had never heard it before. And of those who know the history of the gospel, how few are there who know the nature of that faith, repentance, and holiness which it requireth, or at least, who know their own hearts. . . . I have found by experience, that some ignorant persons, who have been so long unprofitable hearers, have got more knowledge and remorse of

The Present Evangelical Crisis

conscience in half an hour's close disclosure, than they did from
ten years' public preaching.[23]

And so Baxter made the financial arrangements necessary for every
family to have a catechism, and together with his two assistants he would
spend two days of each week, from morning until evening, either having
parishioners in his home or moving from house to house in his parish of
Kidderminster in Worcestershire. Thus he taught, gently quizzing and
sensitively leading his people to Christ through the Scriptures. This was
in addition to the regular Thursday night meeting when he gathered people in his home to discuss the previous Sunday's preaching and its implications and also the weekly meeting for prayer.

Under Baxter's ministry the effect was revolutionary. When he was
installed, perhaps one family in each street was devoted to the Lord and
honored him in family worship; when he left, there were streets where
only one family did not do so.

Of course, the purposes of God and the gifts of Baxter are the explanation for such fruitfulness. But Baxter himself felt that the instrument
of catechizing had been in large measure responsible for the extent and
the quality of the work. He recognized that beginning such an activity
would cause all kinds of inconvenience but argued that anything new has
that effect. Nothing ventured, nothing gained. Better, in his view, to be
inconvenienced now than on the Day of Judgment.

Baxter believed that the chief obstacle to the spread of this vision was
a reluctance to have the reality of the pastor's own life and understanding of the Gospel put to the test. But only then would the quality of his
ministry be seen. Numerically large congregations might turn out to be
small spiritually; eloquent sermons might prove to be unfruitful. But, as
the Puritans realized, apostolic patterns of ministry cannot be adopted
with building materials of wood, hay, and stubble. Ministers are building for eternity and must employ precious stones that will last forever. By
all legitimate means they must gain access to the minds, hearts, and
homes of their people if they are truly to pastor the flock.

These pages have been largely descriptive in character. In many ways,
however, a *descriptive* account of Puritan teaching on pastoral ministry
is already *prescriptive*. Yet we ought not to conclude without asking,

what specifically should we learn from the Puritan view of the ministry? Four basic things should be noted.

1. Ministers must be men of personal godliness. Nothing less than what Samuel Ward called "zeal at the heart"[24] will do.

2. Ministers must have expertise in handling biblical, systematic, and pastoral theology. They should be embarrassed by the expertise expected in the contemporary world of engineers, physicians, and lawyers if they are not themselves seeking to become experts in vastly more important knowledge.

3. Ministers must be men of grace who are called to be gracious in their unreserved and unhesitating devotion to those whom they are called to serve, seeing themselves as divinely responsible to bring the message of the Scriptures home to the life of each person in their flock.

4. Gospel ministers must be marked by a sense of and must live for eternity, as men who see time and the temporal and everything material in its light—and not the other way around.

We do well, then, to listen to the challenge of one of the greatest of the Puritan ministers, Thomas Brooks:

> Such as mind more the humoring of their hearers' fancies, than the saving of their souls, do little consider that of Seneca, *Aeger non quaerit medicum eloquentem, sed sanantem*: Sick men are not bettered by physicians' sugared words, but by their skilful hands. The sword of the Spirit never wounds deep till it be plucked out of the gaudy scabbards of human eloquence. Mr Greenham . . . wisheth that this motto might be written on their study-doors without and walls within, on all their books they look on, on all the beds they lie on, and on all the tables they sit at, &c.: "The price of blood, the price of blood, the price of blood." A preacher's life should be a commentary upon his doctrine; his practice should be the counterpane [counterpart] of his sermons. Heavenly doctrines should always be adorned with a heavenly life.[25]

We have need of such pure and purifying men today!

The Present Evangelical Crisis

NOTES

1. John Bunyan, *The Pilgrim's Progress*, ed. Roger Sharrock (Harmandsworth, England: 1965), pp. 60-61.

2. John Owen, *Works*, ed. W. H. Goold (Edinburgh, 1850-1853), Vol. 9, p. 454.

3. Despite widespread poverty among ministers, it is interesting to note that the two most frequently mentioned ministerial graces were humility and charity. See Patrick Collinson, *Godly People: Essays on English Protestantism and Puritanism* (London: 1983), p. 513.

4. Samuel Clarke, *The Lives of Thirty-Two English Divines*, 3rd ed. (London: 1677), p. 184.

5. See Richard Bernard, *The Faithfull Shepheard* [sic] (London: 1621), p. 75ff.

6. Robert Traill, *Works*, (Edinburgh: 1810), Vol. 1, p. 235.

7. Owen, *Works*, Vol. 9, p. 455.

8. As early as 1580 a conference of Puritan clergy passed a resolution that as a general principle every minister should have a divinity student living with him and train him for the ministry. Patrick Collinson, *The Religion of Protestants* (Oxford: Oxford University Press, 1982), pp. 118-119.

9. Cf. M. M. Knappen, *Tudor Puritanism* (Chicago: 1939), pp. 253-255.

10. For Carter see Clarke, *The Lives of Thirty-Two English Divines*, pp. 133-135.

11. Traill, *Works*, p. 242.

12. Richard Sibbes, *Works*, (Edinburgh: 1862-1864), Vol. 1, p. 54.

13. Cf. Sibbes, *Works*, pp. 317-318; Thomas Brooks, *Works*, Vol. 3 (Edinburgh: 1861-1867), Vol. 2, p. 216.

14. David Clarkson, *Works*, Vol. 1 (Edinburgh: 1864), p. 508.

15. For a modernized version see *The Art of Prophesying*, including Perkins's powerful two-part tract on *The Calling of the Ministry* (Edinburgh: 1996).

16. Sibbes, *Works*, Vol. 7, p. 481.

17. I.e., requiring the taking of pains, painstaking.

18. See "Of the Preaching of the Word," in *The Directory for the Publick Worship of God,* 1645. This is frequently bound together with the Westminster Confession and Catechisms.

19. Anselm of Canterbury, *Cur Deus Homo*, ch. xxi.

20. "Preaching is the chariot that carries Christ up and down the world," Richard Sibbes, *Works*, Vol. 5, p. 508.

21. Traill, *Works*, p. 246.

22. Richard Baxter, *The Reformed Pastor* (1656), ed. William Brown, pp. 178-179.

23. Ibid., p. 196.

Evangelical Ministry: The Puritan Contribution

24. Samuel Ward, *Sermons* (1636) (Edinburgh: 1862), p. 88.

25. Thomas Brooks, The Epistle Dedicatory to *The Crown and Glory of Christianity* (London: 1662).

13

EVANGELICALS AND THE CHRISTIAN MINISTRY: A TRAGIC LOSS

John H. Armstrong

The crisis that presently reshapes the evangelical church—the compromised church—and its missionary institutions becomes obvious when we consider what has been written in the last twenty years or so, by self-conscious evangelical leaders, about the life and identity of the Christian minister. Here we observe a paradigm shift that threatens to direct an entire generation of evangelical ministers, and with them their respective church bodies and missions, down a new path that is dubious at best, and harmful at worst.

Os Guinness, an evangelical who has probed the modern church for fifteen years regarding the inroads of secularization, idolatry, and their connection to the church growth movement, has demonstrated that these changes are nowhere more apparent than in the way we approach the Christian ministry.[1] Historian George Marsden, a scholar plainly not given to rash judgments about crises, sounded a similar alarm over a decade ago when he noted in a leading evangelical publication that "while fundamentalists and their evangelical heirs have erected doctrinal barriers against theological liberalism, more subtle versions of similar sub-Christian values have infiltrated behind their lines."[2]

To address this remaking of the ministry in the evangelical church, now "behind (our) lines" as Professor Marsden puts it, it is imperative that we consider the outcome of this infiltration of ideas into the evangelical mainstream of everyday life and ministry. This we have sought to address in several ways. If a new generation of pastoral leaders and churches, deeply rooted in biblical fidelity for the future, are to lead us, then the entire "royal priesthood" (i.e., every member of the church) must realize its active part in this reforming process. Together, all of us need to examine our faith and practice by the Word of God. Together, we must insist, with informed biblical intentionality, that the church conform all of her practice to the Word of God alone.

The late J. Oswald Sanders, who served God faithfully into his tenth decade, especially as a minister to ministers, gave the church many treasures through excellent books. None can be read with more profit, especially by pastors, than his classic *Spiritual Leadership*. Here Sanders cuts away extensive modern analyses and succinctly observes:

> The supernatural nature of the church demands a leadership that rises above the human. . . . The overriding need of the church, if it is to discharge its obligation to the rising generation, is for leadership that is authoritative, spiritual and sacrificial.[3]

This is my principal point in this present chapter. If the church is supernatural in character, then she needs a supernatural ministry to serve her. This supernatural ministry cannot thrive on talent and degrees alone. It needs God-called men, uniquely gifted and empowered by the Holy Spirit. Such men must be received by the church, as Christ's gifts, for the pastoring and teaching of the flock of God. But this touches the heart of our present problem. We appear to have lost our way with regard to the intention and calling of the pastoral ministry.

There can be little doubt that a great deal of confusion exists in regard to the Christian ministry. This confusion, to my mind, often begins with the idea of a *call* to the Christian ministry. Many ministers, as well as church members, are frankly unsure if there is such a thing as a call. The confusion that results brings significant loss for the congregation.

For over twenty-five years I have served on numerous committees for ordination. In at least half of the ordinations I have participated in personally, I have found the candidate quite unsure of himself with regard to this matter of call. I have discovered, further, in my wide travels among evangelical churches across North America that the average believer is virtually unable to discuss this subject except in extremely mystical and unhelpful ways.

The Present Evangelical Crisis

I believe the confusion of this has left an indelible mark upon a whole generation of evangelical ministers. This mark is not a sign of good health. It needs to be removed if we are to address the present crisis in our churches and seek biblical correction.

A wonderfully useful minister of the last century, F. B. Meyer, once spoke of his own call in a letter to a friend:

> For friendship's sake I do not like to conceal from you, or in fact from any one else, the decision to which I have come. So to be frank, I have decided my future course, and am going, with help from above, to be a minister of the gospel. Now I can imagine your astonishment, but it is a fact. I need only add that it appears to me to be the noblest aim in life to live entirely devoted to the one object of bringing others to know Him who has accomplished so much for us. When weighed against the hereafter, earth and its careers sink into insignificance.[4]

This understanding, common to an earlier era, is less and less heard among evangelical ministers today. Personally I believe the loss is profound.

WHAT IS MEANT BY MINISTRY?

The very expression *ministry* needs serious reconsideration if we are to speak to the present crisis in the compromised church. More precise definition is needed.

The general use of the term conveys an idea that there is some particular and unique work (i.e., "the ministry") that deserves certain, clear designation. This was plainly the way F. B. Meyer spoke in the above quoted personal letter. But is this understanding even valid? Many modern evangelicals apparently think not.

A New Testament Theology of Ministry

There are several dangers to be guarded against in any discussion regarding ministry in the New Testament. One danger is to draw too many precise conclusions with little or no warrant from the text. This approach,

Evangelicals and the Christian Ministry: A Tragic Loss

all too common in some traditions, tends to conclude that we have a rea-
sonably complete knowledge of the nature and function of ministry as
revealed within the New Testament. Leon Morris, a highly regarded
Australian New Testament scholar, concludes:

> While we ought not to minimize what the New Testament has to
> say we ought not to exaggerate it either. And the plain fact is that
> there are many things about the ministry of the early Church
> which we would like to know but about which our documents
> are silent.[5]

An opposite conclusion from Morris's is to assume that since the
New Testament says very little about the nature of Christian ministry, it
says nothing at all. In this approach a growing number of modern evangelicals find comfort. They have a doctrine of the church, sort of, but in
practice they tilt toward the conclusion that Jesus made little provision
at all for a definite understanding of the Christian ministry. The idea that
Jesus might have intended to establish some kind of recognizable leadership structure, uniquely called and set apart, seems inconceivable to such
minds. Leon Morris is a wise guide once again when he points out:

> We can certainly say that there is no evidence that Jesus ever insti-
> tuted an official priesthood. There is no record of any ordination
> conducted by Him. There is no occasion on which He is said to
> have set up an official ministry to which His followers must give
> all due honour. On the contrary He said specifically "All of you
> are brothers," and He forbade His followers to call one another
> "father" or "master" (Mt. 23:8-10). The implication of these
> instructions seems clearly to be that the Christian Church was to
> be a society of equals, a fellowship in which all are brothers and
> none has special privileges.[6]

But as Morris hastens to add, "The story does not end here." Jesus may
not have chosen or ordained a priesthood, but He did select twelve distinct men to be close to Him and to serve, or minister, in His name. The
twelve, named "apostles" (Matt. 10:2), are His "sent ones." They were
men given a special mission by Jesus Himself. Thus Morris further adds:

The Present Evangelical Crisis

They might accordingly be regarded as in some sense His agents, as acting in His name, and accordingly as having some form of official position among His followers. In others words it is easy to see them as forming an initial ministry, or at least as being potentially a ministry.[7]

The significant thing to notice in this matter is the emphasis of the New Testament itself. It is plainly not upon Christian ministry as some part of a pyramidal hierarchy. There is evidence of differentiation in function (and thus calling) among Jesus' followers, but the overwhelming stress of the text falls upon their unity, not their diversity. The historic church seems to have rarely gotten this emphasis right. Morris concludes:

> The really essential thing about the New Testament view of the ministry is that the one basic ministry is that of Christ Himself. Ministers in the Church are never regarded as exercising a ministry by virtue of any inherent power or right of their own. All that they do they do only because of what Christ has done for them. More than that, what they do they do, not only on the basis of that work of Christ, but as a continuation of it.[8]

The Word Ministry

The word *ministry*, and its several cognates, has various uses in Scripture. In the Old Testament the underlying meaning in every case is that of service to or on behalf of another. In the New Testament the same basic idea is evident. Three primary Greek words are used for ministry in the New Testament.

The single word used most frequently to refer to our subject is *diakonos*. Archbishop Trench says this word "represents the servant in his activity for the work, not in his relation . . . to a person." English translations include words such as *servant, minister,* and *deacon.* This is the word commonly used to refer to those servants of the Lord who engaged in the work of preaching and teaching (1 Cor. 3:5). The basic idea to be noted in the word itself is that of a "table waiter." *Diakonos* commonly referred to any kind of lowly service. Words that refer to things such as "authority," "rule," or "office" were all available to the writers of the New Testament; yet the common word chosen to describe the service and ministry of the Word of God to the church is *diakonos*. This idea of lowly service must be brought to the forefront of our thought if we are to regain a biblical understanding of the actual nature of the Christian ministry. A. T. Hanson concludes:

> The pattern is Christ—the ministry—the Church, and the task of the ministry is, not to undertake some specialist activity from which the rest of the faithful are excluded, but to pioneer in doing that which the whole Church must do. And the ministry itself is no originator, but receives its task from Christ. The ordained ministers only exercise the ministry which Christ himself has first exercised, and which he continues to exercise through them, and through their activity in the whole Church also.[9]

Hanson's conclusion is worthy of serious reflection. He seems convinced, as I am, that the Christian ministry is not some kind of caste system that brings leaders into a special privilege that separates them from the priesthood of the entire body. This means ministers have no superior status or power because of any unique position or calling. Ordination, however we understand it, must never be conceived of as setting a person apart from the priesthood of the entire church. Spurgeon surely had it right when he noted, "Ministers do not pretend to be a class of sacred beings, like the Brahmins of India."

On the other hand, Hanson's conclusion that the ordinary believer is called to "ministry" does not rule out the idea that there is a unique calling for service, or ministry, to the church. Actually, the opposite is the case if the evidence is weighed. There clearly is such a thing as the Christian ministry, as Hanson's words indicate. This ministry has a real function, one that has both real importance and real dignity. This biblical ministry does not create a caste system of "special" persons, as we have observed, but it does single out certain men. (I will not argue the point here that this is for males alone, though I believe this to be evidently true based upon the text.) These men are singled out, in some appropriate manner, for the specific task of serving the church through the ministry of the Word of God.

All believers are ministers, in a very important sense. But in another equally real and important sense, not all are ministers in the same manner or with the same function. The conclusion that we are warranted to draw here is that this in no way means all believers are ministers of the Word of God (cf. Phil. 1:1). Affirming the office and calling of every believer does not prevent us from affirming the unique ministry that God gives to ministers of His Word. Our modern American preoccupation with democratizing everything in the church threatens to lose this latter understanding by attempting, falsely, to regain the former. It is this conclusion that I want to challenge.

The function of apostles was called "this ministry" (cf. Acts 1:17, 25). These same men majored in preaching and teaching the whole church. In Acts 6:4 their work was called "the ministry of the word." Here in Acts 6 a major challenge to the work of preaching threatened to change the direction of the entire church. Only the work of the Holy Spirit through wise human agency averted a catastrophe. In 1 Timothy 1:12 (KJV) Paul referred to his own work as "the ministry" (cf. also Col. 4:17, KJV and 2 Tim. 4:5). Most important of all, especially for the church after the death of the apostles, is Ephesians 4:8-12. Here we learn that those who would hold this office in the church must be "able to teach," as we read in 1 Timothy 3:2. This defines the scope of their entire ministry.

The conclusions I have drawn in the above observations are presently under attack within popular evangelicalism. One widely used church growth advocate concludes:

> The idea of every Christian being a minister of Christ is finally dawning upon the American mind. During a long night, growth has been thwarted by the "one minister—one congregation" concept of ministry.[10]

Another widely respected writer, who has influenced many to helpfully consider the plurality of leadership in the local church, concludes even more strikingly:

> The one-man-professional ministry concept is totally unsuited for the body of Christ. Outwardly it may be successful, but in real-

ity it is harmful to the sanctification of the members of Christ's body.[11]

These statements, on the surface at least, appear to offer no more than simple support for the idea of every-member-ministry (or priesthood) noted above. However, something more is plainly going on in these writers. The context of the quotes I have chosen indicates that the author's ideas, in practice, leave little or no room for a *distinct* Christian ministry at all. This is certainly true in terms of a recognizable office or of a called and set-apart ministry, given uniquely by Christ to His church. One contemporary who experienced this kind of thinking in his own ministry, serving as a pastor within a plurality of local church elders, refers to the problems this thinking created in his own experience:

> To recognize distinction in calling and functions between the pastor and other elders was seen by them as evidence of clericalism, hierarchy, and arrogance. For example, the dissident elders were offended when I would encourage young men to consider a call to the ministry. To them this was a put down. They felt I was falsely assuming ministerial prerogatives to myself. They wanted a rotating pulpit, the right to baptize and administer communion on the basis of their calling as elders.[12]

That there has been a lack of uniformity among historic evangelicals regarding the nature of the office of elder cannot be doubted. Some believe the term *elder* refers to one office with two functions—i.e., elders who rule and share in the government of the church, and other elders, "ministers," who rule primarily by the ministry of preaching the Word. Others believe the only elders in a church should be those who are called to preach the Word and are thus ordained to this office. In this understanding, the term *elder* may apply to others, but strictly speaking only those who are actually called to the ministry of the Word, as I will later define this expression, are elders.

Finally, among a growing number there is an understanding that all elders "rule" and all elders "teach" and thus all elders have one and the same office and function. It seems to me that too much of the evidence advanced by the various positions in this debate is made to hang upon slim textual support. This appears to be the reason why Iain Murray, in a fair and evenhanded treatment of this complex issue, concludes:

> The question of the eldership is by no means straightforward. The subject has been handled by a number of the most eminent teachers of the Church including Calvin, Owen, Thornwell, Hodge— to name a few—and none is decisive in establishing a clear scriptural case. They are all unconvincing at certain points and sometimes they are inconsistent in the very views they advance . . . there is ambiguity in the very usage of the word "presbyter" in the New Testament.[13]

Murray wisely concludes that "if the insistence upon *precise* biblical evidence is believed to be required for true church order, then non-preaching 'elders' cannot form a part of that order."[14]

The conclusion I draw from the given biblical information is this: while the term *ministry* clearly has a wide range of uses within Scripture, plainly there is a proper sense in which we can and should speak of the work of preaching and teaching as *the Christian ministry.* If this is true, then it is of vital importance to the health of the church that we are concerned to strengthen the Christian ministry in every way possible. Further, when concern for *precise* forms of church government becomes a dominant concern in evangelical churches, rather than concern for seeing men called by God to preach the Gospel and build up Christ's church in her most holy faith, we are already in a crisis of significant proportions.

BUT WHAT IS MEANT BY CALLING?

The word *apostle* referred to a "sent one." In the strict and official sense it denoted the Twelve (and Paul), all of whom were *immediately* "sent" by the Lord Jesus Christ Himself. Thus Luke 6:13, 1 Corinthians 1:1, 1 Peter 1:1, and 2 Peter 3:2 speak of "apostles of Jesus Christ."

In a more general sense the term *apostle* applies to anyone "sent" through *ordinary* means; thus ministers of the Gospel are described as "sent" individuals. Something of this "sentness" occurs in Matthew 9:38 where we read: "Ask the Lord of the harvest, therefore, to send out work-

Evangelicals and the Christian Ministry: A Tragic Loss

ers into his harvest field." We see the same in Romans 10:15: "And how can they preach unless they are sent?"

The question that arises when we consider this matter of calling to the ministry is: "What exactly is meant by *sent*?" How does this *sentness* relate to *calling* (cf. Acts 13:2-3)? We should observe that the apostle Barnabas was also a "sent one." He was a gospel emissary dispatched by the congregation in Antioch, though not a special or unique apostle; thus even here we have a hint of what such a calling is.

We see, furthermore, in Matthew 10:1 that Jesus gave His disciples *exousia*, which meant "conferred authority, or power to rule in someone's name." This is given, likewise, in Matthew 28:18-19. Here Christ is directly commissioning His apostles. Most New Testament scholars agree that in doing so, our Lord commissioned His church to make disciples. This work of His is done under the ministry of the Word, a ministry given *primarily*, though not exclusively, to those who oversee the church as her pastors.

We need to further note that the term *call* or *called* in the New Testament, with reference to service or ministry, is actually not common. There are only a few examples (e.g., Mark 3:13-14; Acts 13:2; 16:9-10; Rom. 1:1).

I am convinced that, in spite of what a bare word study reveals, the concept of a calling to Christian ministry is to be found in the very *fabric of the New Testament itself*. The repeated occurrence of the word does not specifically argue the case pro or con. We do not draw biblical conclusions on the basis of the number of occurrences of a particular word. Nor should we ignore the inferences and flow of thought by our appeals to lexicons. This is an exegesis of mathematics, a strange practice some adopt through the simplistic use of a Bible concordance.

An actual example of this word, used as I am arguing here, can be seen when Paul was appointed to *special* service to the Gentiles (Acts 9:15). Likewise, Philip was *specifically* called to the Ethiopian eunuch (Acts 8:26-27). Peter was, furthermore, *definitely* called to carry the Gospel to the people in Cornelius' household (Acts 10).

More apropos to our subject are the several seminal texts found in Acts 20:28 and Ephesians 4:8-12. Here, when the above evidence is carefully weighed, I find few willing to debate the idea that some pattern for a specific "calling" to the ministry of the Word can be found in the New Testament. What is ultimately problematic is not the idea of a call itself,

The Present Evangelical Crisis

but the *how* of it. The real question remains: *How is the transmission of this calling understood and received?*

HOW DOES THIS CALL COME?

There have been, essentially, three ideas that have had prominence in the historic church. These are as follows:

The Roman Catholic View

Here there is a "split-life" view in which the priests give "grace" to those in the secular realm, since they alone serve in the sacred realm. A *radical* distinction between the clergy and laity exists in this model. Some Protestant communities did not break with this idea, and it can be seen in certain evangelical communities even today. The clergy have the real spiritual authority. Calling in this view is almost exclusively thought of as *external*.

An Anabaptist Reaction

Here the emphasis is upon a kind of democratic individualism. This is the view that has increasingly dominated the American evangelical scene in recent decades. In this view one's *gifts* are what ultimately matter. Ordination is often downplayed, to varying degrees, usually in response to excessive sacerdotalism. What distinguishes individuals within a particular church or Christian community is *only* one's gift. Church office, or leadership, is conceived of in terms of service *only*. We hear this argument often used today in terms of the women's ordination debate. Advocates of women's ordination argue, "God has gifted women for ministry. The church must therefore make room for the gifts and calling of such women."

The Modern Charismatic View

Here the thing that truly matters is one's *internal* sense of call. This is the Anabaptist view, noted above, joined with the added dimension of the charismatic experience. If the Holy Spirit leads you to preach, then no amount of education, examination, affirmation, or confirmation is really important in the end. The stress here is upon the revelational aspect of "calling." God speaks _directly_ to the person who is supposed to be called, without intermediaries (such as the church) or objective criteria (qualifying gifts).

We see a marvelous cinematic illustration of this in the recent popular movie, _The Apostle._ The lead character, a preacher named Sonny, falls into sin and hard times. He flees to another state, has an argument with God, and starts his entire public ministry over. The first thing Sonny does is privately baptize himself in a river as "The Apostle E. F." No one who joins his new congregation even bothers to inquire about who sent him to preach. The issue is that Sonny believes God ordained him. That is all that really matters.

Most of us, in our present evangelical constituencies, have inherited various parts of these approaches, sometimes without thinking too deeply about how or why. I submit that there is a much more balanced and biblically correct understanding of the divine call to the ministry of the Word.

An Older, Wiser Way

An older, wiser, and more biblical idea is to be found in a large number of evangelical writers from another era. Charles Bridges, an Anglican of the last century, spoke of a divine call to the ministry in this manner:

> We may sometimes trace Ministerial failure to the very threshold of the entrance into the work. Was the call to the sacred office clear in the order of the church, and according to the will of God? . . . Our authority is derived conjointly from God and from the Church—that is, originally from God—confirmed through the medium of the Church. The external call is a commission received from and recognized by the Church, according to the sacred and primitive order; not indeed qualifying the Minister, but accrediting him, whom God had internally and suitably qualified. This call communicates therefore only official authority. The internal call is personal qualifications. Both calls, however—though essentially distinct in their character and source—are indispensable for the exercise of our commission.[15]

Isaac Backus, a pioneer Baptist minister in eighteenth-century New England, expressed the same idea when he wrote:

> I shall lay down this plain assertion, namely, that in order for any man in these days to be truly an ambassador of the LORD OF HOSTS, he must experience essentially the same internal call that all his messengers did of old, both in the Old Testament and the New.[16]

The great Charles Haddon Spurgeon, London minister of the latter half of the previous century, held the same general idea when he stated:

> All are not called to labor in word and doctrine, or to be elders, or to exercise the office of a bishop; nor should all aspire to such works, since the gifts necessary are nowhere promised to all; but those should addict themselves to such important engagements who feel, like the apostle, that they have "received this ministry" (2 Cor. 4:11). No man may intrude into the sheepfold as an undershepherd; he must have an eye to the chief Shepherd, and wait His beck and command. Or ever a man stands forth as God's ambassador, he must wait for the call from above; and if he does not so, but rushes into the sacred office, the Lord will say of him and others like him, "I sent them not, neither commanded them; therefore they shall not profit this people at all, saith the Lord" (Jer. 23:32).[17]

A more recent modern twist has arisen that has profoundly impacted the thinking of many within the evangelical church on this matter of "call." This newer view may not be articulated precisely by many, but it has had a profound influence nonetheless. It is actually a mixture of rationalism and American common sense philosophy. The position I refer to is expressed in the sentiments of popular author, Gary Friesen:

> I had become convinced that Scripture does not require some kind of mystical experience whereby one "hears" God's "inward" call. . . . Rather than waiting for some kind of inward voice, a man should cultivate an inward response to the challenge to serve God in the fullest manner possible. . . . According to the New Testament, a church leader must be a spiritually mature Christian man who

Evangelicals and the Christian Ministry: A Tragic Loss

desires a position of leadership in the church, and is able to lead God's people and teach God's Word. . . . Where the traditional view speaks of a "call," the New Testament speaks of a "desire" or an "aspiration" for the pastoral office. Perhaps the question (about the call at the time of ordination) should be reworded: "Why do you desire to be set apart for the gospel ministry?" . . . (The answer should be:) I want to serve the Lord in the best and fullest way possible. God says that the office of pastor provides a good means for serving Him. So I have consciously aspired to become qualified for that position. The characteristics listed in 1 Timothy 3, Titus 1, and 1 Peter 5 have been my personal goals.[18]

Friesen's approach lacks both a proper view of self as well as an adequate personal awareness of God's dealings with the human soul. It lacks, to put it very simply, the biblical image of the pastor's self-conscious identity. Furthermore, it lends support to the whole idea of ministry as a *mere* profession, entered the way any other profession is embarked upon. If I can make the choice to enter the Christian ministry or not enter it, then in the end I am free to come and go as I feel. This, in the end, is the approach taken within our culture to career development. I believe it is destructive of "the supernatural nature of the church" that Oswald Sanders suggested was so important for real leadership.

Ministers, in distinction from all other Christians, must get their self-identity from texts such as 2 Corinthians 5:20. Here the apostle refers to those who preach as "Christ's ambassadors." Paul seems to have clearly understood that the Lord sovereignly put him "into the ministry" (1 Tim. 1:12, KJV). He noted, further, that it was Christ who sent him "to preach the gospel" (1 Cor. 1:17). If the ministry of the Word is a *continuing* ministry (as I have argued) associated with that of the New Testament, then is the call the Lord issues today any less distinct than what we see in such texts because the *means* have been altered?

Consider this question of *means* for a moment. This actually gets to the nub of the issue. John Wesley, who at times was quite prone to overly subjective approaches to guidance, noted, "God generally guides me by presenting reasons to my mind for acting in a certain way." I am persuaded that what Wesley observed is expressly what happens in the case before us. Our overly mystical notions of guidance have actually created the very problem that Friesen seeks to correct.

The great New Testament example of a distinct "call to the ministry" is seen in the apostle Paul (Acts 9:1-9, 15-16). He heard the direct voice of Jesus and had a commission to "all men" (Acts 22:15), especially to the Gentiles (Acts 26:16-18). Paul knew that God had sovereignly put him into this ministry (cf. 1 Tim. 1:12; 2:7; 2 Tim. 1:11). He was under divine compulsion to preach (1 Cor. 9:16), and this Pauline *sense of compulsion* is still a good model for us who preach today. This sense was confirmed by the congregation (Acts 13:3). Further, in Acts 16:6-8 Paul is actually prevented from going to Asia and is thus brought to Troas. Here he receives his "Macedonian call" in a most unusual manner (16:9).

One thing we can learn from this is that there is considerable variety in God's methods. There were, in some cases, direct words from God (in Paul's experience), and in a few cases God used visions. In other cases there were human mediators—e.g., parents or spiritual leaders.

But does God transmit sovereign appointments today by means of such *direct* communication? How does any kind of subjective call fit into this framework? Note that the question is not God's *capability* but rather God's *purpose*. Direct communication from God, by definition, constitutes some form of *new* revelation. Such revelation would, at least in principle, indicate that the Scriptures were not sufficient or final. Wisely does the venerable Westminster Confession of Faith say:

> The whole counsel of God concerning all things necessary for His own glory, man's salvation, faith and life, is either expressly set down in Scripture, or by good and necessary consequence may be deduced from Scripture: unto which nothing at any time is to be added, whether by new revelations of the Spirit or traditions of men. (Chapter One, Section VI)

Within the pages of the New Testament we have clear cases of *mediated* calls; consider the replacement of Judas (Acts 1), the appointment of Timothy (Acts 16:1ff.; 2 Tim. 1:6), and the ordaining of elders in the churches (Acts 14:23; Titus 1:5). Unless you believe in apostolic succession, you cannot believe the call today must come exactly as it did then. There are no apostles who can appoint or call men today.

Gary Friesen suggests that the idea of *subjective* confirmation of a call to the Christian ministry presents serious difficulties in several cases. He suggests that a subjective call is "an opinion that cannot be substantiated by an objective source of truth." If this definition is accepted, then I agree with Friesen. I believe, however, that we are warranted to think differently about the subjective aspect of a call.

The essence of this mediated call must be understood clearly if we would avoid the pitfalls. The heart of the matter can be seen in one word—*character* (1 Tim. 3:2-7; Titus 1:6-9). But if character is really the issue what is the basis for a subjective call in any sense at all?

I prefer to answer this question by defining what I mean by the subjective aspect: *the moving of God's Spirit within a person's heart that accompanies and is in agreement with an objective source of truth— namely, the Scripture as understood and applied by the presbytery (elders) and the congregation.*

If what Gary Friesen is concerned about is the notion of letting inner impulsion be treated as divine revelation, in some immediate or privatized sense, I completely agree with his concerns. My problem is that his cure creates a new paradigm that may solve the one problem while creating an entirely new one even more serious than the first. I believe this to be especially true in the present church scene, where we focus so much upon talents, gifts, and professional ability to "do the job" while it is increasingly apparent to many that what we really need is God-called men of the Word who know they have been distinctly given to the church by Christ.

First Timothy 3:1 refers to a man "desiring" this work and ministry. The very language used here demonstrates that an inner subjective factor is definitely involved. The balance of this passage, however, states that this alone is never, never enough. The first use of "desires" in verse 1 refers to "reaching out after," while the second means "to stretch oneself towards" (read this verse in the KJV). This second word actually implies a level of emotional response in that the elder sets his heart upon it. The idea is this: the subject does not reach out for ambitious reasons but rather *because* it will enable him to proclaim the glorious Gospel. This strong inclination of the heart cannot be suppressed, even in the face of difficulty (cf. Rom. 1:14-15; 15:20-21).

Is inner desire essential? The apostle Peter says an elder should perform his duties "not because you must, but because you are willing" (1

Pet. 5:2). But does this make it clear, beyond any doubt, that all must have an inner desire to be called of God to serve the church?

One might refer to another case where this desire is not so clearly present. In Acts 14:23 elders are appointed with no mention of this idea. Moses, Gideon, and Jonah seemed to be called of God for specific service before any such inner desire was evidently present. I conclude, then, that inner desire is useful but not necessary.

John Calvin strikingly evidences the point I am making in regard to his own call to ministry in Geneva. Calvin, as you may know, rarely spoke of himself in anything he wrote. A rare glimpse into his own sense of call appears in his *Preface to the Psalms*, where he candidly shares how much he sought to avoid and resist the call of God to preach the Word. Calvin writes:

> Being of a disposition somewhat unpolished and bashful, which led me always to love the shade and retirement, I then began to seek some secluded corner where I might be withdrawn from the public view. But so far from being able to accomplish the object of my desire, all my retreats were like public schools. In short, while my one great object was to live in seclusion without being known, God so led me about through different turnings and changes, that he never permitted me to rest in any place, until, in spite of my natural disposition, he brought me forth to public notice. . . . William Farel detained me at Geneva, not so much by counsel and exhortation, as by a dreadful imprecation, which I felt to be as if God had from heaven laid his mighty hand upon me to arrest me. As the most direct road to Strasburg, to which I intended to retire, was shut up by wars, I had resolved to pass quickly by Geneva, without staying longer than a single night in that city. . . . After having learned that my heart was set upon devoting myself to private studies, for which I wished to keep myself free from other pursuits, and finding that he gained nothing by entreaties, Farel proceeded to utter an imprecation that God would curse my retirement and the tranquillity of the studies which I sought, if I should withdraw and refuse to give assistance, when the necessity was so urgent. By this imprecation I was so stricken with terror, that I desisted from my journey which I had undertaken.[19]

Evangelicals and the Christian Ministry: A Tragic Loss

Calvin was so strongly opposed to any call to public ministry that he did everything he possibly could to avoid it. The end result was that the Spirit of God used a friend, Farel, whose words struck Calvin's conscience profoundly. The issue, as we have noted, is not the means of God's call, per se, but the reality itself.

How Does This Emerge in One's Consciousness?

Is this desire, or divine compulsion, the *direct* work of the Holy Spirit? Or is this put there (by the Spirit) more indirectly by a response to some challenge that is heard, read, or experienced, as seen in Calvin's account? Could an awareness of great need, for example, be the cause God uses? It surely was for John Calvin. Perhaps the best we can say is, "We don't know." Romans 11:33 seems helpful: "How unsearchable his judgments, and his paths beyond tracing out!"

The key factor to note is this: it is the Holy Spirit who issues the call, regardless of the manner in which it comes. The call may come through sheer sensitivity to God's dealing with us personally, perhaps through reading the Scriptures meditatively or hearing Christ-exalting preaching week by week. More than one preacher has received his own call while sitting faithfully under an accurate and searching ministry of the Word. The testimony of the widely used British evangelical expository preacher Alan Stibbs is most instructive here.

During the same period, when I was seventeen [while involved in a Scripture Union group at his school and asked to take leadership] I "discovered," and was arrested by, 1 Corinthians 14. Here I found an injunction to covet spiritual gifts, especially to prophesy (see verses 1, 12, 19). In the light of other statements in the chapter I understood prophesying to mean, not foretelling the future, nor receiving new revelations from heaven, but expounding revealed truth in a manner both intelligible and helpful to the hearer. Such an exposition should be related to men's condition, and should be expressed in words, which they can understand. Its aim should be to bring to the hearers instruction, challenge and encouragement (verse 3).

So I began as a schoolboy of seventeen to pray for this gift, and—on each occasion when I expounded God's Word—to pray for the grace worthily to exercise the gift to the glory of God and the blessing of men. Such prayers I have continued to pray since; and I can humbly testify that God has answered my prayers.[20]

CONCLUSION

What elements, then, constitute this call? How can these elements actually be used to test our desire, or lack of desire, for a divine call to the ministry of the word?

1. The requisite gifts must be present (cf. 2 Cor. 3:6; lit. "God has sufficienced us") in the man who is called.

2. Real and deep conviction is involved in a call (cf. Prov. 16:1). The word "preparations" (KJV) suggests "a placing of things in order" or "a setting of things in battle array." What God appears to do is concentrate a man's thoughts upon a particular matter, causing one idea to predominate in his heart. This can be noted in the case of Nehemiah. He tells us, "I set out during the night. . . . I had not told anyone what my God had put in my heart to do for Jerusalem" (Neh. 2:12). The Lord's servant becomes profoundly aware of duty, an obligation placed upon him by the Lord Himself. This is the same kind of experience testified to by the apostle in 1 Corinthians 9:16b when he says, "I am compelled to preach. Woe to me if I do not preach the gospel!"

3. There will be growing evidence of divine blessing that confirms the call. One may say, "I have a call to preach," but the real question is, "Does anyone have a call to listen?" Usually when a man begins to exercise his gifts, even early on, there will be the evidence of people desiring to listen (cf. Exod. 4:10; John 20:21-22; 2 Cor. 3:5-6).

Several modern concerns grow out of these considerations. (1) Ministers must be viewed, properly, as "elders" in the church. Are "young men" elders? Can they be? Perhaps, but not in the same way. We generally make them such simply because they have attained proper intellectual training and credentials. It is imperative that we understand that a call is never a true call until the church has confirmed it. (2) We must begin to rethink the whole issue of ordination. Colleges and seminaries treat the call as "private" in many cases. This may be due to a hugely competitive marketplace, which causes schools to put stress upon recruiting and training men for the ministry, regardless of what the church has to say about the matter. This thinking needs to be wisely, carefully, and properly challenged. (3) We need to more thoroughly involve the church, as the church, in the whole process.

4. Providence will confirm a true call in due course (Rom. 1:1; Gal. 1:15). The more Paul thought about his own life, the more he realized God had called him before Paul ever conceived of it. Review the past, fellow servants of the Word, and gain true confirmation of God's providential designs in your own case. This will be for the good of both yourself and your ministry.

Charles Bridges reminds us that the old question put to the candidate at ordination was: "Do you trust that you are inwardly moved by the Holy Ghost to take upon you this office?"

This, I believe, is still the *crucial* question. Not voices, dreams, or impressions, but rather, "Is there ample evidence that God's Spirit is moving you into the ministry of the Word?" Charles Bridges says the evidences of such a divine moving are but two: "The two grand combining requisites for this 'divine vocation' may be determined to be, a *desire*, and a *fitness*, for the office."[21] The desire must come from a true sight of God's holiness and of the excellency of Christ joined with the wonder of the Gospel. The true joy in this will come from being used for the edification of saints, the salvation of sinners, and the glorification of God's name.

If you are called to the gospel ministry, the preaching of the Word, you will have a proper calling and a true sense of divine appointment. This will exhibit itself in (1) an amazed humility to even be in the ministry, (2) a sense of authority and boldness in the delivery of God's truth, (3) an endurance in the face of discouragement and opposition, (4) an unusual earnestness and seriousness with true intensity, and (5) the performance of your work with a view to Christ's approval and not man's.

If you are an ordained minister, let your heart dwell often upon gaining God's approval as a steward of His mysteries. If you are thinking about the Christian ministry, ponder these mysteries with much prayer and counsel. If you are carelessly pursuing some type of church ministry (even "youth ministry," as if this were not pastoral ministry), then consider James 3:1 and flee from this unless you are clearly called by God. If you are one of His "saints" (Phil. 1:1), then pray for God-called men to serve your flock. These must be men who are sent by the Master and are

The Present Evangelical Crisis

given true passion by the Holy Spirit. The health of your church depends upon this more than you may know.

NOTES

1. Os Guinness, *The Gravedigger File* (Downers Grove, IL: InterVarsity, 1983); Os Guinness and John Seel, eds., *No God But God* (Chicago: Moody Press, 1992); Os Guinness, *Dining with the Devil* (Grand Rapids, MI: Baker, 1993). These and several more substantial works by Guinness can be consulted to get a sense of the pattern.

2. George Marsden, "Secular Humanism Within the Church," *Christianity Today* (January 17, 1986), pp. 141-151.

3. J. Oswald Sanders, *Spiritual Leadership* (Chicago: Moody Press, 1967), p. 24

4. W. Y. Fullerton, *Life of F. B. Meyer* (London: Marshall, Morgan, and Scott, 1920), p. 17.

5. Leon Morris, *Ministers of God* (London: Inter-Varsity, 1964), pp. 8-9.

6. Ibid., p. 18.

7. Ibid.

8. Ibid., p. 25.

9. A. T. Hanson, *Church Order in the New Testament* (London: S.C.M., 1961), p. 72.

10. Paul Benjamin, *The Equipping Ministry* (Cincinnati: Standard, 1978), pp. 15-16.

11. Alexander Strauch, *Biblical Eldership* (Littleton, CO: Lewis & Roth, 1988), p. 16.

12. Mack Brown, *Order in the Offices: Essays Defining the Roles of Church Officers* (Duncanville, PA: Classic Presbyterian Government Resources, 1993), cited in Iain H. Murray, *Banner of Truth*, August-September 1996, p. 38.

13. Iain H. Murray, "The Problem of the 'Eldership' and Its Wider Implications," in *Banner of Truth*, August-September 1996, pp. 50-51.

14. Ibid., p. 56.

15. Charles Bridges, *The Christian Ministry* (Edinburgh: Banner of Truth Trust, 1967, orig. 1830), pp. 90-92.

16. "A Discourse Showing the Nature and Necessity of an Internal Call to Teach the Everlasting Gospel," in William G. McGloughlin, ed., *Isaac Backus on Church and State and Calvinism* (Cambridge, MA: Harvard University Press), p. 78.

17. Charles H. Spurgeon, "The Call to the Ministry," in *Lectures to My Students* (Grand Rapids, MI: Zondervan, 1972), pp. 22-23.

Evangelicals and the Christian Ministry: A Tragic Loss

18. Gary Friesen, *Decision Making and the Will of God* (Portland: Multnomah, 1980), pp. 315-319.

19. John Calvin, in *John Calvin, Selections from His Writings*, ed. John Dillenberger (Missoula, MT: Scholar's Press, 1975), pp. 26-28.

20. Alan Stibbs, *Expounding God's Word* (London: Inter-Varsity Press, 1960), pp. 9-10.

21. Bridges, *The Christian* Ministry, p. 94.

14

THOMAS BOSTON:
THE EVANGELICAL MINISTER

Philip Graham Ryken

It was an inauspicious beginning. In the autumn of 1699 Thomas Boston (1676-1732) arrived at Simprin to pastor the smallest church in the smallest parish in Scotland. There were fewer than 100 adults in the entire parish, and only seven came to church to hear the new minister.

Though the congregation was small, Boston preached as if his life depended upon it. He expounded a passage that recently had been on his mind: "My people are destroyed for lack of knowledge" (Hos. 4:6, KJV).

The new minister began by preaching to himself, arguing that "the ignorance of a people living under a Christian name, occasioned by the carelessness of their teachers, will be laid to the teacher's charge as well as to their own." In other words, preachers must answer to God for the spiritual condition of their congregations. Indeed, "Ministers by carelessness become the murderers of the souls of their people."[1]

Thomas Boston was determined not to be a careless minister. Nor would he allow his congregation to remain mired in spiritual ignorance for long. He embarked on a year-long series of sermons on the sinfulness and misery of "man's natural estate" and on "Christ the remedy for man's misery."[2] For Boston, the depravity of man and the grace of God in Christ were the fundamentals of true religion.

The subjects of sin and grace occupied Boston's attention throughout his early years in ministry. When he was called to the parish of Ettrick in 1707, he began with the basics once again. This time, however, he organized his preaching on sin and grace into four parts: Innocence, Nature, Grace, and Eternity. Boston traced the history of humanity from created perfection, to the fall into sin, to redemption in Christ, to the eternal realities of heaven and hell. The sermons went through a series of revisions until finally they were published as *Human Nature in its Fourfold State* (1720).[3]

The Fourfold State, as it was called, became the most popular Scottish book of the eighteenth century. More than 100 editions were published in Scotland, England, and America. Because it was a best seller during the Great Awakening (1725-1760), *The Fourfold State* became a foundational document for evangelical theology. Jonathan Edwards (1703-1758) liked it "exceeding well" and considered Boston "a truly great divine."[4] George Whitefield (1714-1770) found it "of much service" to his soul.[5] John Wesley (1703-1791) went so far as to publish an abridgment of *The Fourfold State* in his Puritan library.[6]

Thomas Boston never aspired to international acclaim, nor did he expect it. It was after his death that his writings gained wide exposure. During his lifetime his influence largely was confined to the borders of his own parish, so much so that he sometimes felt "staked down" in Ettrick.

It is Boston's humble surroundings—rather than his posthumous success—that make him a valuable model for evangelical ministry. He did not found his own organization or start his own movement. He was not the head of a megachurch. He was simply the pastor of a small local church.

It was in this pastoral context that Thomas Boston exemplified many of the ideals espoused in this book: reverence for God, confidence in the Bible, simplicity of message, respect for the sacraments, and love for the church, with a passion for its peace and purity.

NONE OTHER GOD BUT ONE

Like most men of Puritan conviction, Thomas Boston was impressed with the weightiness of God. In the words of the apostle, he knew that "there is none other God but one" (1 Cor. 8:4, KJV). His overarching purpose was to magnify the sovereignty and majesty of Almighty God. His preaching thus was suffused with the divine presence.

Perhaps this is what most distinguishes Puritan preaching from the sermonizing of the contemporary church: a surpassing awareness of the

The Present Evangelical Crisis

Godness of God. Too many preachers are preoccupied with meeting felt needs, with immersing themselves in popular culture, or worse, with making people laugh.

An older and better style of preaching valued reverence over relevance. Ministers in this Reformation tradition were concerned primarily to glorify God the Father, Son, and Holy Ghost. They gave precedence to the vertical dimension of preaching (God to man) over the horizontal (man to man). Like Jeremiah (Jer. 9:23-24) and like Paul (1 Cor. 1:31), their boast was in the Lord.

Thomas Boston commended reverent ministry in a sermon entitled "A Heart Exercised unto Godliness, Necessary to Make a Good Minister." The sermon was delivered, as one might expect, at the ordination of a man to the gospel ministry. In it Boston preached what he practiced:

> If the fear of the Lord be not on our spirits, to counterbalance the fear of men, we cannot avoid being ensnared in unfaithfulness. But a heart exercised to godliness, will lead us on to act, as in the sight of God, whether in public or in private, that no souls perish through our default.[7]

His point was that a faithful minister conducts every pastoral duty in the presence of God.

Practicing the presence of God is necessary for all Christians, not just for clergy. A reverent minister longs for a reverent congregation. Boston thus concluded a sermon series, "Of God and His Perfections," with this exhortation:

> Thus we have given you a short description of what God is. Imperfect it is, and imperfect it must be, seeing he is incomprehensible. Do ye study to believe what is taught you of God, and apply to him, through the Son of his love, for further discoveries of his glorious perfections and excellencies; and at length ye shall see him as he is, having a more enlarged and extensive knowledge of him, his nature and ways; though even then ye will not be able to comprehend him. For it was a wise and judicious answer of one that was asked, What God is? that if he knew that fully, he should be a God himself. And indeed that being which we can

Thomas Boston: The Evangelical Minister

comprehend, cannot be God, because he is infinite. O study God and ye will increase in the knowledge of him.[8]

These words capture both a humility about how well God can be known and a hunger to know Him as well as possible.

THE BOOK OF THE LORD

The one true God makes Himself known through His Word. For this reason Thomas Boston was deeply committed to teaching the Scriptures as the Word of God. The Bible is, as he termed it, "The Book of the Lord."[9]

Boston's love for God's Word led to a lifetime of careful study. Since Hebrew was not then part of the divinity curriculum at Edinburgh, he assembled a library of grammars and concordances to teach himself how to read the Old Testament in the original. Eventually he became a skillful enough Hebraist to publish a learned Latin treatise on the accentuation of the Hebrew text.[10]

Boston held, of course, to the inerrancy of the Bible in its original autographs. This defining doctrine of evangelicalism was held (almost) universally until the nineteenth century. As Boston asked rhetorically in his exposition of 1 Peter 1:20-21, "If all scripture was given by inspiration, if no scripture be of private interpretation, nor came by the will of man, but holy men spake as they were moved by the Holy Ghost, how can there be any error in any passage of scripture?"[11]

The inerrancy of Scripture was more than simply a theory; it was a matter of practice as well as faith. God's Word was given so that God's people might become godly.

> What then remains . . . but, that we diligently read the holy scriptures as being the word of God, and the rule which he hath given to direct us both as to faith and practice; and that we fervently pray to God, that he may give us his holy Spirit to enlighten our minds in the saving knowledge of the word, without which we will remain in the dark, and the word will be but a dead letter to us?[12]

In answer to Boston's question, the only thing that remained was to preach the Word of God. Bible exposition was at the center of his min-

The Present Evangelical Crisis

istry. Worship services included prayers, of course, and also the singing of psalms, but mainly they consisted of the reading and preaching of the Bible. In addition to preaching a sermon, Boston regularly lectured on a Scripture reading.

The centrality of the Word of God was emphasized by the architecture of the Ettrick kirk. Like many church buildings, it was built on a rectangular plan. However, the large, canopied, wooden pulpit stood along one side of the church. The preacher was thus surrounded by the congregation on three sides. The effect was to bring the people of God into the greatest possible proximity to the Word of God.

Once Boston mounted the steps of his pulpit, he preached in the Puritan style.[13] He took a single verse for his text, or sometimes only a phrase from a verse. He began by making several exegetical observations about the text. Next he stated its central doctrine in propositional form. After explaining and expounding this preaching proposition, he concluded with the "use" of the doctrine.

"Use" referred to the usefulness of the doctrine for practical Christian living. This often took as much as half the sermon. The Word was not simply to be heard or preached; it was carefully applied.

> If we would be good Christians, or good ministers, we must study this, not simply as a book of knowledge, that we may speak of the truths contained in it; but as a book of saving knowledge, that we may feel the power of the truths of it on our hearts.[14]

Boston never tired of reminding his congregation (or himself) that "Religion is not a matter of mere speculations to satisfy men's curiosity, but a matter of practice."[15]

PLAIN AND SIMPLE

Boston's belief in the utility of God's Word led him to strive for simplicity in his preaching. He was wary of "vain ostentation" in the pulpit, preferring to "stoop to the understanding of the meanest, and not to give the people a comment darker than the text."[16] This concern for "simple and plain speech" was another characteristic of Puritan preaching.[17]

As Boston observed, however, it was first and foremost a character-

istic of the teaching ministry of Jesus Christ, who taught "plainly and per-
spicuously" in the Gospels. In the same way Jesus used words and images
adapted "to the low and dull capacities of men," so "he would have his
ministers to preach."[18]

Despite his breadth of reading, Boston rarely quoted from learned
divines or repeated anecdotes from classical sources. Partly he was afraid
of anything that would distract from the biblical message. Early in his
ministry he wrote:

> I have been helped to speak to the people by similitudes; but
> exacting an account of the sermon from the people, several of
> them told me the earthly part, but quite forgot the heavenly part;
> which was very wounding to me; so that I know not how to
> preach so as they may be profited.[19]

This shows the value of soliciting sermon critiques. Boston did not
simply assume his message was getting through; he checked to be sure.
This also poses a familiar homiletical conundrum: parishioners remembering the illustrations but forgetting what they illustrate!

Some might expect that Boston's decision to eschew anecdotes would
lead to dull or uninspiring sermons. However, his preaching retained two
sources of imaginative appeal. The first, of course, was biblical imagery.
Boston gravitated toward the metaphors and narratives of Scripture.
Often he used a single image to organize an entire sermon. A particularly
vivid example is his exposition of Song of Solomon 2:3 ("I sat down
under his shadow with great delight, and his fruit was sweet to my taste,"
KJV), which he called "Suitable Improvement of Christ the Apple Tree."[20]

Second, Boston derived analogies from the common experiences of
life on the farm. The daily tasks of a rural community afforded a rich field
for illustrating the truths of Scripture. In one of his first sermons, Boston
exhorted his people to learn how to read "the book of creation." "When
you dight it, sow it, plough, harrow, &c. ye may learn much."[21] Or as he
asserted on another occasion, "Every pile of grass is a preacher of the lov-
ing-kindness of the Lord."[22]

Fourfold State exemplifies many of the virtues of Boston's preaching.
To begin with, the book has a simple structure. Its organizing principle
comes from Augustine's *Treatise On Rebuke and Grace*, in which

Augustine (354-430) distinguishes between the grace God gave Adam to be able to not sin (*posse non peccare*) and the grace he will give the saints in heaven not to be able to sin (*non posse peccare*).[23] The great Medieval systematician Peter Lombard (ca. 1095-1169) took this idea and expanded it into four states or conditions of humanity: innocence, fallen nature, grace, and glory.[24]

Boston's innovation was to preach through these four states. He wanted his people to know their origins (Creation) and their destiny (Eternity). He especially wanted them to recognize their sin (Fall) and to come to Christ for salvation (Grace). The basic structure of *Fourfold State* provides a simple, systematic, memorable framework for understanding Christian life and doctrine.

Fourfold State makes frequent use of the stories and similes of Scripture. Its treatment of the doctrine of union with Christ is a good example.[25] Boston took John 15:5 for his text: "I am the vine, ye are the branches." He then used this simple metaphor to show how justification, sanctification, adoption, glorification, and all the other benefits of salvation flow from Christ to the Christian. This organic metaphor was doubly appropriate for parishioners in Ettrick, since it was agricultural as well as biblical.

One other feature of Boston's preaching seems worthy of mention: his sermons were short. The long sermon is sometimes considered the hallmark of Puritan homiletics. True, some Puritans did preach two hours or longer. But not Boston. He carried an hourglass with him into the pulpit; when half an hour was up, he stopped. Later he would mark an *x* in his manuscript to remind himself where to begin the following Lord's Day.

Thomas Boston kept things simple. He did not try to entertain his congregation. He was not a people-pleaser. But he did strive to preach so people could understand and apply the Word of God. His gift for simplicity was greatly admired by his ministerial colleagues, who lauded his "peculiar talent for going deep into the mysteries of the gospel, and at the same time for making them plain."[26]

Simplicity was one key to Boston's success. His published works were not for pastors or theologians primarily, but for Christians of the common sort. One nineteenth-century historian described *Fourfold State* as the "gospel of the peasantry."[27] Its unexpected popularity was due in no

Thomas Boston: The Evangelical Minister

small measure to Boston's frequent prayer that the Holy Spirit would give him "plainness in treating of gospel-mysteries."[28]

Holy Fairs

Thomas Boston was a minister of sacrament as well as of the Word. Here we encounter a paradox: the Lord's Supper was celebrated rarely in eighteenth-century Scotland, yet it remained at the center of Scottish church life.

This seeming contradiction arose from the practice of "communion seasons." Instead of observing weekly Communion, many congregations hosted annual eucharistic services. One church historian describes them like this:

> Sacramental occasions in Scotland were great festivals, an engaging combination of holy day and holiday. They were, as one divine said, "fair-days of the gospel," festal events in a Reformed calendar otherwise dominated by the week-to-week observance of the Sabbath. In them religion and culture, communion and community, piety and sociability commingled. Regularly times of renewal and revival, they were the high days of the year.[29]

Once the date for the Lord's Supper was set, preparations began in earnest. Other ministers were invited to participate, as were their congregations. Church members opened their homes as guests from other parishes began to arrive.

Services generally were held out-of-doors—sometimes under tents or pavilions—and followed a conventional pattern. Thursday was a fast day. On Friday communicants were examined by their elders. This was a primary means of church discipline in the Scottish church. In order to receive the sacrament, communicants were required to present a Communion token from their elders. The token certified that the holder was a confessing sinner and a professing Christian.

A preparation service was held on Saturday, at which congregants were challenged to confess their sins before receiving the body and blood of Christ. The Lord's Supper itself was finally celebrated on the morning of the Sabbath. Communicants came in groups to sit around a common

The Present Evangelical Crisis

table. This practice helped symbolize the Lord's Supper as a covenant meal.

The Communion service was followed by services of thanksgiving on Sunday evening and again on Monday. Communicants celebrated their salvation in Christ and pledged to live in new obedience to Christ. Given the pattern of repentance, faith, and new commitment, it is not hard to recognize the roots of American revivalism in these "holy fairs."

Thomas Boston regularly participated in Communion seasons throughout southern Scotland. He took the sacrament seriously, only coming to the Lord's Table after careful self-examination. One early diary entry gives a glimpse of the way he prepared himself. After citing a variety of Bible verses describing the heart-desires of a true Christian, he reasoned:

> 1. I am content to part with all sin, and take Christ to follow him. . . . 2. I desire union and communion with Christ. . . . 3. I desire a whole Christ, and would as fain have sin subdued and mortified, as guilt taken away. 4. I esteem Christ above all; give me Christ, and take from me what thou wilt. 5. Sin is a burden to me, especially my predominant lust. 6. I endeavour, in some measure, to seek after Christ; Lord, thou knowest. Therefore I have true faith.[30]

There are obvious disadvantages to infrequent Communion, but this shows one advantage: the Communion season was a time to scrutinize one's spiritual life.

As his reputation grew, Boston often was asked to preach at Communion seasons in nearby parishes. This he was happy to do. Many of the sermons in his published works were first preached during a "holy fair." On one such occasion he was deeply affected by the spiritual realities represented in the sacrament:

> The elements after consecration being declared to be no more common bread and wine, but sacred symbols of the body and blood of Christ, I felt in my spirit a sensible change accordingly; I discerned the sacramental union of the signs and the thing signified, and was thereby let into a view of the mystical union. I saw it, I believed it, and I do believe it to this day. I do not remember

myself ever to have been so distinct in the view and faith of this glorious mystery; and that with application, for I do believe that Christ dwells in me by his Spirit, and I in him by faith.[31]

Boston's last Communion season at Ettrick must have been a thrilling occasion. "A great day of the gospel," he would have termed it. Wave upon wave of communicants approached the Lord's Table; some 777 tokens were distributed in all.[32] The presiding minister had come a long way from his first service at Simprin, when only seven came to hear him preach.

BAPTIZED INTO THE DEATH OF CHRIST

"The sacraments," taught Boston, "are external means of spiritual washing, and are made effectual by the Spirit, being received by faith." This is true of baptism as well as Communion. Baptism is a sign and a seal of union with Christ and all His benefits: remission of sins by the blood of Christ, adoption into the family of God, regeneration by the Holy Spirit, and resurrection unto life eternal. It is also a sign and seal of "our engagement to be the Lord's, to be his only, wholly and for ever."[33]

As a devout Presbyterian, Boston believed in the validity of infant baptism. However, he was careful to point out that baptism in and of itself does not save. It was partly for this reason that Boston refused to conduct private baptisms, even when a newborn seemed to be dying. He was convinced that the sacraments belong in the public worship of God. To ride from manse to barn every time a baby was ill would only encourage a superstitious view of the efficacy of baptism.

This was not merely a theoretical issue for Boston. The infant mortality rate was high in those days, and a minister buried children as often as he baptized them. This is perhaps the appropriate place to mention how deeply Boston himself was scarred by personal tragedy. Six of his ten children died in infancy. One diary entry hints how heavy a burden he carried for his loved ones: "I came home . . . and found my family, by the mercy of God, no worse than when I left them."[34]

The death of one son was especially tragic. Boston had already lost a son named Ebenezer, meaning "Hitherto hath the Lord helped us" (1 Sam. 7:12, KJV). When his wife delivered another son, he considered naming that child Ebenezer also. In effect, the boy would be a second pillar of faith set up in praise to God. Yet Boston was troubled by the thought, "What if he dies too?" That would be a blow almost too bitter to bear. It was only "after no small struggle" that he decided to name the boy Ebenezer. This was an act of courageous faith. Nevertheless, the boy was sickly, and Boston describes going out to the barn to intercede for his newborn son:

> . . . there I renewed my covenant with God, and did solemnly and explicitly covenant for Ebenezer, and in his name accept of the covenant, and of Christ offered in the gospel; and gave him away to the Lord, before angels, and the stones of that house as witnesses. I cried also for his life, that Ebenezer might live before him, if it were his will.[35]

But Ebenezer never recovered. As Boston gently put it, "It pleased the Lord, that he also was removed from me."[36]

Only a grieving parent can understand the agonies Boston endured at the death of his second Ebenezer. Yet he did not despair. He entered instead into deeper and fuller intimacy with God, as his description of his son's burial reveals:

> When the child was laid in the coffin, his mother kissed his dust. I only lifted the cloth off his face, looked on it, and covered it again, in confidence of seeing that body rise a glorious body. . . . I see most plainly, that sovereignty challenges a latitude, to which I must stoop, and be content to follow the Lord in an untrodden path; and this made me with more ease to bury my second Ebenezer than I could do the first. . . . I learned not to cry, How will the loss be made up? but being now in that matter as a weaned child, desired the loss to be made up by the presence of the Lord.[37]

These painful events taught something of what it means to be baptized into the death of Christ Jesus (Rom. 6:3-4). Since the man cannot be separated from the ministry, the trials were woven into the tapestry of Boston's pastorate. He entered into the kind of ministry the apostle Paul desired, knowing both the power of Christ's resurrection and the fellow-

Thomas Boston: The Evangelical Minister

ship of sharing in his sufferings (Phil. 3:10). To put it another way, he carried out his life and ministry in union with Christ.

THE SHEPHERD OF ETTRICK

Thomas Boston was a compassionate minister, deeply devoted to the flock under his care. In addition to ministering to the sick and bereaved, he maintained an ambitious schedule of pastoral visitation. Traveling by horseback and ranging over territory covering some 100 square miles, he visited every home in his parish twice annually.

The purpose of these visits was to promote the spiritual welfare of every member of the congregation. Boston prayed, read Scripture, catechized children, and generally inquired how each household was growing in its love and knowledge of Jesus Christ. By doing so, he was following the directives of the General Assembly of the Church of Scotland, which instructed ministers to "be painful (i.e., careful) in catechising, frequent in visiting of families, and in private personal conference with those of their charge about the state of their souls."[38]

Recognizing that they were living in ungodly times, members of the Assembly also reminded elders and pastors of the necessity of church discipline. They lamented the "growth of profanity, ignorance, and irreligion, that is too manifest in this land, and the woeful decay of the life and power of godliness, with the small success of the Gospel, that is to be observed every where at this time." The Assembly thus recommended "the vigorous, impartial, and yet prudent exercise of Church discipline against all immorality, especially drunkenness and filthiness, cursing and swearing, and profaning the Lord's Day."[39] Since discipline begins in the pulpit, Boston often preached against these and other sins. Where necessary, flagrant sinners were reproved individually, as his Session minutes reveal.[40]

Although Thomas Boston was not afraid to reprove sin, he greatly preferred to promote righteousness. One way he did so was by starting a small group shortly after arriving in Simprin. Notes from the group's first meetings have survived, and their title explains their purpose: "Cases of Conscience discoursed on at the weekly meeting for prayer and Christian fellowship."[41]

These meetings for prayer and fellowship began with a question about the Christian life: "What may be the marks of true and saving

The Present Evangelical Crisis

faith?" Or, "How prayer is to be gone about so as it may be accepted of God." Finding answers to such questions made for the most inductive of Bible studies. Members of the group gave answers and suggested relevant Scripture passages for study. Boston carefully wrote down each answer, as well as references to any Bible passages the group consulted.

The idea for these small groups may have come from the Puritan Isaac Ambrose (1604-1663). Boston owned a copy of *Prima, Media, & Ultima*, in which Ambrose provided careful guidelines for the establishment of such "Christian Societies."[42] Small groups and home Bible studies are sometimes considered a recent phenomenon. Ultimately, of course, they go back at least as far as the house churches of the New Testament. Yet small-group Bible studies have more immediate antecedents among the Puritans. Then, as now, Christians practiced the communion of the saints by meeting in one another's homes for prayer and Bible study.

HOW TO MINISTER DURING A CRISIS

The present volume arises out of grave concern for the spiritual health of the evangelical church. The situation is a crisis not because all has been lost, but because all will certainly be lost if the church does not return to its true calling.

The signs of evangelical compromise and crisis are everywhere. The worship of God is casual and irreverent. Ignorance of biblical doctrine is widespread. The sacraments have been marginalized. The local church is no longer a lifelong commitment but a consumable good. As a result, Christianity no longer exercises a culture-shaping influence on western civilization.

Thomas Boston faced a similar crisis in the Scottish church of the early eighteenth century. Ungodliness was epidemic. As a young minister he lamented the "great ignorance prevailing" in the parish of Simprin.[43] Later he drew a comparison between Ettrick and Corinth "in her three grand evils, self-conceit, a divisive temper, and sins of uncleanness."[44] His estimation of the spiritual condition of the nation was (if possible) even lower:

> The land is defiled with idolatry, superstition, sinful swearing, Sabbath breaking, unfaithfulness in all relations, murders, uncleanness, dishonesty and fraud, lying, and covetousness.[45]

Thomas Boston: The Evangelical Minister

At the same time, liberal theology was gaining its first foothold in the Scottish universities. This was most evident in the prolonged heresy trials of John Simson (1667-1740), who was Professor of Divinity at the University of Glasgow. Simson was accused of a number of theological errors, the most egregious of which concerned the person of Jesus Christ.

Another controversy—known as the Marrow Controversy (1718-1723)—showed that the Scottish church was in danger of losing its grip on the Gospel. The controversy arose from a book Boston himself discovered: *The Marrow of Modern Divinity*. *The Marrow*, as it was called, was a short summary of Reformation theology written in 1645. Boston found it helpful on a number of topics, especially in its opposition to legalism, its emphasis on the assurance of faith, and its insistence on the free offer of the Gospel. Eventually *The Marrow* was condemned by the General Assembly, but the controversy helped make Scottish preaching more explicitly evangelistic.

Much more could be said about the crises Boston faced during his ministry. A series of droughts caused widespread famine. There was war in Scotland and England between Protestants and Catholics, especially during the Jacobite Rebellion of 1715.

What is perhaps more important than the crises themselves is the way Boston handled them. When the crisis was outside the church—such as war or famine—he called his people to public prayer and fasting. Fasting has become a neglected spiritual discipline. Contemporary Christians would rather feast than fast; yet both have their place in the Christian life.

In addition to fasting himself, and calling his congregation to fast, Boston wrote perhaps the church's finest work on the subject: "A Memorial Concerning Personal and Family Fasting and Humiliation."[46] In the memorial he defined fasting as

> . . . a religious exercise, wherein a particular person, having set apart some time from his ordinary business in the world, spends it in some secret place by himself, in acts of devotion tending to his humiliation and reformation, and particularly in prayer, with fasting.[47]

The cause for reformation could be either personal or national.

When the crisis was inside the church, Boston was a reluctant but

The Present Evangelical Crisis

active participant. During the Simson affair he pleaded with the General Assembly to defend the deity of Jesus Christ by removing Simson from the ministry. He was also a central figure in the Marrow Controversy, writing documents, testifying before committees, speaking on the floor of the Assembly, even publishing a carefully annotated edition of *The Marrow* itself (1726).

In all these disputes Boston distinguished himself by behaving honorably and peaceably. Then, as now, ministers vowed before God and presbytery to maintain the peace and purity of the church. These virtues often appear to be diametrically opposed. On the one hand, doctrinal purity has a way of disturbing the peace. Theological rigor often leads to disputes and divisions in the church. On the other hand, peace can come at the expense of purity. Naive tolerance of doctrinal error means the death of theological truth in the church.

It is a rare Christian who has equal concern for both the peace and the purity of the church. Boston's colleagues considered him such a rarity. Shortly after his death they praised his

> . . . joint concern for purity and peace in the church; no man more zealous for the former and at the same time more studious of the latter; having observed and felt so much of the mischief of division and separation, was exceedingly cautious and scrupulous of any thing new or unprecedented, until he was thoroughly satisfied of its necessity and ground. It was his settled mind, that solidly and strongly to establish the truth, was in many cases, the best, the shortest, and most effectual way to confute error, without irritating and inflaming the passions of men, to their own, and to the truth's prejudice; on all which accounts, he was much respected and regarded, by not only his brethren that differed from him, but generally by all sorts of men.[48]

This is a remarkable epitaph for a remarkable minister. Never have his virtues been more urgently necessary than in these post-Christian times when the church needs men and women to seek its peace and defend its purity.

Thomas Boston loved the church in his time, as we must in ours. He was greatly impressed by Paul's commendation of King David: "David

. . . served his own generation by the will of God" (Acts 13:36, KJV). Boston used this verse to define "generation work" as the particular call of God to every Christian in every generation. His words form a suitable conclusion for both my chapter and this book, as well as a call to action for everyone who reads it:

> Our generation-work . . . is the work we have to do for God and the generation in which we live, that we may be useful not for ourselves only, but for our God and fellow-creatures. . . . There are, by the wise dispensation of God, several generations of men in the world, one after another; one goes off the stage, and another succeeds. Each generation has its work assigned it by the sovereign Lord; and each person in the generation has his also. And now is our time of plying of ours. We could not be useful in the generation that went before us; for then we were not: nor can we personally in that which shall come after us; for then we shall be off the stage. Now is our time; let us ply it, and not neglect usefulness in our generation.[49]

Amen.
Soli Deo Gloria.

NOTES

1. "MSS of Thomas Boston of Ettrick," Aberdeen University Library, MS.3245/2, p. 157 (hereafter, "Aberdeen MS").

2. Thomas Boston, *The Complete Works of the Late Rev. Thomas Boston of Ettrick,* ed. Samuel M'Millan, 12 vols. (London, 1853; repr. Wheaton, IL: Richard Owen Roberts, 1980), Vol. 12, p. 153.

3. The most readily available edition is Thomas Boston, *Human Nature in Its Fourfold State* (Edinburgh: Banner of Truth, 1964; repr. 1989).

4. Jonathan Edwards, *The Works of Jonathan Edwards*, ed. John E. Smith, (New Haven, CT: Yale University Press, 1957), Vol. 2, p. 489.

5. George Whitefield, in Donald Fraser, *The Life and Diary of the Reverend Ralph Erskine* (Edinburgh: 1834), p. 317.

6. Thomas Boston, *The Doctrine of Original Sin*, ed. John Wesley (London, 1774).

7. Boston, *Works*, Vol. 4, p. 79.

8. Ibid., Vol. 1, p. 130.

The Present Evangelical Crisis

9. Ibid., Vol. 1, p. 56.

10. Thomas Boston, *Tractatus Stigmologicus, Hebraeo-Biblicus* (Amsterdam, 1738).

11. Boston, *Works*, Vol. 1, p. 30.

12. Ibid., Vol. 1, p. 37.

13. Ibid., Vol. 2, p. 649.

14. Ibid., Vol. 4, p. 76.

15. Ibid., Vol. 2, p. 649.

16. Ibid., Vol. 1, p. 420.

17. Irvonwy Morgan, *The Godly Preachers of the Elizabethan Church* (London: Epworth, 1965), p. 28.

18. Boston, *Works*, Vol. 1, p. 419.

19. Ibid., Vol. 12, p. 99.

20. Ibid., Vol. 3, p. 165-179.

21. Boston, Aberdeen MS, p. 175.

22. Boston, *Works*, Vol. 1, p. 203.

23. Augustine, *De Correptione et Gratia*, J. P. Migne, ed., *Patrologiae Cursus Completus*, Series Latina, 44 (Paris, 1863), cols. 915-946 (X. 28).

24. Peter Lombard, *Sententiae in IV Libris Distinctae*, Spicilegium Bonaventurianum, IV-V, 3rd ed. (Rome, 1971), II.25.2. The history of the fourfold state is traced in Philip Graham Ryken, *Thomas Boston as Preacher of the Fourfold State*, Rutherford Studies in Church History (Carlisle, England: Paternoster, forthcoming).

25. Boston, *Works*, Vol. 8, pp. 177-231.

26. Ibid., Vol. 12, p. 451.

27. Henry Grey Graham, *The Social Life of Scotland in the Eighteenth Century*, 2 vols. (London: Black, 1900), Vol. 2, p. 80.

28. Boston, *Works*, Vol. 12, p. 262.

29. Leigh Eric Schmidt, *Holy Fairs: Scottish Communions and American Revivals in the Early Modern Period* (Princeton, NJ: Princeton University Press, 1989), p. 3.

30. Boston, *Works*, Vol. 12, p. 40.

31. Ibid., Vol. 12, p. 262.

32. Ibid., Vol. 12, p. 435.

33. Ibid., Vol. 2, pp. 476-477.

34. Ibid., Vol. 12, p. 388.

35. Ibid., Vol. 12, p. 206.

Thomas Boston: The Evangelical Minister

36. Ibid., Vol. 12, p. 205.

37. Ibid., Vol. 12, p. 207.

38. *Acts of the General Assembly of the Church of Scotland, 1638-1842* (Edinburgh, 1843), p. 280.

39. Ibid.

40. "Simprin Kirk Session Minutes—1699-1714," Scottish Record Office, CH 2/346/1.

41. Boston, "Aberdeen MS," pp. 77-82.

42. See Isaac Ambrose, *Prima, Media, & Ultima* (London, 1674), pp. 243ff.

43. Boston, *Works*, Vol. 12, p. 103.

44. Ibid., Vol. 12, p. 459.

45. Thomas Boston, *A Collection of Sermons, Shewing the Grounds of the Lord's Controversy with this Church and Land* (Edinburgh, 1772), p. 16.

46. Boston, *Works*, Vol. 11, pp. 341-393.

47. Ibid., Vol. 11, p. 349.

48. Messrs. Calder, Wilson and Davidson, "Sketch of the Author's Character," in Boston, *Works*, Vol. 12, p. 452.

49. Boston, *Works,* Vol. 5, p. 254.

General Index

Index

The Present Evangelical Crisis

Index

The Present Evangelical Crisis

Index

The Present Evangelical Crisis

Index

The Present Evangelical Crisis

Index